The Foolproof COOKBOOK

The Foolproof COOKBOOK

Mary Norwak

Illustrations by Lorna Turpin

B. T. Batsford Ltd, London

ISBN 0 7134 3907 6 (cased)
ISBN 0 7134 3908 4 (limp)

Typeset in Hong Kong by Graphicraft Typesetters
and printed in Great Britain by
The Anchor Press Ltd
Tiptree, Essex

for the publishers
B. T. Batsford Ltd
4 Fitzhardinge Street
London W1H 0AH

Contents

Introduction

'Some are born great, some achieve greatness and some have greatness thrust upon them' — Shakespeare's wisdom certainly applies to amateur cooks. A few are truly born cooks, analysing a dish by sight and taste, knowing just how much to vary a seasoning, how to achieve a golden doneness, and how to make everything appetising in colour, smell and flavour. Many competent cooks learn their skills painstakingly over the years, and with luck, care enough about food to gain some of the knack which is a rare natural gift.

Most cooks, however, are forced into their calling by the necessity of feeding themselves and/or their families at regular intervals for every day of their lives. To many of them, cooking can be agonising with ill-balanced menus, pallid casseroles, lumpy sauces and soggy cakes. I spend a lot of time answering readers' letters to magazines, demonstrating to women's groups and instructing small classes, and find that there are a number of faults common to the cook who is not naturally skilled or has not had the advantage of specialised culinary education.

Many intelligent people find the language of cookery difficult to follow, and cannot discover the exact technique and nuances of such processes as grilling or baking. Published recipes rarely give details of how a dish should look or feel during preparation, and some are indeed regrettably vague. What is an unskilled cook to make of the sort of instruction which reads 'line the tin with the pastry, put in the filling and bake till done'? This quotation is not an exaggeration, but comes from one of our most respected cookery writers. To succeed, the unskilled cook needs to know the size of the tin, the heat of the oven, and the time necessary to achieve a good result, and is also entitled to expect some idea of what the finished dish will look like.

Many published recipes give poor results even in the hands of a skilled cook, so that the nervous one needs to know how to choose a foolproof recipe, and will then be encouraged by a good result. This will be achieved only if the correct equipment is used in the recommended sizes, and ingredients are carefully chosen and measured.

As I teach, I stress these points, and find that so many people do not realise that a different-sized cake tin can affect cooking time; that a blunt knife is a cook's enemy; that there are many different types of fat and flour which can substantially alter texture and flavour, and so on. In my classes, I explain these details with illustrations and encourage my pupils to cook dishes which incorporate the points they have raised. At the end of half a dozen lessons, they have perfected perhaps a dozen dishes, and have become enthusiastic cooks, building on these recipes and the techniques involved to create many more delicious meals. They find that once they have studied the niceties of making a perfect spongecake, a mousse or a sauce, they can develop variations themselves, and are also better able to assess the value of printed receipes which take their fancy.

Quite apart from these life-long 'family' cooks, there are now many more people who live on their own — the young student, the executive man or woman and the formerly married who may be coping with a single household in middle age or later. While they may have the will and the necessity to produce good meals, they may be hampered by poor equipment or a lack of basic knowledge of ingredients and techniques or by ill-chosen recipes.

I sent my son to his first job and London flat, and thought that he was a competent cook since he had always cooked marvellous breakfasts. After a couple of days, there was an anxious telephone call. 'How do you cook a potato? It's a big one?' Not easy to explain the technique on the telephone, but I managed it. He has always taken potatoes for granted, and the bed-sitter cookbook with which I had equipped him was silent on the subject. He didn't much care for finding that a dish needed toasted hazelnuts either — not part of the store cupboard for a school-leaver, and soon the book was abandoned in favour of my telephoned instructions.

This book is therefore for all enquiring cooks, whether they are beginners, or have muddled along for many years, in the hope that I have answered their questions and given them a repertoire of dishes for everyday use and for entertaining, and it is in effect a guide to other recipe books.

My thanks are due to the publishers, B.T. Batsford, who felt that such a book was needed; to Jo Pennington-Legh for research, and to Carolyn Newman for her patient and competent typing. Above all, thanks are due to all those pupils and audiences who asked the questions, and to my family who put up with my ill-temper as I struggled to provide perfect answers.

Basic Ingredients, their Storage and Planning a Meal

Perfect ingredients do not automatically mean perfect dishes, as anyone who has eaten in a restaurant will recognise. However, if care is taken with shopping and the initial choice of all ingredients, the cook's skill will be enhanced greatly.

A shopping list is essential, and it is a good idea to keep a list in the main store cupboard or larder of items which are needed, so that a good basic store of goods is maintained for everyday and emergency use. With care, dried, preserved and processed foods need be bought only every 2-3 months; frozen foods every 3-6 months, according to the size of family and freezer; and fresh food every 3-4 days, or even once a week if storage facilities are adequate.

Deliveries are adequate for dairy products and some groceries, but good shoppers and cooks prefer to choose their own fresh foods in shop or market. This means that they can buy food which is in season, and therefore at a reasonable price at the peak of quality, and in the required quantities. Bulk-buying is a practicable proposition when there are four or more people in a household, or where there is ample space for storage. Otherwise foods may grow stale, you may get tired of them, or prices may actually go down. The most suitable items for storage by bulk-buying are dry goods such as beverages (e.g. teabags, instant coffee) which will not deteriorate, and which are in regular use; paperware; and cleaning and washing equipment.

When carrying food home, get it back as quickly as possible, label for storage if necessary and arrange in place. It is wise to buy frozen or chilled food last on a shopping expedition, and to unpack it first so that it does not thaw, melt or spoil in a hot car or train.

Consult the following storage chart for advice about short-term and long-term keeping. There are four main storage areas: the refrigerator for short-term keeping; the freezer for long-term keeping of

fresh produce and cooked dishes; the larder for fruit and vegetables and for fresh food (e.g. cheese) which does not benefit from refrigeration; and cupboards for dried goods, cans and packets. When a larder is not available, all perishables have to be stored in the refrigerator. Storage places must always be kept clean and tidy, with the food organised so that it is eaten within the recommended storage time. The refrigerator should be defrosted regularly, and the interior washed with a cloth wrung out in warm water containing a teaspoon of bicarbonate of soda to each 1 pt (600 ml). A larder and/or cupboards should be kept fresh and insect-free, and have easily cleaned shelves or paper linings which can be discarded as they become dirty. The best storage areas are cool and dark, so avoid cupboards in a warm part of the kitchen, or those which contain a large window which faces the sun for a large part of the day.

Since it is not possible to finish ingredients each time they are opened, they should always be stored

```
┌─────────────────────────────────────┐
│       ┌──────────────────┐           │
│       │    TO STORE      │           │
│       └──────────────────┘           │
│   Food Freezer  [✱ ⊂•⊃] 3 months     │
│ 'Star' marked Frozen Food Compartment│
│  ⊂••⊃ 3 months   ⊙ 1 month  ⊙ 1 week │
│      Ice making Compartment 3 days   │
│         Cool Place 24 hours          │
└─────────────────────────────────────┘
```

carefully after use. Open packets should be closed and sealed or tightly folded over. Jars and bottles should have lids screwed on tightly. Canned foods should be transferred from open cans and placed in the refrigerator. All refrigerated foods should be covered with foil or film so that they do not dry out and deteriorate, or pick up flavours from other food. Dry goods and cans should be dated immediately when purchased so that they are used in turn and not pushed to the back of the shelf.

Storage Chart

Food	Recommended storage	Storage life
Meat (red or white)	Remove wrappings, put on a clean plate and store in refrigerator.	3 days
Offal and minced beef	Remove wrappings, put on a clean plate and store in refrigerator.	1 day
Sausages	Leave in packet, or wrap in film and store in refrigerator.	1 day
Ham and bacon (whole)	Remove wrappings, put on clean plate and store in refrigerator.	5 days
Bacon (wrapped and sliced)	Unwrap, store in polythene box and keep in refrigerator. If vacuum-packed, keep sealed until first used, then proceed as above.	7-10 days
Poultry and game	Unwrap, put on a clean plate and store in refrigerator.	2 days
Fish	Unwrap, put on a clean plate and store in refrigerator.	1 day
Butter and other fats	Keep in wrappings and store in door of refrigerator.	1 month
Eggs	Store in door of refrigerator or cool larder.	1 week
Cheese	Hard cheese should be covered lightly with a cloth (or keep in a covered cheese dish) and stored in larder. Keep cream or cottage cheeses covered in refrigerator.	1 week
Bread	Store in bin or crock in cool place.	1-2 days
Cakes	Store in airtight container. Fatless sponges do not store well. Butter-iced cakes will remain fresher in freezer storage than in a box or tin.	Plain cakes 7 days; fruit cakes up to 6 months, according to richness
Pastry and biscuits	Store in airtight containers. Do not store with bread or cakes, for the pastry and biscuits will become soft and the cakes stale.	Pastry 3 days; biscuits 4 weeks

Food	Recommended storage	Storage life
Sugar	All kinds in a cool, dry cupboard.	Indefinitely
Tea	All kinds in a cool, dry cupboard.	4 months
Coffee	All kinds in a cool, dry cupboard.	Ground and vacuum packed: 2 years
Cocoa	All kinds in a cool, dry cupboard.	1 year
Cereals and grains	All kinds in a cool, dry cupboard.	1 year
Pasta (dried)	All kinds in a cool, dry cupboard.	Indefinitely
Pulses	All kinds in a cool, dry cupboard.	1 year
Jams and pickles	All kinds in a cool, dry cupboard.	1 year
Spices	All kinds in a cool, dry cupboard.	Whole: 1 year; Ground: 6 months
Herbs (dried)	All kinds in a cool, dry cupboard.	6 months
Bottled sauces	All kinds in a cool, dry cupboard.	6 months
Canned foods	All kinds in a cool, dry cupboard. Fruit Vegetables Cooked meats Fish in oil Fish in sauce	 18 months 18 months 18 months 5 years 2 years
Cream	Keep in sealed container in refrigerator. If opened, or in jug, cover with film and use quickly.	3 days
Vegetables	Store root vegetables in larder or a cool place. Do not wash before storing. (They may be kept in salad crisper of refrigerator for 5 days, but take up a lot of space.) Store green vegetables in the salad crisper of refrigerator. (They may be kept in a cool, dark place for 2 days if refrigerator space is limited.)	3 days
Salads	Clean and dry them and store in salad crisper of refrigerator.	4 days
Fruit	Store in cool, dark place. Soft fruit (e.g. straw-berries) are best kept in the refrigerator 1-2 days. Melons must be chilled before eating, but should be wrapped in polythene or the smell pervades other foods.	7 days
Frozen food	Store in freezer, or in ice-making compartment of refrigerator, according to star-markings on cabinet and time recommended on packages.	
Ice-cream	Store in freezer, or in ice-making compartment of refrigerator, according to star-markings on cabinet and time recommended on packages.	

The Store Cupboard

The selection of ingredients for a store cupboard must be a matter of personal taste, but there are some basic items such as flour and sugar which are necessary in most households. It is worth keeping a few extra ingredients, however, to make emergency meals, or to extend everyday ones for additional guests. This list gives the *essential* ingredients for good basic cooking.

Flour	Plain, self-raising, strong plain
Sugar and sweeteners	Granulated, caster, icing, soft brown and demerara sugar, golden syrup, black treacle, honey
Raising agents	Baking powder, bicarbonate of soda, cream of tartar, dried yeast
Setting and thickening agents	Gelatine, table jellies, cornflour, arrowroot
Rice	Long-grain rice, short-grain
Pasta	Spaghetti, macaroni
Pulses	Dried peas, beans, lentils
Tea	China tea, Indian or Ceylon tea (loose and bags)
Coffee	Vacuum-packed ground coffee, instant powder or granules, essence
Chocolate	Cocoa, drinking chocolate powder, plain slab chocolate
Canned foods	Fish: tuna, red or pink salmon, sardines, anchovies Vegetables: kidney beans, sweetcorn, tomatoes Fruit: apricots, black cherries Soups: consommé
Dried fruit	Currants, sultanas, raisins, glacé cherries, apricots, dates, prunes
Nuts	Almonds (whole and ground), hazelnuts, walnuts, unsweetened chestnut purée
Jams and jellies	Apricot jam, red currant jelly
Pickles and sauces	Walnuts, cocktail onions, olives, tomato sauce, high-quality mayonnaise, fruit chutney, horse-radish, cranberry sauce or jelly
Herbs	Mint, sage, thyme, parsley, basil, chives, chervil, tarragon, bay, marjoram, dill, rosemary
Spices	Ginger, cinnamon, nutmeg, mace, cloves, allspice, black and white pepper, salt, mustard (powder and prepared), paprika, chili powder, curry powder or paste
Oils and vinegars	Olive oil, sunflower oil, wine vinegar
Essences and flavourings	Vanilla, almond, lemon, sherry, brandy, liqueurs

See page 33 for a checklist of 'emergency' stores.

Basic Ingredients

Flour
Wheat-grain flour is graded according to the amount of bran and wheat germ left after milling. The most common method now is to grind the grain with rollers. Stoneground flour is prepared in the traditional way between flat, rotating stones marked with grooves, which gives a coarse flour of 100 per cent extraction containing all the wheat germ. It may be sieved and sold as 81 per cent stoneground flour which indicates that some of the wheat germ has been removed. Some proteins in flour form gluten when mixed with water, and when dough is kneaded the gluten toughens and makes the dough pliable and elastic. Some flours are high in gluten-forming proteins, but the bran and wheat germ in wholemeal and wheatmeal flours weakens the gluten, and doughs made from them have less volume and a close texture. A mixture of white and wholemeal flour will give a lighter and more open texture, and paler colour, but is more acceptable to some people.

Flour should be stored in its own bag on a cool, dry shelf, rather than in a bin, and old flour should not be mixed with fresh.

Wholemeal Sometimes known as 'wholewheat', this is the flour from which nothing is taken away after grinding by rollers or stones, and is always described as being 100 per cent extraction. It may be coarse, medium or fine ground.

Wheatmeal Often known just as 'brown' flour, this contains about 85 per cent wheat grain. It may be coarse, medium or fine ground.

White Many types of white flour are available, from which the bran and wheat germ have been removed. A range of flours should be in the store cupboard, as they have specific uses and will produce differing results. The names and labels of white flours should be studied carefully before purchase.

Strong (or bread) flour contains a high proportion of gluten-forming proteins and is the flour to use for bread and other yeast doughs. It is also the best to use for puff, flaky and choux pastry. If you are not sure that your flour is suitable for bread making, squeeze a handful gently and open your hand. Strong flour will remain flowing freely, while soft flour will remain in a lump.

Soft (or weak) flour is made from a different type of wheat, and has less gluten-forming proteins, but more starch. It is suitable for cakes, sponges, puddings, biscuits, batters, shortcrust pastry, and thickening purposes.

Plain flour is preferred for all purposes, with a raising agent when necessary, but self-raising flour is convenient for a few cakes and puddings. It contains the equivalent of 4 teaspoons baking powder for every 1 lb (450 g) flour. Super-sifted flours make light cakes, and will not go lumpy when thickening, but pastry made with them becomes rather tough and biscuit-like.

Other flours Flour may also be made from rye, oats and barley and may be specified in a few recipes. They may also be useful for dietary purposes when gluten is prohibited, as rye flour contains few gluten-forming proteins, while barley and oat flour contain none. Rice flour is finely textured and used in some cakes and biscuits, and for thickening. Potato, pea, soya and sago are obtainable, and may be used for some recipes and for thickening, but they are not essential to the basic store cupboard.

Cornflour This is made from maize, and is very finely textured. It is used in some baking recipes and for shaped puddings such as blancmange and for sweet sauces. If used for thickening gravy or savoury sauces, a glutinous jelly-like result can be unpleasant.

Sugar, syrup and honey

Sugar may be made from cane or sugar beet, and is refined before sale to extract impurities. White sugar goes through more refining processes than other types.

Granulated sugar Sugar with medium-sized crystals which is used for most sweetening purposes may be used for some baking, but often leaves brown specks on the surface of cakes and biscuits where the grains have not dissolved completely and have caramelised. This makes granulated sugar unsuitable for fine-textured cakes such as sponges. Use for sweetening fruit, milk puddings and custards, sweet making, drinks, jams and pickles.

Preserving sugar Often recommended for jam and jelly making, this sugar has larger crystals and is more expensive than granulated sugar. It dissolves more slowly without forming a thick layer in the cooking pan, and so needs less stirring and also produces less scum. It does not improve the setting quality or clarity of jam.

Caster sugar This fine-textured sugar dissolves quickly and is best for making cakes and biscuits, for sprinkling on pies and sponges and sweetening raw fruit. It is also the sugar most often used for meringues and meringue toppings.

Icing sugar Sometimes known as 'confectioner's sugar', this is powdered and dissolves quickly. It is used for all types of icing and buttercream, for some meringues and may be used for sweetening drinks and cooked fruit.

Cube (lump or loaf) sugar Shaped sugar cubes which are convenient for sweetening drinks. Occasionally used in recipes for removing the strongly flavoured zest from the rinds of citrus fruit which is used for adding a true flavour to cakes, etc.

Coffee sugar Irregularly shaped large crystals which dissolve slowly and are used only for sweetening coffee. May be brown, white or coloured.

Raw cane sugar Sugar which is derived only from the cane and which has not been extensively refined. The sugars are dark, soft and sticky, with rich colour and flavour suitable for many culinary purposes. Sometimes known as 'natural brown sugar', each variety has a special purpose. Muscovado or Barbados sugar is fine-grained and dark and rich in natural molasses, which makes it suitable for fruit cakes, gingerbread, toffee and puddings made with dried fruit which need a dark colour and rich flavour. Light Muscovado is cream-coloured, with less molasses, and is more suitable for light-coloured cakes and puddings. Molasses sugar, sometimes known as 'Black Barbados' or Demerara Molasses, is stronger in flavour and colour than the other two, being very rich and almost black, with a sticky texture and flavour like treacle toffee. Demerara sugar is richly flavoured with a crunchy texture and is good for using in crumbles, or for sprinkling on raw or cooked foods. All these sugars may be used for sweetening cooked dishes, mulled drinks and for making chutney.

Soft brown sugar This may be labelled according to colour, e.g. light or dark, and is manufactured sugar made from sugar and molasses which has been more highly processed than raw cane sugar. These sugars are less sticky than the raw variety and are milder in flavour. They may be used for baking, chutneys and all general sweetening purposes.

Demerara sugar If this is not labelled as a natural brown sugar, it has been manufactured from white or washed cane sugar, coloured and flavoured with molasses and consisting of large, golden crystals. It may be used for sprinkling on raw or cooked foods, and for general culinary purposes.

Black treacle This is the residue left after manufactured sugar has been crystallised from the cane or sugar beet. It is quite thin and has a rich toffee flavour, and is used for gingerbread, and for darkening and flavouring rich fruit cakes and puddings. It may also be added to wholemeal bread, and to some savoury dishes to add colour and richness.

Molasses Similar to black treacle, this is made from the cane, and is thicker, stronger and more bitter than black treacle.

Golden syrup Made from the residue after white sugar has been crystallised, it is very sweet. It may be used for many varieties of cakes, biscuits and puddings, and for general sweetening purposes.

Cane syrup Natural, unrefined pure syrup from Barbados sugar cane, which may be used in recipes instead of molasses or black treacle.

Maple syrup The sap of the maple tree which is imported from Canada and the USA and is rather expensive. It has a delicious and distinctive flavour and is mainly used on pancakes or waffles, but may be a flavouring for cakes and ices. Cheap substitutes may be a sugar syrup with artificial flavouring, so read the labels carefully.

Honey Honey is easier to digest than sugar, and may simply be used on bread or toast to give quick energy. It has been a natural food and sweetening ingredient for thousands of years, and may be used for all sweetening purposes and for baking. In pickles and chutneys, substitute honey for half the sugar in the recipe; in baking substitute only up to one-quarter of the sugar content or the recipe may not be successful. Cakes may be a little darker, but will keep longer. Honey may come from a single country, even an individual region or town, or it may be blended. Blended honey is usually cheaper and suitable for culinary purposes; individual flower-flavoured honey is delicious and is used as a spread. There is no difference between clear or thick honey, but very thick-set honey may be difficult to spoon out and measure.

Fats and oils

There are many different fats and oils available which vary in flavour and texture, and which also have specific uses in the kitchen. A wide range is essential in the store cupboard and refrigerator for preparing successful and delicious recipes.

Butter Available salted and unsalted, home-produced and imported. Richly flavoured, unsalted French butter is considered the finest for table use. Unsalted Danish and Dutch butters are best for baking cakes and biscuits and for sauces as they have a delicate flavour. Regional British butters have distinctive flavours for table use, while Australian, New Zealand and blended butters are suitable for both table and culinary use.

Margarine Block and soft margarine are available, which may be made solely with vegetable oils, or with a mixture of animal and vegetable oils, and vitamins A and D are added. Margarine may be used as a spread, but is not suitable for frying because of its high water content. Hard margarine is excellent for pastry and cake making; soft margarine makes all-in-one cakes, sponges and puddings which are very light.

Spreads Brand-name butter, margarine and low-fat spreads have a high water content. Many spreads are low in calories and eaten for dietary purposes. Because of the high moisture content, they may not be suitable for baking or cooking and labelled information should be studied carefully.

White cooking fats These are sold under brand names and are made in a similar way to margarine but contain no liquid. They are suitable for frying, pastry and cake making.

Lard Refined white pig fat with a smooth texture which is suitable for frying, roasting and pastry.

Dripping Fat of beef, lamb or pork which has been melted down. Beef fat has the best flavour and is used for frying and roasting and may be used in some pastry, cakes and biscuits. Pork fat is also acceptable, but lamb fat is little used as it has a strong flavour and waxy texture. Chicken dripping is used in some recipes; goose and duck dripping are excellent for frying, particularly potatoes, and may be used in pastry. Bacon fat is suitable for frying bread or vegetables, and is required in one or two salad dressings.

Suet Hard white fat which surrounds the kidneys. Beef suet is most generally used and may be grated or chopped to use in pastry and puddings. Suet is, however, usually bought ready-shredded and mixed with a little flour, to keep it free-flowing.

Corn oil Made from maize, this is a mild-flavoured oil which can be heated to a high temperature and is useful for deep-fat frying. It may also be used for specially formulated cake recipes.

Sunflower oil A light oil made from sunflower seeds which has a pleasant flavour and is suitable both for frying and for salad dressing. The oil is high in polyunsaturates and is therefore often recommended for dietary purposes.

Groundnut (peanut or arachide) oil This oil has a slightly nutty flavour and is good for dressings and oil-based sauces. It is also good for frying and gives a distinctive and pleasant flavour to batter dishes such as fritters.

Soya bean oil Another useful oil for frying and dressings.

Blended oils These are sometimes sold as 'cooking oil' or 'salad oil' and are blends of oils. Choose with care as some have a very strong and unpleasant 'fishy' flavour.

Olive oil Distinctively flavoured oil pressed from crushed olives, which may be thick and almost green in colour, or thin and golden. The best French oil comes from Provence and is very fragrant; Spain, Italy and Greece also produce the oil. Use for mayonnaise and other salad dressings and for dishes from the Mediterranean region. Olive oil may be used for shallow frying, but does not reach a high enough temperature without burning to be used for deep-fat frying.

Nut oils Walnut and almond oils are the best known of these, and are very expensive. Walnut oil has a delicate nutty flavour and is used for salad dressings, but should be bought in small quantities as it does not keep well. Almond oil has a delicate flavour, but is rarely found or used in Britain.

Vinegar

There are a number of different vinegars on the market, and fine cooking depends on their correct choice for table and culinary use, and for pickling.

Malt vinegar This is a strong, brown vinegar made from barley and is cheap. It is suitable for pickling but the flavour is too strong for salad dressings. Very cheap vinegar may in fact be 'non-brewed condiment', which is coloured with caramel and has a very sharp flavour.

White (distilled) vinegar The flavour is as sharp as malt vinegar from which it is distilled but the liquid is colourless. This makes it suitable for pickling vegetables and fruits which look more attractive than in brown vinegar.

Spiced vinegar Malt vinegar which is ready-spiced and therefore quick and easy to use for pickling vegetables.

Wine vinegar Made from red or white wine, this is a more expensive vinegar with a finer flavour, which is used for salad dressings and mayonnaise, and in some recipes. There is no difference between red and white wine vinegars except the colour, but they may be bought ready-flavoured with garlic, tarragon, fennel and other herbs.

Cider vinegar This is made from apples and may be used in the same way as wine vinegar. It is also often used for dietary purposes as some authorities consider that it can aid slimming.

Rice

There are thousands of rice varieties and a number of useful products prepared from the grain. Since rice may be used as the basis of a complete meal or dish, or as an accompaniment to savoury foods, it is worth keeping a few different types in store.

Long-grain (Patna) rice This is the rice to use with savoury dishes such as stews, curry and salads. The grains are long and slim and should be light and fluffy when cooked.

Short-grain (Carolina) rice The short grains of this rice have a slightly chalky appearance. When they are cooked they become sticky and cling together, and are therefore generally used for milk puddings and moulds. This may be packaged and labelled as 'pudding rice' but may be used for risottos and other European savoury dishes as it closely resembles Italian rice.

Italian rice Another short-grain rice with slightly fatter grains, which is used for risottos. Arborio rice from northern Italy is also a risotto rice with a very good flavour.

Basmati rice High-quality, long-grain Indian rice,

with a very good flavour which is perfect with curry and other spiced dishes.

Brown rice Unpolished long-grain rice with just the husk and a little bran removed, and a nutty flavour. The germ of the grain is kept, so this rice has more protein, minerals and vitamins than other rice. It takes longer to cook than white rice.

Wild rice This is not a true rice, but a wild grass seed, which is rare and expensive, but very good with game dishes.

Easy-to-cook rice Usually sold under a brand name, this is an easy rice for the amateur cook as it produces separate, tender grains. The rice has been partly cooked under steam pressure, and in the kitchen must be added to a carefully measured amount of water. It has the advantage that it can be cooked in a covered casserole in the oven, which may save space on a crowded stove top. This ensures that there is no burning or boiling over, and the rice can be prepared in an oven-to-table dish.

Instant rice This has been cooked and dehydrated before packing, and is reconstituted with hot water.

Ground rice Rice grains which have been ground coarsely or finely, and which can be used in milk puddings, or baked in cakes and biscuits.

Flaked rice Large, irregular white flakes processed from rice grains. They cook quickly and make good milk puddings. May also be used to thicken savoury dishes, and for fillings in fruit pies.

Pulses

Dried beans, lentils and peas are known as pulses and are a staple protein food, also containing calcium and vitamin B. It is worth keeping a few varieties in the cupboard to make soups, salads and casseroles. Dried beans should be soaked in cold water for 3-4 hours before cooking, but they should not be soaked longer as they may begin to ferment and become slightly toxic.

Adzuki beans Small, round, red beans with a sweetish flavour, much used in Chinese cookery. May be used for sprouting as a salad.

Black beans These are used a great deal in Caribbean cooking and some Chinese dishes, and combine well with spicy sauces.

Black-eyed beans Small white beans with a black mark and a strong flavour which go well with other strongly flavoured food such as ham, spinach and garlic dishes.

Boriotti beans Brown or white and tender, these cook to a soft floury consistency, and are much used in Italian recipes. Saluggia beans are similar but smaller.

Broad beans These may be dried; if so, they need soaking and long cooking before they are tender enough to use. They should be skinned to use in salads and in Greek recipes.

Brown Dutch beans A type of haricot bean which is coloured a rich brown and is fully flavoured. May be used instead of haricot beans.

Butter beans Large, white beans with floury texture which may be served as an accompaniment. They are rather inspid and are improved by a sauce such as one flavoured with tomato.

Egyptian brown beans Small, round brown beans used in Middle Eastern cooking, particularly when dressed with oil, lemon juice, parsley and garlic in a salad.

Flageolets Small pale green haricot beans with a delicate flavour. Good as a hot vegetable or salad, or as a purée, particularly served with lamb.

Lima beans Similar to small butter beans, these are white or very pale green. Much used in American cooking, and may be substituted for haricot beans.

Navy (and pearl) beans Similar to haricot beans and good in dishes such as baked beans which need long, slow cooking.

Red kidney beans Bright red, shiny beans used in Spanish and Mexican cooking, and good for soups, salads and highly spiced dishes. May be bought ready-cooked in cans.

Soya beans May be bought whole or ground into flour. Very nourishing, and often used as a meat substitute.

White haricot beans Small, white beans for soups, salads or as an accompaniment, or herb-flavoured purée.

Lentils There are more than sixty varieties of lentils, including red, pink, green, white, black, yellow and mottled. They are good for soup, salads and purée, and go extremely well with pork and ham, and with herbs and spices. Lentils need soaking for 3-4 hours before cooking.

Chick peas Small, very hard peas which need 24 hours soaking and 3 hours cooking to make them palatable. They may be white, black or red, and are much used in Arab cooking as well as in South America and in some Mediterranean countries.

Split green peas Small green peas which have been skinned, split and dried, and are good for soups and purées. They need soaking overnight before cooking.

Split yellow peas Similar to split green peas, but golden yellow in colour. Popular in Swedish and Indian cooking.

Whole, dried peas Large, marrowfat peas which have been dried whole and look rather pale and wrinkled. They need soaking overnight before cooking, and are good for soups and purées. Often served with pork or fish.

Herbs

A range of herbs is essential for the imaginative cook, and these may be used fresh, frozen or dried. A few basic herbs may be grown in the garden, in a tub, on a balcony, or on the kitchen window-sill so that they may be freshly cut when needed throughout the year. Herbs may be dried on a dry day in summer when they are just about to flower. They should be tied loosely in small bunches and hung up to dry in a warm, shaded place, then stripped from the stems to store in dark glass bottles so that they do not lose colour and flavour. Thyme, sage, savory and marjoram are best dried this way. Use up dried herbs before the spring when fresh ones are available. Be careful when buying commercially dried herbs as these may be very old, dry and flavourless.

Soft-leaved herbs such as mint, parsley, tarragon, fennel and basil may be frozen although they lose some subtlety of flavour. Just chop them finely and pack into ice-cube trays with a few drops of water. Freeze solid and then wrap each cube in clingfilm for storage in a freezer bag.

These are the most useful herbs which are likely to be mentioned in recipes:

Basil Best grown freshly each year. Strong flavour like cloves which is delicious in tomato dishes, in sausages and in soups.

Bay An evergreen shrub which can be grown in a tub. May be bought dried. Flavouring for fish and meat, casseroles, soups, milk puddings and custards.

Chervil An annual plant which looks like fine-leaved parsley and has a delicate flavour. Use for soup, salads, eggs and fish.

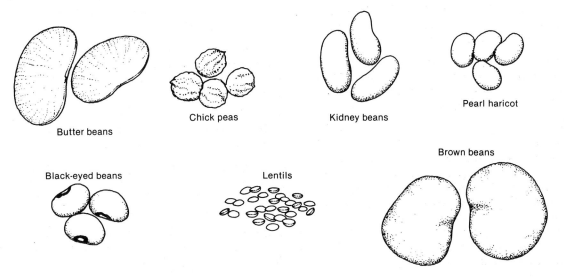

Butter beans

Chick peas

Kidney beans

Pearl haricot

Brown beans

Black-eyed beans

Lentils

Chives These grow like a cluster of tiny onions. The finely chopped tops give a mild onion flavour to salads, soups, eggs and cheese dishes.

Dill Easily grown annual herb with feathery leaves. May be bought dried as dill weed or seed, and has a delicate flavour when used with cucumber, fish and new potatoes.

Fennel A perennial plant which looks similar to dill and has a strong aniseed flavour. Use in fish dishes.

Garlic A head of small 'cloves' with strong individual onion flavour. Keep heads uncovered in a basket or strung up in a cool, dry place. Peel individual 'cloves' for chopping or crushing into other ingredients.

Marjoram Easily grown and available in a number of varieties, including the strongly flavoured oregano. A richly scented plant which gives flavour to chicken, lamb and Italian-style, tomato-based dishes such as pizza and pasta.

Mint Easily grown and very fragrant plant with many varieties. Use in sauce for lamb, in tomato dishes and fresh fruit salad.

Oregano See Marjoram.

Parsley Annual plant often used for garnish. Flavour is excellent in sauce to serve with ham or broad beans.

Rosemary Aromatic shrub with spiky leaves. Good with rabbit and roast lamb, beef and pork.

Sage Fragrant shrub with strongly flavoured leaves used with onions, pork, duck, goose and sausages.

Savory Summer savory is an annual plant, and winter savory an evergreen perennial, but they have similar flavours. Good with eggs, poultry, lentils and bean dishes.

Tarragon Perennial plant with slightly aniseed-flavoured leaves. Good in salads, chicken dishes and many classic sauces.

Thyme Many varieties of this small shrub may be grown. Scented and has a light flavour, suitable for stuffings and stews.

Herb mixtures

Bouquet garni A mixture of two or three stalks of parsley, a sprig of thyme and a bay leaf, sometimes bound together with the green leaf of a leek and including a dried clove. A sprig of marjoram may be added if liked. This mixture may be made up at home from fresh herbs (spare bunches may be frozen). Also available dried in small, muslin bags.

Fines herbes Parsley, chervil, chives and tarragon chopped finely and used fresh or dried for salads, omlettes and egg dishes.

Mixed herbs A mixture of sage, parsley, thyme and marjoram, which may be fresh or dried. Use in stuffings, in meat and in fish dishes.

Spices, flavourings and colourings

As with herbs, a range of spices is necessary for successful cooking. They may be bought in whole

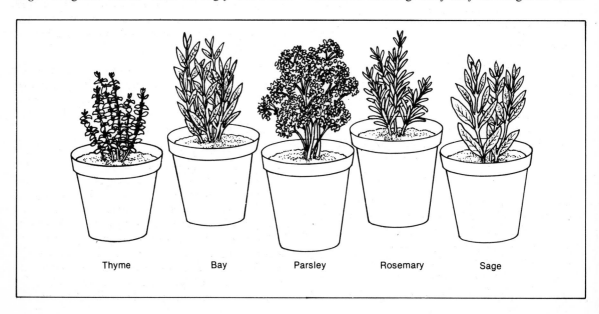

Thyme   Bay   Parsley   Rosemary   Sage

and ground form, but are best bought in small quantities from spice specialists or quality grocers, as ground spices in particular become musty and tasteless after long storage. Whole spices are best for pickles and chutneys, drinks and savoury dishes. Ground spices are for cakes, biscuits and pastries, but can make other dishes cloudy.

Allspice Sometimes known as 'Jamaica pepper' and sold whole and ground, but not to be confused with 'mixed spice' which is a mixture of spices mainly used for cakes and puddings. Allspice subtly combines the flavour of cinnamon, nutmeg and cloves and may be used in savoury and sweet dishes. Whole allspice (which looks like black peppers) is for soups, fish and meat dishes, pickles and preserves. Ground allspice is for cakes, puddings, drinks and fruit mincemeat.

Caraway Seeds are used for flavouring cakes, bread, biscuits, cream cheese and cabbage dishes. Ground caraway may sometimes be bought, and is useful for those who like the flavour but find the small seeds irritating.

Cardamom Sold in pods or as seeds, or ground. The lightly scented spice is used in curry powder, meat dishes, cakes and pastries (it is used frequently in Eastern and Scandinavian dishes). Also adds flavour to hot wine punches and to coffee.

Cayenne Very hot pepper which must be used sparingly. It lifts the flavour of cheese, fish and tomato dishes.

Celery seeds They have a delicate flavour of celery which is useful in soups, sauces, salads, pickles and egg dishes. Celery salt and celery flakes are also available.

Chillies Small, thin peppers which may be used fresh or dried, or ground. Use for curries and rice dishes.

Cinnamon Sold in sticks, as pieces, rough bark or ground. Use sticks or bark for flavouring drinks, preserves, cooked fruit and sugar. Ground cinnamon may be used for cakes, biscuits, pies and milk puddings.

Cloves Sold whole or ground. Use whole cloves in fruit pies, fruit pickles, wine punches and when garnishing hams. Cloves are stuck into a peeled onion when making stock and some sauces. Ground cloves may be used in cakes and biscuits, and improve the flavour of gingerbread.

Coriander Whole or ground spice with a lightly fragrant lemon taste. Used in curry, cakes, biscuits and dishes à la grecque.

Garlic powder Handy if no fresh garlic is available for flavouring meat dishes, poultry and pâté. Garlic salt is also available.

Ginger Dried root and ground ginger are both useful. Use the root well bruised to release the flavour for preserves and wine punches; ground ginger is for cakes and biscuits. Fresh ginger may be bought often in greengrocers and markets and may be frozen — it is mainly used in Chinese and Indian dishes. A small jar of ginger preserved in syrup is useful for adding to cakes, puddings and sauces.

Juniper The berries, which look like peppercorns, smell of gin. Whole berries are used in marinades, but are usually crushed to include in pâtés, and in game and poultry dishes.

Mace The outer husk of nutmeg, which has a similar flavour. The pieces of husk are known as 'blades' and the spice is also sold ground. Whole or ground mace may be used in savoury dishes, preserves, pickles, cakes and biscuits.

Mustard May be sold as seeds, powdered or ready-made. Mustard seeds are used for pickles and ground mustard for pickles and sauces. Made mustard may also be used for flavouring sauces and other savoury dishes.

Nutmeg Sold whole or ground, but the flavour is best when the whole nutmeg is freshly ground for each recipe. Use for meat dishes, particularly cold meats such as pâté and brawn as nutmeg highlights their flavour. Also use on creamed potatoes and on green vegetables, in milk puddings and junkets, in cakes and wine punches.

Paprika Mildly hot and slightly sweet spice ground from sweet red peppers, used to give colour and flavour to meat dishes and cheeses. Useful garnish sprinkled on pale foods such as eggs, fish, chicken and on cocktail canapés.

Pepper Dried black and white peppercorns are sold whole and ground. It is best to grind peppercorns freshly in a peppermill as the packaged ground pepper loses flavour quickly. Whole peppercorns are often used in pickles and savoury dishes. Ground white pepper should be used for delicate pale sauces and dishes as the dark flecks of black pepper look unsightly. Soft green and pink peppercorns preserved in liquid are available in jars and cans and give a delicious flavour to meat, poultry dishes and to sauces.

Saffron A very expensive spice used for colouring and flavouring. It may be bought in powder form (though this may sometimes be adulterated) or in threads or stamens which are soaked in a little water before use to extract flavour and colour. Use in rice dishes, soups and cakes.

Salt This has the quality of bringing out and intensifying the flavour of both savoury and sweet dishes. Sea salt and rock salt have the finest flavour which enhances food, and these are best for table use as well as for cooking. Free-running table salt may be used, but contains a chemical to keep it free-running and this makes it unsuitable for use in pickles, when block salt should be used. Flavoured salts, such as those with celery, garlic and onion, are available, and may be used in savoury dishes.

Oils and essences Many flavoured oils and essences are available, and are particularly useful when making cakes, biscuits, puddings, ices and confectionery. Essences are cheaper, but may be synthetic and impart poor flavour. Oils are expensive and may have to be ordered from a chemist, but only a drop is needed to impart a true flavour. Almond, lemon and peppermint flavouring are most commonly needed.

Colourings A small range of colourings is needed for cakes, puddings and confectionery. Cochineal is the most usual colouring for pink tints. Buy pure vegetable colouring or bottles which are specially labelled for food colouring — yellow and green are the most useful in the kitchen.

Beverages

A range of dry goods, squashes, juices and alcohols is necessary in the kitchen, not only for drinking purposes, but also for recipes. These need not be purchased all at once, but the stock may be increased gradually as need arises.

Coffee Coffee beans should be bought in small quantities and freshly ground. They may be bought loose or in sealed packets, which are more convenient if coffee has to be stored for more than a few days. Choose a breakfast blend for everyday use and a more heavily roasted after-dinner blend. Ground coffee may also be purchased loose or in sealed packs, and choice will again depend on how long it must be kept. Instant coffee may be powder or granules, and there are more-strongly flavoured varieties for after-dinner use. Decaffeinated coffee is available as natural coffee beans or in instant form, and is useful for those who like the flavour of the drink, but find that caffeine does not agree with them. Instant coffee powder or granules may be

dissolved in water for flavouring purposes, or liquid coffee essence may be used. This is sometimes made into drinks, but is very sweet.

Tea A range of leaf teas gives variety to this pleasant drink. Indian or Ceylon tea is for day-round drinking; China teas are very delicately flavoured and usually chosen for the afternoon or at the end of a meal. China tea, or a scented blend, such as Earl Grey, is also suitable for flavouring ices and creams. Teabags are prepared from many different teas and are useful for individual drinks.

Chocolate Cocoa is unsweetened chocolate powder which may be made into a drink, and this is usually the chocolate powder intended for recipe use in cakes and puddings. Drinking chocolate includes dried milk and sugar and is intended for drinking. It should not be substituted for cocoa in recipes as it will produce pale, oversweetened results unless the recipe has been specially formulated for its use.

Juices Fruit and vegetable juices may be packed in cans, cartons or bottles. It is important to check whether these are natural or sweetened when they are to be used in recipes. Frozen, concentrated juices are handy to store as they come in small packs and can be quickly reconstituted for drinking or cooking (some recipes specify the use of undiluted juice). Packet juices of dried powder which has to be reconstituted may be kept in the store cupboard, but these are not usually pure juices and the packet label should be studied carefully.

Alcohol and liqueurs The two alcoholic liquids most often specified in recipes are sherry and brandy. A medium sherry will be most suitable for adding to soups, pâtés, cakes and puddings. A cheap brandy will be good enough for use in both savoury and sweet dishes. One or two liqueurs are often specified in recipes — an orange-flavoured one such as Grand Marnier is the most useful, but miniature bottles of others such as Cherry Brandy and Crème de Menthe may be kept in stock.

Milk, cream and yogurt

Dairy products may be easily obtained fresh each day, but it is often useful to keep milk, cream and yogurt in stock and there are many varieties which serve specific purposes.

Fresh milk Milk which is delivered or available in many shops is usually *pasteurised*, which means that it has been treated with mild heat and will keep up to 3 days in the refrigerator. It will not sour naturally, and is not suitable for making soft cheese, but is useful for all table use and recipes. This milk is distinguished by a silver top, but richer milk from Channel Island and south Devon herds has a gold top. *Untreated* milk will sour quickly and naturally, and will keep only for 2 days in the refrigerator. This milk is packed with a green cap, or with gold-striped green if it comes from Channel Island and south Devon herds. *Homogenised* milk with a red cap has been treated so that the cream remains blended into the milk instead of rising to the surface, and will keep for 3 days in the refrigerator. It is suitable for all purposes except making junket. *Sterilised* milk has been homogenised and then heated for about 20 minutes before cooling. This increases the keeping quality to 7 days in the refrigerator, but the milk slightly loses some vitamin content. It looks richly creamy, but has a slightly 'cooked' flavour. It is good for cooking, but cannot be used for junket, and may be used at the table by those who like the flavour; it is distinguished by a blue foil or crown cap.

Skimmed milk This is available from some dairies and shops, and has the cream removed, so that it is useful for dietary purposes.

Buttermilk Not often available, this is a by-product from butter manufacture. It may be sweet or sour, according to whether fresh or ripened cream has been used for the butter. It may be used for drinking, and is good for some cake, scone and pancake recipes. Cultured buttermilk is a refreshing, fermented drink.

Long-life (UHT) milk This is homogenised milk which has been subjected to very high heat treatment for a short time and which is packaged in cartons. It will keep for many months without refrigeration, and is date-stamped.

Evaporated milk Unsweetened full cream or half-cream milk which has been pasteurised and evaporated until reduced to 60 per cent volume, then homogenised and canned before sterilisation. May be diluted with water to use in drinks and in some recipes. May also be used undiluted as a substitute for cream for table use, ice-creams, sauces and other recipes.

Condensed milk Prepared in a similar way to evaporated milk but with 15 per cent sugar added before evaporation. It is very thick and sweet and rarely used at table, but is suitable for some recipes and confectionery.

Dried milk Milk powder is produced by the evaporation of water from milk by heat or other means. It may be skimmed, partly skimmed, or contain a proportion of cream, so read the labels carefully if you are using it for dietary purposes. The dried powder may be added to beverages, or may be reconstituted with water for table or culinary use. Dried milk powder may be stored in airtight containers for many months, but may deteriorate if left exposed to air. When reconstituted, the milk should be treated like fresh milk.

Single cream This has a minimum fat content of 18 per cent. It may be used for beverages and recipes, but cannot be whipped.

Half (or coffee) cream A light pouring cream with a minimum fat content of 12 per cent. May be used in beverages, but cannot be whipped.

Whipping cream With a minimum fat content of 35 per cent, this is thinner than double cream and whips to a light, fluffy texture. It may also be used in recipes in place of double cream, which can make a dish cheaper although less rich.

Whipped cream Ready-whipped cream with a fat content similar to that of whipping cream, but sweetened. It is sold from chilled cabinets and freezers.

Double cream This has a minimum fat content of 48 per cent, and whips very well. Very fresh cream looks thinner than that which has been in storage for some days. May be sold frozen. Some packs contain 'pieces' of cream, so that only a small portion may be used at a time.

Extra thick cream With the same fat content as double cream, this is homogenised and cannot be whipped.

Clotted cream Thick golden cream, with a minimum fat content of 55 per cent, from the West Country. The cream has been heated and then cooled and the thick top 'crust' taken off for packing in pots, jars or freezer containers. Bottled cream should last up to 10 weeks, but check date markings carefully. Use with fruit, puddings, or with scones.

Soured (or cultured) cream Cream with a minimum fat content of 18 per cent which has been soured by a culture so that it is light and smooth with a sharp fresh taste, and set consistency. Use for baking, cheesecakes, salad dressings, etc.

Canned cream Thick cream which can be kept as an emergency supply for table use and for recipes. It has a slight 'cooked' flavour.

Long-life (UHT) cream Prepared like UHT milk

and packed in handy containers, this cream may be stored without refrigeration, and is date-stamped. Single, whipping and double cream are available, and may be used in the same way as their fresh counterparts.

Non-dairy creamers Substitutes for cream made from non-dairy fats and packed in the form of granules in packets or jars. These are intended for use with coffee and are not for recipe use, but they are very economical to use for the person living alone, or for mass catering, so that liquid milk is not over-ordered and wasted.

Yogurt A cultured milk product which may be natural or fruit-flavoured. All yogurt is 'live' unless the label specifies that it has been pasteurised. Natural yogurt does not freeze well, but fresh fruit yogurts may be frozen for up to 3 months, or may be bought ready-frozen. Check labels to see if yogurt is 'low fat'; fruit yogurts are often heavily sweetened and may be high in calories for those who are dieting. Use yogurt for recipes and for thickening.

Fresh foods

It is wise to buy fresh food at frequent intervals to ensure that it is in peak condition. The most enjoyable meals are those based on food which is in season (e.g. soft fruit in July, red cabbage in the autumn), and seasonal food is also the best value for money, when it is cheap, plentiful and of high quality. It is, for instance, better culinary sense to serve a salad of celery, carrots, cabbage, apples and nuts in the middle of the winter rather than to buy tomatoes, cucumber and lettuce which are expensive and tasteless.

Seasonal Food Calendar

January	
Vegetables	Brussels sprouts, cabbage, cauliflower, celery, chicory, parsnips, turnips.
Fruit	Early rhubarb, cranberries.
Fish	Cockles, cod, haddock, mackerel, mussels, scallops, sprats, whiting.
Meat, poultry and game	Hare, pheasant, pigeon.

February	
Vegetables	Brussels sprouts, cabbage, cauliflower, celery, chicory, leeks, parsnips.
Fruit	Cooking apples, grapefruit, Seville oranges for marmalade, early rhubarb.
Fish	Cockles, mussels.
Meat, poultry and game	Hare.

March	
Vegetables	Broccoli, Brussels sprouts, cabbage, cauliflower, celery, parsnips.
Fruit	Early rhubarb.
Fish	Cockles, mussels, mackerel, scallops.
Meat, poultry and game	Spring lamb.

April

Vegetables	Broccoli, Brussels sprouts, parsnips, spinach.
Fruit	Rhubarb.
Fish	Cockles, mackerel, prawns, whitebait.
Meat, poultry and game	Spring lamb.

May

Vegetables	Asparagus, broccoli, carrots, cauliflower, peas, spinach.
Fruit	Rhubarb.
Fish	Crab, herring, plaice, prawns, whitebait.
Meat, poultry and game	Spring lamb.

June

Vegetables	Asparagus, broad beans, cabbage, carrots, cauliflower, corn on the cob, French beans, globe artichokes, peas, potatoes, spinach, tomatoes.
Fruit	Cherries, gooseberries, loganberries, peaches, raspberries, rhubarb, strawberries.
Fish	Crab, herring, plaice, prawns, shrimps, whitebait.

July

Vegetables	Asparagus, aubergines, broad beans, cabbage, carrots, cauliflower, corn on the cob, courgettes, French beans, globe artichokes, herbs, peas, peppers, potatoes, spinach, tomatoes.
Fruit	Apricots, black currants, cherries, figs, gooseberries, loganberries, melons, peaches, plums, raspberries, red currants, strawberries.
Fish	Crab, haddock, plaice, prawns, shrimps.

August

Vegetables	Aubergines, cabbage, cauliflower, corn on the cob, French beans, globe artichokes, peas, peppers, runner beans, spinach, tomatoes.
Fruit	Apples, blackberries, damsons, figs, melons, peaches, pears, plums.
Fish	Crab, haddock, plaice, prawns.
Meat, poultry and game	Hare.

September

Vegetables	Aubergines, Brussels sprouts, cabbage, cauliflower, celery, corn on the cob, courgettes, leeks, onions, parsnips, peppers, runner beans, spinach, swedes, tomatoes.
Fruit	Apples, blackberries, damsons, grapes, peaches, pears, plums.
Fish	Cockles, crab, haddock, herring, mussels, plaice, prawns.
Meat, poultry and game	Hare, pheasant.

October

Vegetables	Brussels sprouts, cabbage, celery, leeks, parnips, spinach, swedes, turnips.
Fruit	Apples, blackberries, damsons, grapes, nuts, pears, pomegranates, pumpkins, quinces.
Fish	Cod, haddock, herring, mackerel, plaice, scallops, sprats.
Meat, poultry and game	Hare, pheasant.

November

Vegetables	Brussels sprouts, cabbage, celery, Jerusalem artichokes, leeks, parnips, swedes, turnips.
Fruit	Apples, cranberries, grapes, pears, pomegranates, tangerines.
Fish	Cockles, cod, haddock, herring, mackerel, mussels, plaice, scallops, sprats, whiting.
Meat, poultry and game	Hare, pheasant.

December

Vegetables	Brussels sprouts, cabbage, celery, parsnips, swedes, turnips.
Fruit	Apples, grapes.
Fish	Cockles, cod, haddock, herring, mackerel, mussels, plaice, scallops, sprats, whiting.
Meat, poultry and game	Hare, pheasant.

Meat

Meat may be bought from the butcher or the chilled cabinet of a store (or ready-frozen to be transferred at once to the freezer cabinet). Try to choose a cut of meat which is suitable for the way in which you wish to cook it, and allow 4-6 oz (100-150 g) boneless meat or 8-10 oz (225-300 g) meat on the bone per portion.

Beef Beef comes from a larger and older animal than other meats, and the carcass is hung for 6-10 days to develop full flavour. Beef should look fresh and slightly moist, with firm, dry fat. Roasting joints should be smooth and velvety in texture; coarse lean indicates stewing meat, but very coarse beef will be extremely tough. Meat from the front of the animal has developed stronger muscles as this is the active part of the body, so forequarter cuts need long, slow cooking with added liquid, to tenderise them. The more expensive cuts for roasting are sirloin, fillet, rump, topside, fore ribs, wing ribs and back ribs. Sirloin, fillet, rump and thin cuts of top ribs may be grilled as steaks. The economy cuts are top rump (sometimes called thick flank), flank, brisket and silverside for pot roasting; shin, leg, neck and clod, chuck, blade and skirt for stewing. Chuck, blade and skirt are best for pies and puddings. When buying mince, check that it is not full of fat as this will spoil dishes and be wasteful, as so much melted fat must be drained off — it is better to choose a piece of steak and mince it yourself although this will be more expensive than buying mince prepared by the butcher.

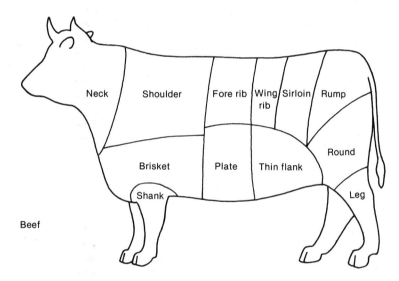

Beef

Veal This is very lean and has a delicate flavour, and is most suitable for moist methods of cooking with the addition of fat or cream. It should be moist, finely grained and pale pink in colour. It is not hung before use, but only chilled. Joints need additional fat for roasting, and the shoulder, leg and breast may be boned and rolled before roasting. Pie veal is cut from the leg, shin and neck and may also be used for stews. Thin slices from the leg may be fried and finished with sauce, or stuffed, rolled and braised. Escallops are thin slices cut across the grain, and used for frying.

Pork Pork is not hung, but chilled only before sale. It should be eaten as fresh as possible, and the flesh should be firm, dry and pale pink, with a thin covering of creamy white fat and smooth, supple rind. If you like crisp crackling on joints, ask the butcher to score the rind with a sharp blade. All cuts of pork are excellent roasted on the bone or boned and rolled. Leg, loin and shoulder are used, and may easily be divided into smaller joints. The loin may also be divided into chops. Beneath the loin is a long, round strip of lean meat called the tenderloin which may be roasted, fried or enclosed in pastry. Spare rib chops are cut from the shoulder and give portions of lean meat on the bone; spare ribs for Chinese cookery are rib bones with a thin covering of meat and fat. Other economy cuts are the hand which comes from the lower end of the shoulder and may be roasted or cubed for pies and casseroles (when attached to the trotter this is known as 'hand and spring'). Streaky belly pork may be roasted whole as a joint, cut into slices for grilling or frying, or used in a casserole.

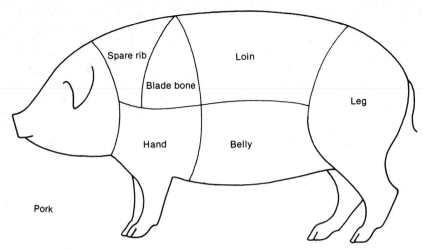

Pork

Lamb This meat is hung for 5-7 days before sale. English lamb is in season from June to the end of the year; New Zealand lamb arrives then' and continues through the spring. English lambs tend to be a little larger than imported ones. Very young lamb has pale pink lean, and this darkens to deep pink as an animal ages; fat should be white and firm. A hogget is a year-old lamb, and joints are larger with a rich, full flavour. Mutton from an older animal is seldom seen, but can be very good roasted and in pies. The leg is the prime roasting joint and may be divided into two smaller joints. The shoulder is an economical joint with more bone and fat, and the meat may also be used cubed in recipes. The loin may be roasted whole, or halved, and can also be boned and stuffed, or divided into loin chops. Larger chump chops come from the leg end of the loin. Best end of neck consists of 5 or 6 cutlets which may be divided for grilling or frying, or left whole as a joint. The whole neck consisting of scrag and middle neck is suitable for casseroles and hot-pots. The breast has tasty meat containing rib bones and may be boned, stuffed and rolled as a joint, or cut into pieces for recipes, but it is a rather fatty cut.

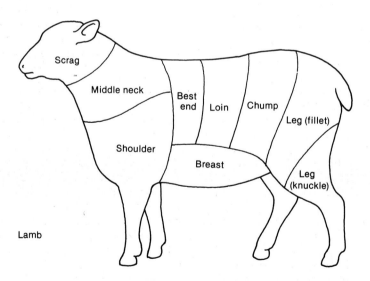

Lamb

Offal This is lean and nutritious, and must be cooked within 24 hours of purchase. While it is all delicious, there are some variations according to the animal from which the offal has been obtained.

Liver may be bought in the piece or ready-sliced. Calf's liver is the best with a fine texture, and it is tender and full of flavour. Lamb's liver is slightly coarser. Pig's liver is darker in colour and stronger in flavour, but is very good for baking and for making pâté. Ox liver is coarse and strongly flavoured but very cheap. It may be used for casseroles and braises, but is not suitable for frying or grilling. *Kidneys* are richly flavoured and delicious when grilled, fried or used in casseroles. Lamb's kidneys are small, weighing 1-2 oz (25-50 g) each, so each person will need two or three. The kidneys should be very fresh and free from smell when purchased. Pig's kidneys are slightly larger, about 3-5 oz (75-125 g) each, and with a firm texture and stronger flavour. One kidney should be enough for each person. Veal kidney is larger and consists of segments joined to a central core, and has a delicate flavour. These are the most expensive kidneys, but each person will need only about 4 oz (100 g). Ox kidney is also segmented, and is large, dark and strongly flavoured. These kidneys are not suitable for grilling or frying, but are best when mixed with steak for a pie or pudding — allow 6 oz (150 g) kidney to 1 lb (450 g) steak. *Hearts* are very lean and give good value for money. Lamb's hearts are quite small, about 4-8 oz (100-225 g), and one will be enough for each person. They are usually stuffed and braised or pot-roasted, in the same way as pig's hearts, which are double in size, so that one heart will give two servings. Calf's heart is about three times the size of lamb's heart, so allow about 6-8 oz (150-225 g) per serving. Ox heart is very large and may be sold in slices or large pieces. The meat needs very long, slow cooking, and 6-8 oz (150-225 g) will make a good portion with vegetables.

Oxtail is sold by weight, and 12 oz (350 g) should be allowed for each portion. It is cut into sections and usually a whole tail is tied together for sale. *Tripe* is the stomach lining of an ox and is sold blanched and partly cooked. It may be plain in texture or with a deep pattern like a honeycomb, and it is extremely nutritious and cheap. Allow 6 oz (150 g) per person, and just rinse in cold water before preparing a recipe. *Sweetbreads* are the pancreas glands of lambs and calves and have a delicate flavour and texture. They must be bought very fresh or frozen, and 4-6 oz (100-150 g) is enough per person.

Tongue is lean tender meat and it is much cheaper to prepare at home than to buy in cans or from a delicatessen. Ox tongue weighs 3-4 lb (1.5-2 kg) and is usually sold salted so that it must be soaked for 2-3 hours before cooking. Allow about 6 oz (150 g) per person. The same quantity is needed of lamb's or calf's tongues which are sold fresh, usually by weight, and which are of course far smaller than an ox tongue.

Ham and bacon For all practical purposes, ham and bacon are the same thing — cured pork. The ham is the upper part of the leg, and is sometimes described as gammon. Bacon may be cut from this area or from the back, and may be in a joint or rashers. Any joint makes good economic sense, as it can provide a hot meal and a number of cold meals, and every piece can be used. *Streaky* bacon comes from the belly and combines fat and lean in about equal proportions. A joint is excellent for boiling, and rashers may be grilled, fried, or used for paté. *Back* rashers are lean, and are best for grilling or frying, but may be cut thick to use as chops, or cubed for use in casseroles or pies. *Middle or throughcut* rashers combine back and streaky bacon, and give a large double rasher for grilling or frying; the cut may be rolled and used as a joint. *Collar* bacon may be used as an inexpensive joint, or can be cut into rather large, ungainly rashers. *Middle gammon* is the upper leg and is lean and meaty, but quite expensive. It may be used as a joint, or cut into thick rashers or steaks for grilling and frying. *Gammon hock* is a succulent joint with plenty of lean, while *prime forehock* is a shoulder joint which is a good mixture of fat and lean.

Salt beef and pork Salt beef makes an excellent meal when boiled with vegetables, and is just as good cold. *Silverside* and *brisket* are the two joints usually salted, but it is important to give the butcher some idea of when you will want to collect the meat so that he can allow enough time to salt your chosen joint. *Salt pork* makes a good meal on its own when boiled, but is more often used as the base for pâté, soups or other recipes. The hock and belly are most often salted.

Delicatessen meats Many ready-cooked meats are now available from butchers and chilled counters in stores. Vacuum-packed meats are handy for outdoor meals, but the contents are often heavily salted. Freshly sliced meat or sausage should come from fresh-looking pieces which are not dried out or discoloured. By law, they should not be displayed anywhere near uncooked meats, because of cross-infection, so beware of shops where these meats are carelessly handled. The slices should also be lifted out with tongs or a wide knife, not with the assistant's hands.

Poultry and game
Poultry may be chosen fresh or from the freezer cabinet. Game is usually bought complete with feathers or fur, but a game dealer will prepare it for the table for a small extra charge.

Turkey   Turkey is economical for entertaining, as there is plenty of flesh in proportion to bone — the larger the bird the higher proportion of lean. Be sure that the turkey that you buy will fit your oven. A 10-13 lb (5-7 kg) bird will serve 10-12 people for one hot meal. When buying a fresh bird, avoid one which looks dark and scrawny, but choose one with a broad breast, and if possible choose a hen bird, which has a finer flavour. If using a frozen bird, avoid one which has areas of browning, 'freezer burn', which can indicate long and improper storage, or dehydration. Remember that frozen turkeys need a long time to defrost (about 36 hours for a 9 lb (4.5 kg) bird).

Goose   Goose will probably be fresh rather than frozen. Make sure that it is a plump young bird with supple yellow legs and traces of down, and a soft underbill. A goose loses half its weight in cooking, and a 10 lb (5 kg) bird will feed 8 people.

Duck   Duck may be fresh or frozen, and a bird should be broad-breasted as the carcass is large in relation to the amount of flesh carried. When buying a fresh bird, look for one with soft webbing between the feet and a soft underbill. A young bird about 8 months old is best for eating and a 5 lb (2.5 kg) bird will serve 4 people if carved carefully.

Chicken   Fresh or frozen, chicken is an economical choice as it may be used for hot and cold meals and soup, and all scraps of flesh can be used. A chicken of 3 lb (1.5 kg) will feed 4 people for a hot meal and leave enough for a second dish. A 5 lb (2.5 kg) bird should feed 6 people well with plenty of leftovers. At Christmas, a large capon of 8 lb (4 kg) weight will provide a good alternative to turkey. Remember that a *broiler bird* is one which has been intensively reared; a *boiler* is an elderly bird suitable for slow, moist cooking, which is usually cheaper than a roasting bird, and is excellent for casseroles, pies and made-up dishes. Poultry may also be bought cut into pieces. A single piece of chicken or duck is enough for one person, while a turkey piece will usually feed 2 people. It is also possible to buy sliced breast meat and boned, rolled poultry joints, which can be useful for making up recipes, or where a large quantity of meat is not needed.

Game   Game is available only in specified seasons of the year (except pigeon and rabbit which are classed as vermin), and is bought from a registered game dealer, who may also be a butcher or a fishmonger. Most game has to be hung to tenderise and develop full flavour, and it is important to know when birds or animals have been shot and whether the dealer has already hung them for the required time. *Grouse* (12 August to 10 December) is best roasted, unless very old or badly shot. One young bird will feed 2 people; an older bird will do for 3. The young birds have pointed wings and rounded spurs. *Pheasant* (1 October to 1 February) are the easiest game for the amateur cook to tackle, as chicken and pheasant recipes are nearly all interchangeable, with the well-hung pheasant tasting like a slightly more 'gamey' chicken. A young cock bird has rounded spurs in the first year, short pointed ones in the second year, and sharp long ones when older. A young hen bird has soft feet and dark feathers, and is smaller than the cock, but less dry and more tender, with a good flavour. One large bird will feed 4 people, but do not use an old bird for roasting. *Partridge* (1 September to 1 February) is not seen so often at the dealer, but is a delicious bird. First-year birds have the first flight feather pointed at the tip, not rounded, and as with other game, the young birds are best for roasting. One bird will serve 2 people. *Venison* (late June to January) is a very lean meat, tasting like rich beef, and may be bought fresh and well-hung, or is often found in freezer cabinets. Large joints come from the haunch for roasting; smaller pieces are best casseroled, cooked in pies or other made-up dishes, but all venison needs marinading before use, and joints may be larded as there is little natural fat. *Hare* (September to February) is a large animal and sometimes single pieces may be bought. The young hare has pointed teeth and fresh-looking fur; older animals are scruffy-looking, with cracked brown teeth. A hare will easily feed 10 people, and the saddle can be roasted; other joints are usually casseroled, used in soup or in pâté. *Rabbit* has a more delicate flavour than hare, and a young one may be roasted. Single leg joints may be boned and fried in breadcrumbs and they taste like chicken, but rabbit pieces may be casseroled, used in pie or pâté. *Pigeons* are lean birds with dark, rich flesh, and one bird will feed 1-2 people, according to recipe. Fat, young birds may be roasted, but larger ones will be dry and are better for pies, casseroles and pâtés.

   Wildfowl may be found in some areas, and there are geese, members of the duck family, snipe and widgeon to be enjoyed. The flesh of these birds is rich and strongly flavoured, and they are best roasted, but may be braised or casseroled. Small birds (e.g. teal, snipe, widgeon) will feed 1 person; duck 2-3 people; goose 4-5 people.

Fish

Fresh fish may be bought from the fishmonger, although frozen fish is available in freezer cabinets. The latter is ready to eat, and portions will be indicated on packets.

What is often described as 'wet' fish is divided into two categories — white fish (e.g. plaice, cod, haddock) and oily fish (e.g. herring, mackerel, salmon). All fresh fish should be firm, with scales firmly attached and bright, shiny eyes. Gills should be clear red, not greyish in colour. If white fish looks slightly blue or green, it is stale, and this can also be recognised if the piece has a rank, 'fishy' smell. When buying a white fish, allow for each portion 10 oz (300 g) whole, ungutted fish; or 8 oz (225 g) gutted fish with the head on; 6 oz (150 g) fish steaks; or 5 oz (125 g) fillets. For oily fish, allow 8 oz (225 g) whole, ungutted fish; 7 oz (175 g) gutted fish with head; 5 oz (125 g) steaks; and 4 oz (100 g) fillets.

Smoked fish such as mackerel, trout, kippers and salmon may be freshly prepared or frozen (some 'fresh' fish may have been thawed for sale, so check carefully if you want to freeze it yourself). Smoked fish should be firm and bright and fresh-looking, not dried-up and dark. Allow 1 whole trout or kipper per person; 2 kipper fillets or 1 mackerel fillet will be enough for a single portion.

Shellfish are divided into crustacea (e.g. crabs, lobsters) and molluscs (e.g. mussels, cockles) but all must be very fresh when bought and eaten in 24 hours. *Crustacea* are normally sold cooked and dressed ready for table except in seaside areas. One small crab is a single portion, but larger ones may be shared into 2-3 portions. A small lobster may be a single portion, but generally half a lobster is served. Prawns and shrimps are bought by the 1 lb (450 g), and portions are best judged by eye, according to appetite. *Molluscs* may be sold live or prepared, and may be sold by weight or by the pint (600 ml) measure. When buying mussels in the shell 1 pt (600 ml) will be one portion; as with smaller crustacea, the small molluscs such as cockles and winkles must be judged by eye according to appetite, unless a quantity is specified in a recipe. Mussels should be tightly closed when bought, and it is always wise to buy shellfish from a reliable source and not from casual sellers.

Cheese

Always try to buy cheese from someone who takes a pride in selling it, and who stores it properly in cool, but not refrigerated conditions. Look for hard cheese (e.g. English farmhouse or Dutch) which can be cut from a large cheese, and avoid small, plastic-wrapped portions which become sweaty and evil-tasting. Buy small pieces of cheese regularly rather than one large piece, as it is not easy to store in perfect condition. Soft cheeses deteriorate quickly and should be bought in peak condition or when slightly under-ripe rather than when runny and smelly. 1-2 oz (25-50 g) cheese will be enough to serve at a snack meal, or after a main course. If catering for a party, allow 3-4 oz (75-100 g) per head.

Vegetables and salads

Because so many vegetables are now imported, most can be obtained throughout the year, but there are still guidelines for buying good quality items. Broad, French and runner beans are best when young and small. Peas should be bright green and full, without any wrinkling or yellowing of the pod. Cabbages of various types should be crisp, bright green and firm; sprouts should be small, firm and dark green, without being overblown, wilting or yellow. Cauliflowers and broccoli should have bright green, fresh leaves and creamy-looking curds. When choosing leeks, look for firm, straight medium-thick ones, which have been trimmed at the top; onions should have papery skins and no green shoots. Root vegetables should be firm with no soft brown patches or green crowns, and no cracks or spade damage. Potatoes should be clean, without damage or green patches.

Lettuce should be crisp and green, without wilted or discoloured leaves. Tomatoes should be firm and bright red, but not over-ripe or squashed. Chicory should be crisp, fat, and white with pale yellow tips (when the tips turn green, the chicory has been packed for some time and is too old). Cucumbers should be firm and well-coloured without soft ends.

Fruit

As with vegetables, many fruit are now available all the year. Citrus fruit should be heavy for its size, but be careful when buying thick-skinned fruits as there is often very little flesh inside. Bananas should be golden yellow and firm as they ripen very quickly in a warm room and quickly develop a dark-spotted skin and a very soft flesh. Grapes should have a soft bloom on the skin, and look firm, without any bad fruit on the bunch. Apples and pears should be crisp but well ripe and well shaped — there is considerable wastage when small fruit has to be peeled and cored for recipes. When buying plums, apricots, cherries, and peaches, look for good-sized fruit which is ripe but not squashy, has a bloom on skins, and has no soft brown patches. Look over soft fruit carefully, as if containers are stained, it usually means that the fruit has been picked for some time and the lower layers are soft and unattractive. Melons must be chosen carefully if they are to be used at once. Gentle pressure at the base away from the stem should give a slight yielding indentation when the fruit is ripe; brown patches indicate that it is over-ripe. Pineapples should be richly golden all over without green or soft brown patches. When buying avocado pears, it is wise to buy slightly under-ripe and firm ones a few days before use as they ripen to perfect softness at room temperature, but are seldom in peak condition in the shops.

Alternative Ingredients

Cream or yogurt
Yogurt can be used as an alternative to cream but is too unstable to be used without treatment and should therefore be stabilised.

For approximately 2 pt (1.2 litre) stabilised yogurt, put yogurt into pan and beat. Fold in 1 stiffly beaten egg white, 1 tablespoon cornflour mixed with a little water and $\frac{1}{2}$ teaspoon salt. Bring slowly to the boil and simmer for about 10 minutes, stirring to stop burning on the bottom of the pan. Cool and use. Yogurt cannot be used instead of whipped cream but only generally where cream is needed as a thickener or to finish a dish. It has a more acid flavour than cream, which should be borne in mind when balancing the flavours.

Yogurt made with skimmed milk is a very low fat alternative to cream, in low cholesterol diets. It may be used in its stabilised form for sauces, ice-cream, and other dishes which usually contain a lot of cream. Stabilised yogurt can be used as an alternative to milk in such dishes as baked custards, sauces and soups.

Unsweetened evaporated milk can be used as an alternative to cream. It will whip if boiled in the tin for 20 minutes, then allowed to cool in a refrigerator for 24 hours before use.

Wine or cider
In most recipes which include wine, the wine is actually cooked and thus the alcohol content is vaporised. Therefore the difference between the alcohol content of cider and wine does not make any difference to the cooking process. The difference lies in the taste achieved by their addition to the dish; and to a very limited extent in the acid content of the two liquids. When the liquor is cooked, the alcohol disappears and a form of 'essence' is left behind with the concentrated taste of the liquor. This is the main reason for using wine

or cider so that they can be used as alternatives. Where one is indicated in a particular recipe, it is usually with the final taste of the dish in mind. Experiment is the best answer to the use of these two liquors as alternatives.

The use of wine or cider in marinades is also related to the final taste achieved. The slight difference in the acidity of the two liquors makes little or no difference in the tenderising or preserving quality of the marinade.

Wines and ciders come in varying degrees of dryness and sweetness and if one is being substituted for the other it might be as well to try to balance these attributes of the liquor. When a little wine is added to a dish at the last minute, as in consommé, cider is not a suitable substitute.

Chocolate or cocoa
Both chocolate and cocoa derive from the seeds of the cacoa tree. Chocolate is a 'paste' or 'cake' formed from the roasted and ground seed and sweetened. Cocoa is the unsweetened powder from the roasted and ground seeds. Pale coloured or 'milk' chocolate is chocolate with the addition of milk or milk extracts. The basic differences are that chocolate is solid and sweetened and needs to be melted in most cases before use in cooking, whereas cocoa is an unsweetened powder and needs to be dissolved in a liquid such as milk or water before it is used in cooking.

When cocoa is to be substituted for chocolate in cooking, it needs to be sweetened to the same degree as chocolate. If chocolate is indicated by weight in the recipe, the substituted cocoa should be calculated with all its additions, not as dry powder. Chocolate contains a small amount of 'cacoa butter' which is a vegetable fat. When substituting cocoa for chocolate the addition of a very small amount of butter or vegetable fat gives a smoother and more chocolate-like result.

If chocolate is being substituted for cocoa in a recipe, it should be remembered that weight for weight the cocoa powder is much stronger than block chocolate. This means that if an amount of chocolate is added to a recipe equal to that of the cocoa indicated, the result will be much weaker in flavour. If a recipe indicates the use of dry cocoa powder, it should be remembered that melted chocolate will produce some liquid. This should be allowed for by the slight reduction of any liquids such as milk, water, wine or spirits in the recipe. It should also be remembered that chocolate already contains some sugar and therefore the amount of sugar in the recipe should be slightly reduced as the balance of the recipe will be otherwise upset.

Stock or stock cubes

When stock is indicated in a recipe, an equivalent quantity of stock may be made up using stock cubes or concentrate to the quantities indicated on the package. Cubes can be crumbled directly into the other ingredients, but the correct amount of liquid should also be added, as the flavour will otherwise be too concentrated and the dish will be spoiled. Stock cubes and concentrates tend to be more salty than stock and seasoning should be adjusted to allow for this.

A better result can be obtained from the use of stock cubes and concentrates by simmering them with a mixture of roughly diced root vegetables for a minimum of 30 minutes. If this method is used, allowance should be made for the evaporation of water during the process, otherwise the stock will be very strong in flavour.

Alternatives to stock can include (a) the strained water from vegetables; (b) cider or wine and water; (c) commercial consommé thinned with water or wine. In a few cases, such as some soups, milk or milk with water may be used.

The juices from meat cooked in the oven or on top of the stove may be mixed with water and make a good substitute for stock. While the pan is still hot, swill it round with hot water, or the strained water from cooked vegetables. Check the seasoning carefully as the salt content will be higher than in an ordinary stock and pour off any excess fat.

Fresh/canned/dried fruit or vegetables

When canned fruit or vegetables are substituted for fresh, strain off the liquid from the can before use. Make an allowance in the seasoning for the fact that many vegetables are canned in a brine and will therefore be more salty than their fresh counterparts.

Canned vegetables and fruit have already received a certain amount of cooking during processing and will therefore require very little more than gentle heating in a recipe. They will otherwise collapse and in general they should be added late in the cooking. This holds true for canned pulses although they will stand a greater amount of cooking.

Canned fruits are generally processed in a heavy sugar syrup. When substituted for fresh fruit, they should be drained of this liquid and rinsed in clean water to remove any excess. Even with this treatment, a small amount will remain, and a slight reduction should be made in the amount of sugar in a recipe to retain a balance. The flavour of canned fruit and vegetables will be somewhat different from that of their fresh equivalents and will

therefore affect the final flavour of the dish. This should be allowed for when adding seasoning or other flavour-enhancing ingredients.

When dried fruit or vegetables are substituted for fresh, in most cases they should be soaked before addition to the recipe. An equivalent soaked weight rather than dried weight should be added. Reconstituted fruit and vegetables will be more delicate than fresh, and will rarely require as long a cooking time. The flavour will also be different, and so slightly different results can be expected.

Dried reconstituted fruits very often have a higher sugar content, which should be balanced by a reduction in the sugar required in the recipe. Some dried vegetables can be added directly to a recipe, although allowance should be made for the amount of extra liquid from the recipe which will be absorbed by them while they reconstitute. Check the package label to make sure that the contents can be added to a recipe without soaking.

Tomatoes: fresh/canned/concentrate/juice

There is no substitute for raw fresh tomato in such dishes as salads, as the tinned varieties are too soft to be presented in this way.

In cooked dishes, tinned tomatoes may be used as an alternative to fresh, and plum tomatoes are best for this purpose. They should be strained of all their juice (if not required) and then used as the recipe indicates. Plum tomatoes can be chopped or used whole as they will retain their shape and texture almost as well as fresh tomatoes. Good quality canned tomatoes are best as they tend to be less damaged in the preserving process.

Concentrated tomatoes (tomato purée) should be used sparingly as an alternative to fresh or canned tomatoes since as much as 4 lb (2 kg) tomatoes are used to make 1 oz (25 g) purée. Most purées have only a little preservative added. Canned or fresh tomatoes may be used as a substitute for purée, by reduction over a low heat until they reach the required concentration.

Tomato juice may be used as an alternative to canned or fresh tomatoes although it lacks their concentration of flavour and bulk. Salt may have been added to the juice, and allowance should be made for this in the ingredients. Juice cannot generally be used as an alternative to concentrate because of its thinness. The juice can usually be used when the recipe calls for a large proportion of liquid, as in stews. Juice may be concentrated by boiling, but much of the flavour will be spoiled.

In an emergency a little tomato ketchup can be used to give colour and flavour. It does, however, contain many ingredients other than tomatoes, including sugar and acid and these will change the flavour of the dish.

Baking powder or self-raising flour

If plain flour is indicated in a recipe, self-raising flour should not be used as an alternative, as it contains a raising agent, and will radically alter the result of the recipe.

Self-raising flour may, however, be substituted for a combination of plain flour and baking powder and vice-versa. The basic equivalents for 1 lb (450 g) self-raising flour are:

1 lb plain flour plus 4-5 level teaspoons baking powder	Fruit Cake
1 lb plain flour plus 2 level teaspoons baking powder	Madeira Cake
1 lb plain flour plus 5-6 level teaspoons baking powder	Light Sponge

Baking powder can be substituted with bicarbonate of soda with tartaric acid, or cream of tartar. The proportion is generally 3 parts bicarbonate of soda to 2 parts cream of tartar. The proportion of cream of tartar is slightly less if there are other acid ingredients in the recipe such as yogurt or soured cream.

The raising agent in self-raising flour is designed to work quite slowly so that the flour can be stored without deterioration. Baking powder or the soda and cream of tartar mixture will start to react immediately in contact with liquid. Recipes using these ingredients should therefore be placed in the heat of the oven as soon as possible after mixing, or the raising abilities of the mixture quickly begin to fail.

Thickening agents

In many cases, thickening agents are interchangeable. However, care should be taken to understand their properties in relation to the cooking process used, as they may react badly sometimes.

Flour is very rarely added directly to a mixture to thicken as it will cause lumping if added directly to a hot liquid. It is usually combined in one of the following ways:

- *Flour and water* A small amount of flour is mixed to a smooth paste with water and is added slowly and carefully to just-boiling liquid, stirring vigorously all the time. This can be a difficult process and can lead to small, very hard lumps in the liquid. The mixture should be kept at boiling point for at least 5 minutes to ensure that the starch granules have all burst, releasing the starch to act as thickener. If this is not done, an 'uncooked' floury flavour will be present in the food.

- *Beurre manié* Flour is worked together with margarine or butter until a soft, malleable mixture is achieved. This is broken into small balls and stirred vigorously into liquid just under boiling point. Again this mixture should be kept at boiling point for at least 5 minutes to ensure the flour is cooked. This method is particularly effective when a sauce or gravy is found to be too thin, as a little can be added at a time.

- *Roux* (see page 129, Sauces).

- *Tossing meat in flour* This has the advantage of cooking the flour early in the process, ensuring that it is fully absorbed into the flavours and texture of the finished dish. This method is particularly used when preparing a stew.

Cornflour needs to be mixed with water to a very smooth paste before it is added to either hot or cold liquids. If the mixture is left after mixing before it is cooked, it will separate, forming a thick layer in the bottom of the mixing bowl, and this will need to be remixed. Cornflour used as a thickener creates a much more glutinous texture and is more transparent than any flour mixture. Cornflour can be boiled when it has been mixed with liquids.

Arrowroot is much less stable than cornflour, and is generally used as a thickening agent in very light foods, or in diets of people with very delicate stomach conditions. It should not be boiled more than momentarily, as it will separate from the liquids losing its ability to act as a thickener.

Egg yolks are useful thickeners and use may be made of leftover yolks. 4 egg yolks will thicken 1 pt (600 ml) liquid to a thin custard consistency, which will set firm when cold. Once added to liquid the mixture should not be boiled, as this will coagulate the protein in the yolk, causing separation or curdling. The texture and consistency of liquids thickened by egg yolk is completely different from any of the flour combinations, being non-glutinous, smoother and less stable.

Very thick cream can be used as a mild thickener. Like egg yolk, it should never be boiled once added to a liquid, unless there is some flour in the mixture which acts as a stabiliser. The thickening effect of cream is very limited, and needs very careful handling to prevent curdling.

Gelatine is best known as a thickener or setting agent for cold dishes. However, a gravy or meat soup may be thickened to a certain extent if gelatinous bones or pork skin are added in the early stages of cooking. These can be removed before the dish is served.

Emergency Meals

There are many occasions when an emergency meal is needed and there may be little fresh or refrigerated food available. Sensible use of the store cupboard and freezer can ensure a quick meal which is pleasant to eat.

The store cupboard

Pasta	Spaghetti, tagliatelli, cannelloni, dried or canned ravioli
Canned vegetables	Petits pois, tomatoes, tomato purée, sweetcorn kernels, button mushrooms, pulses (e.g. chickpeas, red kidney beans), new potatoes
Canned fruit	Peaches, pineapple, apricots, black cherries, pears
Dried milk	
Canned meats	Ham, pâté, mince, stewed beef
Canned fish	Sardines, tuna, mackerel, salmon, shrimps
Dried goods	Vegetables, fruit, instant potato
Flavourings	Herbs and spices in airtight, light-free containers, gherkins, capers, olives, lemon juice
Packets	Soups, stuffings, sauces
Canned soups	Cream soups, consommé
Parmesan cheese	

The contents of the store cupboard will largely depend on whether a freezer is available, as cooked dishes and a wider range of raw materials may be kept in the freezer. Keep a checklist of quick shortcuts (see below) and emergency recipes pinned inside the store cupboard door. Always replace emergency stores as quickly as possible.

The freezer

Cook extra quantities of such dishes as stews and casseroles, and pack the surplus for the freezer. Small chicken portions and pieces of fish can be cooked from frozen as can small quantities of good quality minced meat and thin slices of meat. Freeze leftover portions of meat or poultry in gravy or sauce. Freeze fruit and vegetables when cheap and in season.

Freeze basic sauces such as béchamel and brown sauce bases as long as they do not contain cream or egg yolks as these will curdle when unfrozen and reheated. Concentrated frozen stock can be used as a base for soups and sauces.

Pasta dishes and Shepherd's Pie may be made or bought for the freezer. Keep a small variety of ice-creams and sorbets, with containers of home-made sauces. Puff and shortcrust pastry to extend portions of meat, poultry or fish are very useful. Keep a variety of bread and rolls, including sliced bread which toasts straight from the freezer.

Quick recipes

Tinned or packet soups can be made very much more interesting with the addition of extra ingredients.

- Add a little sherry to consommé when it has been heated.
- Add some sweated onion and leek to cream of vegetable or chicken soup, with some chicken stock to give a lighter, more tasty result.
- Add some cream, lemon juice and finely chopped parsley to tomato soup and serve with freshly made croûtons.

Canned meat can be improved with the addition of a few freshly fried mushrooms, herbs and a dash of wine or brandy, *or* with the addition of a little tomato purée, chopped parsley and finely chopped and sweated onion. These meats can be quickly made into a pie with a covering of puff pastry glazed with egg yolk. If pastry is not available, cover with thin slices of bread soaked in a mixture of mustard and milk, and placed in the oven to dry and brown.

Canned tuna can be served cold, dressed with mayonnaise, chopped parsley, celery and walnuts. It may be mixed with a little cold cooked pasta, parsley, mayonnaise and a generous dash of lemon juice.

Canned sardines can be placed in a dish, covered with a layer of breadcrumbs mixed with finely chopped garlic and parsley and grilled until the top is crisp and brown and the sardines hot. They can be served cold as an hors d'oeuvre with a vinegar-and-oil dressing garnished with sliced gherkins and capers.

Canned fruit is enhanced if drained and allowed to soak in wine or liqueur before serving ice cold with plenty of cream. Half peaches, with the centres filled with soft brown sugar and a tiny dash of brandy and placed under a very hot grill provide another quick pudding.

Small additions to packet stuffings and sauces can completely change their flavour and character. Try a little grated orange or lemon rind or juice;

fresh melted butter; a little cream; Parmesan cheese; fresh finely chopped herbs; freshly ground spices; crumbled cooked ham or bacon.

Overcoming Disasters

Even the best cooks are faced with disaster sometimes. Many calamaties may be retrieved at once although a few are better abandoned for later treatment.

Curdled sauces

Mayonnaise Curdling usually occurs because the ingredients are too cold or are of different temperatures. They should all be at room temperature. The yolks may not have been beaten enough initially, as they should be whisked until foamy and pale before adding the oil.

The emulsion may not occur because the oil has been added too swiftly in the initial stages. Add the first 4-5 fl oz (100-125 ml) oil very slowly, beating hard after each addition to ensure a good emulsion.

Mayonnaise curdles when the mixture does not start to thicken very soon after the first additions of oil or when the mixture appears thin and flecked with light yellow in darker yellow (the separated yolk and oil). If left, the constitutent parts separate and cannot be whisked together.

When mayonnaise has curdled:

a) Stop adding oil immediately. First try slowly adding 1 tablespoon very hot water, beating all the time.

b) If the above does not work, thoroughly beat another yolk in a clean bowl, then slowly add the curdled mayonnaise.

Hollandaise Curdling occurs because the clarified butter has been added too swiftly in the initial stages of forming the emulsion. Add the first 4-5 fl oz (100-125 ml) very slowly, beating well between additions. If the yolks have been heated too much before the clarified butter has been added, curdling may occur. This can be rectified by starting again with a fresh yolk, adding the mixture slowly when it has been well beaten, but this will not work if the yolk has become at all hard. If the yolk and butter mixture is allowed to become too hot during mixing, or the mixture is kept for too long and at too high a temperature before serving it may curdle also and will not look like mayonnaise. When hollandaise has curdled, follow the same remedies as for mayonnaise.

Roux sauces (béchamel, velouté, etc.) Curdling is rare, but may occur because the fat and flour mixture for the roux was not thoroughly amalgamated and cooked. Stir in small pieces of beurre manié (see page 85) slowly over the heat. Allow the sauce to thicken and add extra liquid to regain correct consistency.

Lumpy sauces

These usually occur because (a) the flour and fat have not been well amalgamated and cooked before the liquid is added; (b) the liquid was added too quickly without thorough mixing with the roux; (c) the liquid added was too cold and the roux not mixed thoroughly so that when heated to thickening point, pieces of roux remain, forming hard lumps.

This can be overcome by one of the following ways.

- Beating the mixture well over a low heat until the lumps break up and are absorbed by the liquid.

- Straining the sauce through a fine sieve, and working the remaining lumps through the sieve with the back of a wooden spoon (never a metal spoon as this will cause a reaction with the sieve, giving the sauce a tainted flavour). Return the sauce to the heat and beat until smooth over a low heat.

- In cases where the lumps are too hard to pass through the sieve, strain the sauce and discard the lumps. Make a small quantity of roux, making sure it is well amalgamated and cooked, add in the remaining strained sauce and continue with the recipe.

Collapsed puddings

If a pudding collapses when turned out, consider serving it in a different form. Spoon the mixture into individual serving dishes, arranging it as attractively as possible. Dress with whipped or piped cream, a topping of pouring cream or a little fruit if this was included in the original dish.

Broken meringues

Small pieces of broken meringue can be used as a topping for cold puddings. They can also be folded into an ice-cream mixture, just before it reaches freezing point, to give an unusual and interesting texture. If the pieces are added too early, when the mixture is still rather liquid, the meringue will collapse and the effect be ruined.

Burnt cakes

Cut off the burnt parts. What is left may be good enough to be eaten as it is or the remains can be used in a trifle or as a pudding base. The cake may be made into crumbs (see below). If, when the burnt parts have been removed, the cake can be eaten whole, but looks unattractive, it may be covered with icing or marzipan or coated in jam and rolled in coconut or chopped nuts.

Leftovers

Egg yolks

Store in refrigerator with a little cold water to cover in order to stop them drying. Alternatively, store in freezer with a little sugar or salt to prevent coagulation and label carefully so that you know which has been used. They can then be used for: egg custard; mayonnaise; with cream to finish soups; glazing pastry; scrambled egg (with the addition of a little water, milk or cream); making cakes (add the equivalent in milk to the yolks, unless the recipe is for yolks only); pastry cream; choux pastry; egg nog.

Egg whites

Store in grease-free containers in refrigerator (earthenware is best as this allows a small amount of liquid to evaporate, thus making the whites easier to whisk). Whites may be frozen without treatment. They can be used for: meringues; clarifying consommé; cake making (very light sponges in which it takes the place of raising agent); glazing pastry (with a tiny sprinkling of caster sugar). They may be added to puddings where a light frothy consistency is needed; royal icing; as extra whites for soufflés and whipped into cream to make it go further.

Vegetable trimmings

In general these should not be stored, but may be kept for a short time in a plastic bag in the refrigerator. They can be used for: vegetable stock; and when fried with meat trimmings form the basis for a brown stock. Certain trimmings such as Brussels sprouts and carrots can be used for the basis of a soup.

Biscuit and cake crumbs

Store in an airtight container until required, or in polythene bags in the freezer. They can be used for: making uncooked cakes such as Rum Truffles and Swedish Apple Cake; cheesecake base (biscuit crumbs). Sweet cake or biscuit crumbs may be scattered as a contrasting topping on creamy puddings such as fools and may be layered with fruit as an emergency pudding.

Cheese ends

These are best stored in an airtight container to retain moisture or they may be grated and frozen. They can be used for most cooking purposes. The cheese should be finely grated as it will tend to be harder and will not melt as quickly as fresh cheese. It can be added to sauces; used for soufflés; sprinkled on top of dishes and browned; used as part of a stuffing for pancakes or omlettes; added to scone mix to give cheese scones.

Stale bread

Use as soon as possible before mould occurs. It can be used for: breadcrumbs for stuffing or bread sauce; breadcrumbs baked until golden for use as coatings. Slice bread thinly for Apple Charlotte, Bread and Butter Pudding, Queen of Puddings. Bake leftover bread crusts and slices in low oven to use as rusks with soup.

Stock making

This can be made with vegetable trimmings (root vegetables are best as they do not cloud the stock), meat trimmings and bones (cooked or uncooked). If a brown stock is required, uncooked bones should be fried or placed in the oven until brown, and then used. Onion skins also help to give a good colour to stock; bacon rinds, herb stalks and tomato skins also add to the flavour of stock.

Orange and lemon skins

These can be used by removing all the pith and drying them in a very cool oven (after it has been used for other purposes). They can be stored in airtight containers and added to bouquet garni, cooked fruit, syrups and sauces.

Fruit syrups
Juice drained from canned fruit may be stored in the refrigerator for 1 week, or frozen. Use for poaching fresh fruit, or sweetening raw fruit in fruit salads.

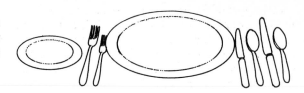

Cream
Whip surplus cream with a little sugar and freeze — it may be piped into rosettes and frozen on a flat surface before freezing. Rosettes will thaw in 30 minutes if placed on a pudding at room temperature.

Wine
Put in covered container in refrigerator and use within a week for marinades or gravy. It can be frozen in cubes and added to stews.

Planning a Meal

When planning a menu, give consideration to the occasion for which it is being chosen. Priorities will be different for family, guests, the type of occasion and the money available. A good well-planned meal does not have to contain many courses or elaborate dishes. How many courses are there to be? The traditional order for meals of many courses is: hors-d'oeuvre, soup, fish, meat dish, sorbet, roast dish, sweet course, savoury course, cheese, fruit, petit fours. The occasions when all eleven courses are served are very rare and any combination of the courses can be used, but should traditionally be served in the order given. More often the courses offered are: hors-d'oeuvre or soup, a main fish or meat course, and a sweet course and/or cheese and fruit.

The balance of the menu is particularly important and includes a consideration of variety, texture, palatability, digestibility and appearance.

Variety This refers to the non-repetition of a main ingredient in a number of courses. For example, fish (smoked or fresh) in both starter and main course (unless of course this is part of a special 'fish meal') or cream or eggs appearing in every course. Pastry, potato, tomato, and garlic are other ingredients which can easily appear too often, as can a favourite combination of herbs. Try to make each course different from the others, whilst retaining their complementary nature.

Texture There is nothing more unattractive than eating a meal in which all the textures are the same. Sometimes everything is soft and covered in sauces, vegetables are overcooked and mushy and served with an unidentifiable stew, and followed by soft, collapsed pudding. This is so easily avoided

by a little thought and planning. Many recipes have built into them a certain amount of variety of texture. Even the simple stew with light, fluffy dumplings can contrast the rich, tender qualities of the meat dish. Very often the dressing of a dish will provide contrast between hot and cold, crisp and soft, smooth and crunchy, and for that reason should not be ignored. Attention should be given to those dishes which will have a cleansing effect on the palate. such as raw ingredients, on sharp ingredients such as orange, lemon, grapefruit or vinegar.

Palatability This aspect and that of texture are very closely related. The food should not have a sameness about it but should provide a variety of tastes, textures and temperatures to excite the taste buds. It also refers to the acceptable qualities of the food in terms of edibility. Sauces that are too thick; baked goods which are too hard or undercooked; certain combinations of tastes and over-seasoning all lead to lack of palatability and mar the enjoyment of the meal.

Digestibility Some foods are very much more difficult to digest than others. This is particularly true of fatty foods. If a high proportion of fried foods or foods dressed with oil or served with cream are included in the menu, this will probably lead to indigestion. This is caused by the greater difficulty of the stomach acids acting through the layer of fats on the foods eaten, and the resultant length of time in which the food stays in the stomach. Very hard boiled eggs, tough meat and any overcooked protein are hard to digest. Very acid foods can also cause indigestion. If these foods are to be served, it is best to serve something with them that will counteract their action. In the case of fatty foods the inclusion of an acid element in the menu will help, such as lemon served with fried fish; bread, pasta or potatoes will help to counteract very acid dishes.

In the case of cooking for invalids, it is best to remember that raw foods, overcooked protein and large amounts of carbohydrates are the most difficult ingredients to digest, and lightly cooked foods tend to be more suitable when normal diet is not possible.

Appearance This includes texture, colour, decoration and service of the food. Colour can be very important in attracting an eater to the dish. English cooks are renowned for serving 'white' or 'brown' meals and this is completely unnecessary. Colours need not be garish but there is nothing more pleasing or attractive than, for example, fillets of white fish, served with a delicate white sauce, but garnished with ice-cold, pale green skinned grapes. There is no excuse for the perennial quarters of lemon or tomatoes with large wilted lettuce leaves. The imaginative use of chopped herbs, sieved egg yolk, chopped egg white, gherkins, capers, small shaped glazed vegetables, crystallised fruits, nuts and delicate piped cream can add instant appeal to a dish. There is, however, no point in trying to disguise a dish with clever decoration.

New recipes

If a new dish is to be used for a menu, allow for this (as extra time and trouble will probably be needed) by arranging for simple or familiar dishes to accompany it. It is as well to consider one cold dish which can be made in advance, or a hot dish which can be made in advance and kept hot without damaging it.

Equipment and cooking space

Keep these in mind when choosing the constituent parts of the menu. Many recipes give the equipment needed, but if they do not, work out carefully what will be required and if certain items are not available consider alternatives. It is not worth getting some specific items if they will not be regularly used. Cooking space is a prime consideration, and there is little point in compiling a complicated menu if the oven is not large enough or if there is nowhere to keep food hot. There are answers to a lack of hot storage, such as pressure cookers with several compartments; steamers; or saucepans with separate removable sections. Care should be taken when using these that flavours do not become too intermingled.

Cost

Cost should be related to the type of menu being prepared. To keep cost down on a 'guest' menu, keep the major part of the menu interesting but inexpensive, spending perhaps more on one particular special item which may be the centrepiece of the menu. When pricing a menu allow for all the additions and small items. These can very often create a cost equivalent to that of the main items, particularly when they include cream, anchovies, olives and other accompaniments which may not usually be kept in store. Expensive items do not necessarily make a better dish, and certainly in most cases do not add to the nutritional value of the meal. Carefully cooked and attractively presented cheaper cuts of meat can be as appetising and interesting as the more expensive.

Economic use of the cooker

If the oven is to be used in the preparation of a menu, make sure that it is not being wasted. One small item baked in the oven can prove to be very expensive. If at all possible, use the whole of the oven, even if it means preparing dishes for another meal at the same time.

Remember that the heat in the various parts of the oven varies quite considerably, so that dishes requiring different temperatures can often be cooked at the same time. Items needing a slightly lower temperature to that at which the main dish is being cooked can sometimes be placed in the oven at the same time without damage, by placing the cooking vessel in a pan of cold water, which will lower greatly the cooking temperature of the item.

Quantities and the Number of Servings

It is difficult to give precise quantities of food required per person, due to very different eating habits, but a general guide can be given in terms of 'average servings'.

Meat

As a general rule allow for each serving:

2-3 oz (50-75 g) cooked meat
4-6 oz (100-150 g) uncooked, without bone
8-10 oz (225-300 g) uncooked with bone
1 kidney
4-6 oz (100-150 g) liver
4 oz (100 g) sausage (i.e. two large sausages)

3 lb (1.5 kg) chicken will serve 4-6 portions
Duckling may serve up to 4 portions but many ducklings are only large enough for two portions
Goose will serve 8-10 portions
12 lb (5 kg) turkey will serve 14 portions
Pheasant will serve up to 4 portions, depending upon the size of the breast
Rabbit will serve 4-6 portions

Fish

As a general rule allow for each serving:

6-8 oz (150-225 g) filleted fish
8-10 oz (225-300 g) whole fish or unfilleted (cutlets)
1 small crab

10-12 oz (300-350 g) lobster
1 pt (600 ml) molluscs (mussels, cockles etc.)
$\frac{1}{2}$ pt (300 ml) small crustacea (prawns, shrimps, etc.)

Vegetables

In general allow 4 oz (100 g) cooked vegetables per portion. When fresh vegetables are used the unprepared weight will vary considerably. For fresh vegetables allow:

6-8 oz (150-225 g) root vegetables (potatoes, carrots, swedes, turnips, kohlrabi, Jerusalem artichokes, parsnips, beetroot)
10-12 oz (300-350 g) broad beans and peas
8-12 oz (225-300 g) French or runner beans
6-8 oz (150-225 g) brassicas (cabbage, broccoli, Brussels sprouts, kale, spring greens, green tops)
8 oz (225 g) spinach
$\frac{1}{2}$ head celery
3-4 oz (75-100 g) chicory
10-12 oz (300-350 g) vegetables with high water content (pumpkin, marrow, courgette, leek)
2-4 oz (50-100 g) mushrooms

Fruit

Allow for each serving:

6-8 oz (150-225 g) fruit for cooking (the higher level generally applies to fruits with very high water content such as rhubarb, blackcurrants, blackberries)
3-4 oz (75-100 g) strawberries, raspberries
4-6 oz (100-150 g) melon or watermelon
2-4 oz (50-100 g) fresh grapes
3-4 fresh plums, greengages, other small fruit
1 piece large fruit (apple, pear)
2-4 oz (50-100 g) shelled nuts

Prepared foods

Allow for each serving:

$\frac{1}{8}$-$\frac{1}{4}$ pt (75-150 ml) sauce
$\frac{1}{4}$ pt (150 ml) custard
$\frac{1}{2}$ pt (300 ml) soup
2 oz (50 g) flour in the basic mix for pastry, cakes and puddings

Dairy produce

Allow for each serving:

$\frac{1}{4}$ pt (150 ml) cream for pouring (allow less for whipping cream, e.g. 1 pt (600 ml) for 6-8 portions
1-1$\frac{1}{2}$ oz (25-40 g) butter or margarine
2-3 oz (50-75 g) cheese. (This will vary quite considerably with the type of cheese. For hard cheese, it may be more; soft cheese less. The ripeness of the latter will also affect the portion as it will be more difficult to serve if very soft and ripe.)

Doubling Recipes

There is no rule of thumb when it comes to doubling recipes. Some will double directly from the recipe, while others need to be carefully re-balanced.

The addition of liquids and seasoning

Liquids in this context may be water, wine, spirits, stock, oil, melted butter, milk, cream, eggs, syrup or juices. In most cases, less liquid is required in a doubled recipe to achieve the same consistency as that of the original. When doubling a recipe, therefore, add the liquid carefully, not all at once, and check the consistency regularly. Doubling seasonings, especially spices, can lead to an overpowering flavour. There is no guiding rule but it is best to cut down slightly on seasoning and learn from experience by tasting carefully and adjusting seasoning accordingly.

Baking recipes

Doubling baking recipes can bring a large number of difficulties. Very light mixtures, particularly those using white of egg as the raising agent, should be made in small quantities, as the handling required for larger amounts can lead to disappointing results. If sponge mixtures are to be doubled, do not try to place in larger tins without altering the consistency and time of cooking. In these cases the mixture needs to be slightly thicker and an extra 10 to 15 minutes added to the cooking time at a slightly lower temperature. Fruit cakes can be easily doubled, but again the cooking time should be longer and at lower temperatures. For double quantities, baking tins should be wider rather than taller. For a fruit cake, tie two or three layers of brown paper or newspaper around the outside of the tin to prevent either burning or drying the cake.

Timing a Meal

Work backwards from the time the meal is to be served, allowing for both cooking time and preparation time. Work out how long each dish will take to cook, placing them on a list with the longest time first, noting the actual hour at which it should be placed in the heat of the oven or hob. Allow time for the oven to heat up to the temperature required.

Work out the order in which the preparation has

to be done. Certain dishes may need to prepared just before they have to be cooked, others may be prepared well in advance, even the day before. It is best when planning a dinner/lunch party to design the menu in such a way that much of the preparation is done well in advance, taking the pressure off the day of the party and giving time for attention to other details. Work as closely as possible to the plan, using a timer if needed to remind you when things should be started or finished.

If a new recipe is being tried, allow a little extra time (particularly at the preparation stage) to be sure that pressure of time does not lead to mistakes. If guests are to be greeted, make an allowance in both planning and timing for this activity.

Serving each part of the meal should not be complicated if the timing plan has been well worked out. All serving dishes, plates, bowls, etc., should be placed ready and warmed if necessary.

Keeping food warm There are various methods which allow food to be kept warm without spoiling, giving some leeway to the time at which the meal is to be served.

Soups can be kept just below boiling point on the hob. If allowed to become too cool, a skin may form on the top. This should be removed before reheating, as it will create lumps in the soup. If a soup has cream or egg yolks added it should never be boiled when being reheated as the cream will curdle and the yolks become hard.

Some egg dishes can be kept waiting. Scrambled eggs can be partially cooked and placed in a container in a *bain marie*. This is a shallow

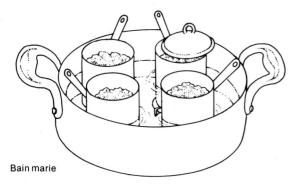

Bain marie

container of hot water which is placed either in a cool oven or on a slow hob, into which other containers are placed containing dishes which are too delicate to be kept warm through direct heat. If the eggs have become rather more cooked than desired, one or two raw eggs should be beaten in. The heat of the remainder of the eggs will cook the

added eggs without their becoming in any way hard. Poached eggs can be partially cooked in water, to the point at which they can be handled. They are then removed and placed quickly in very cold water to stop cooking. When they are required they should be placed in slowly boiling water to heat and finish the cooking process. This does not lead to tough eggs.

Pasta can also be treated in the above way. Cook the pasta until almost done, remove from the water and rinse well with very cold water. Leave well-covered with cold water until needed. Drain well and place in boiling water until hot and cooked.

Most vegetables can be treated in this way, even the green leafy ones. The secret is to be sure that they are plunged very quickly into very cold water, and that they are completely cold before leaving. If there is the slightest warmth left in the vegetables, cooking will continue, giving a soggy texture to the reheated food, as well as an unpleasant flavour and appearance. Vegetables can be kept for several hours once they are cold and placed in plenty of cold water to wait reheating.

Meat dishes can be kept warm in a cooling oven with the door slightly ajar, so that the heat does not allow for further cooking. Roast foods and those with a browned top should not be covered as this will cause the crispness of the top or outside to become soggy.

Soufflés can also be kept for a short while, though the time should be limited to not more than about 10-15 minutes. Leave the soufflé in a warm oven, with the heat still turned on, but with the door slightly open so that the heat does not build up.

Sauces keep well if placed in a *bain marie* as this will not change the consistency markedly, as will keeping the sauce hot over the direct heat of the hob. The steam created by the *bain marie* will also slow the process of skin forming on the top of the sauce. This can be slowed further by sprinkling a small amount of butter over the top to form a very thin layer of oil; or by placing a double layer of greaseproof paper slightly damped with cold water over the sauce.

Reheating Food

Food which is to be reheated should have been stored preferably in a refrigerator not longer than 2 days. If there is any sign of contamination, the food should be discarded. Do not be tempted to remove the contaminated part, as it is almost certain that the rest of the food is contaminated to a certain extent. It is most important therefore that food is thoroughly heated right through. If possible, and especially in the case of meat products and meat mixtures, the food should be brought to boiling temperature, and held there for at least 3 minutes to kill off the bacteria.

Most foods when reheated will loose a lot of their flavour, and will become dry if not treated properly. Reheating should therefore be as rapid as possible, and the food should have moisture added in some form. It is as well to cut large items for reheating into small pieces, so that the process is speeded up, e.g. meat cut from a joint should be sliced and reheated in gravy. A little extra liquid should be added to stews and other dishes with a thick gravy, as the reheating will cause the evaporation of some of the original liquid.

Vegetables can be tossed in butter and steamed for a short time, with the lid on the pan, but it should be remembered that reheated vegetables will lose the majority of their vitamins. Soups and sauces should be heated slowly, and thoroughly boiled except in the case of sauces to which egg yolk has been added, as this will curdle the egg yolk.

If fresh ingredients are to be added to the mixture being reheated, these should be cooked first and then added and the whole dish heated together thoroughly. This allows the added food to be fully cooked, and prevents the overcooking of the reheated food.

Never reheat a dish more than once. The risk of contamination by bacteria is greatly increased and the nutritional value of the food will be very low. Reheated foods are best served with a dish high in vitamin and mineral content to compensate for their loss in the reheating process.

Special Diets

If a member of the family is placed on a diet for medical reasons ask your doctor for advice and the address of an appropriate group such as The British Heart Foundation who can supply further information and recipes. If you are entertaining a guest with a dietary problem these guidelines may be useful.

Diabetic

The major form of diabetes is created by the malfunction of the islets of Langerhans which are responsible for making use of the sugars taken in by the body and produced by the digestion of carbohydrates. The condition is now generally controlled by the introduction of insulin to the body. Even so, the diabetic has to be careful with

his diet. It is best to ask the advice of the diabetic prior to the visit for he or she will have been given dietary instructions by his doctor. However, in the majority of cases, carbohydrates are considerably cut, especially the sugars, and those carbohydrates which are easily transformed to sugars within the body. Proteins vary little from normal diet. To aid the diabetic there are various proprietary goods on the market including jams and marmalades, chocolate and other sweets as well as starch-free bakery goods, which are available from good chemists. Fats generally have to replace carbohydrates as the source of energy. Base a menu on high protein content and have plenty of fruit and vegetables as it is easy enough for the diabetic to add carbohydrates if needed.

Salt-free

While the implications for this type of diet are obvious (heart disease, high blood pressure, some kidney and liver disorders), it should be remembered that all seasoning with salt has to be stopped, in meat dishes, vegetables, pastry, etc., and it is very easy to forget this. There are few types of food which have to be given up altogether, but among those which should be treated with care are sea foods and produce grown close to the sea which may have absorbed a higher than average proportion of salt. Other foods to be watched carefully are tinned, dried, packaged and prepared goods and concentrates. Check carefully on the wrapping as the ingredients should be listed, although the salt content may not be mentioned. If unsure, do not use, or consult a dietitian. There are commerical alternatives (bought from chemists) to salt which the person on a salt-free diet may use.

Fat-free

This diet may be of two types: animal fat-free or total fat-free.

Animal fat-free This means the use of skimmed milk for all drinking and cooking purposes; vegetable oil based margarine to spread on bread; and vegetable oils as alternatives to butter, lard dripping or suet for cooking. Meat should be trimmed of all fat, and preferably grilled to melt out any remaining fat. Grilled foods can be basted with vegetable oil to retain a certain amount of moisture. Any frying can be carried out with the use of vegetable oil. White fish may be eaten, but not oily fish such as herring, mackerel and salmon. Eggs should also be cut down to an absolute minimum. Most diets allow for 1 egg per week. Cream should not be eaten, but can be substituted by yogurt made with skimmed milk. This can be stabilised to substitute for cream in cooking (see page 30). Purchased goods should have their ingredients checked for animal fats.

Completely fat-free diet As above, but no vegetable fats (margarine) or oils should be used in any cooking process or included in dressings such as mayonnaise or vinaigrette. Seasoned skimmed milk dressings can be used as alternatives.

Vegetarian

This type of diet will depend on the individual as it may or may not include the use of dairy produce such as milk, yogurt, cream, cheese and eggs. Check with the individual first. The vegetarian gets his protein from vegetables and the combination of pulses with grains. The highest level of protein is found in soya beans. Nuts of all sorts also produce an excellent source of protein in the diet and can be usefully included in either raw or cooked state.

A certain amount of imagination is required to produce a good, balanced vegetarian diet, as with a meat-based diet and with careful planning none of the essential nutrients need to be missed. Each meal should include a protein source and an energy source (in the form of fats or carbohydrates), and a selection of vegetables to provide vitamins and minerals. If a correct vitamin balance is provided there is no need to supplement the diet with vitamin tablets.

Various commodities are available on the market for the vegetarian, including soya preparations such as tofu, although those which are designed to take the place of meat (i.e. have meat flavouring and meat-like appearance) are usually eschewed by the serious vegetarian.

Skills and Techniques

Chopping and Shredding

These are skills which are very basic to cooking, and to the attractive appearance of finished dishes. It is essential to use a wooden board to prevent food from slipping and to protect working surfaces. It also stops the knife or other cutting instrument from being blunted too quickly. It is most important to have a very sharp cutting instrument. A knife with a blade which is deeper than the handle makes the job much easier. A mandolin, or electric appliance such as a food processor or shredder, will help to make the job easier, and give a fine, regular end-product. There are many reasons for chopping and shredding, but perhaps the most important is the fact that a finely chopped or shredded item will cook more quickly, causing less damage to the texture, and minimum loss of vitamins and minerals. The appearance and easier management of the dish at table is also of great importance.

Chopping

Chopping is made easier if the hand actions are well co-ordinated, and the relationship between the knife and the holding hand is correct. The knife should be held lightly in one hand by the handle. The other hand should hold the item to be cut in such a way that the knife can be brought up against the knuckles, which are used as a guide for the movement of the knife. The chopping action should be swift, and straight up-and-down, with the cutting edge of the blade kept level in most cases.

For small items, e.g. herbs, a slightly different action is required. In this case the herbs should be piled in the centre of the board, and the knife placed across them. The tip of the blade should be held down in position with the fingers of one hand, and the handle moved up-and-down swiftly to bring the blade through the herbs. The point should not be moved, but the knife swivelled across the herbs, back and forth in the chopping motion, until they are chopped finely enough.

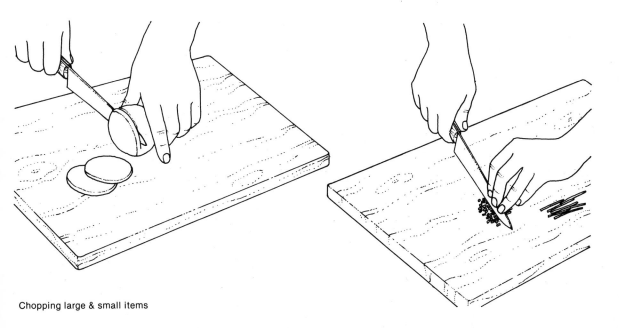

Chopping large & small items

Onions can be chopped very finely, after halving from top to bottom, placing the cut edge on the board. Cut several times horizontally towards the root end, but not cutting right through. Finally cut vertically through the bulb to give a fine result, of small squarish pieces. Larger vegetables can be cut finely by cutting into slices first, then making cuts at right angles to these cuts to produce sticks. Finally cut at right angles again to form small cubes. Round articles are very much easier to chop if a thin slice is removed from one side so that there is a flat surface which can be placed on the board to stop movement during chopping.

Shredding

This is the reduction of food to a fine, and usually long shape, such as cabbage for a salad. Shredding is usually carried out against the 'grain' of the food so that the fibres are short and more easily masticated. This is an easy job if a mandolin is used, which can be set to cut very finely. Many electrical appliances now have very efficient shredding attachments. If a knife is used, the item

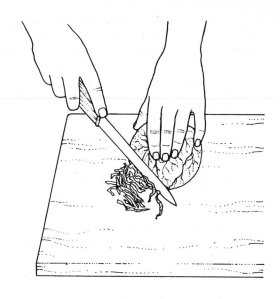

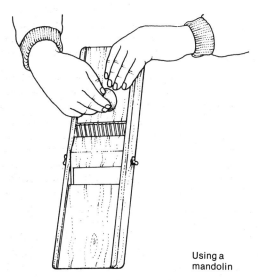

Using a mandolin

to be shredded should be held with the grain at right angles to the knife blade. It must be held with the fingers in such a position that the area between the central joints of the fingers is at the same angle as the flat of the blade, and can be used as a guide to its direction. The width of the cut can then be regulated by the distance that the fingers are moved back along the length of the item being shredded.

Creaming

This is a method of introducing air into fat (or a fat and sugar mixture), and it is one of the basic methods of introducing air into a cake or sponge mixture. Before starting to cream, the fat should be soft but not oily and it is advisable to take the fat out of the refrigerator the night before it is to be used. If the fat is not soft before creaming begins, a great deal of energy is needlessly used in softening it at the start of the creaming process. Fats are described as having a creaming quality if they have the ability to absorb a large quantity of air during the creaming process. The fat (or fat and sugar mixture) is stirred swiftly, keeping the wooden spoon, spatula or fork on the surface of the mixing bowl, so that the fat is softened. In the case of a fat

and sugar mixture, the sugar is absorbed by the fat. As the fat begins to soften, air is introduced. The more the mixture is creamed, the lighter in colour it becomes, indicating the greater absorbtion of air. If not creamed adequately there will be a limited amount of aeration of the final mixture which will not rise when cooked — particularly disastrous in the case of sponge cakes.

Whisking

Another method of introducing air rapidly, it is sometimes referred to as 'whipping'. It is usually applied to ingredients that are fairly liquid such as cream or egg whites. Whisking by hand is carried out with a fork, balloon whisk or rotary whisk. The action of using a fork or a balloon whisk is a rapid circular motion with the emphasis on the lifting movement. Whisking should be done from the wrist, not using the whole arm as this is tiring and unnecessary. The finer the wire of the balloon

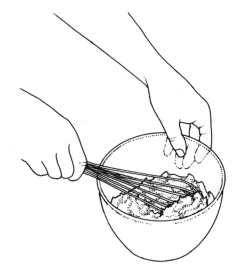

whisk, the faster the air is beaten and the smaller the bubbles introduced. This is very important in some recipes where a very even mix is required when the whisked ingredient is added to other ingredients. This should be borne in mind when deciding what tool to use when whisking. Whisking with a rotary whisk, or an electric beater, while faster, does not have the emphasis on the lifting motion. Although good enough results can be obtained, the end result is not as light and airy as a mix beaten with a balloon whisk. Egg whites are easier to whisk if they have received a little previous attention:

Separate the whites from the yolks the day before they are to be used and place in an

earthenware dish if available, and then in a cool place where there is a slight draught. This is to evaporate a small amount of the water present in the albumen. This has the effect of concentrating the albumen, which will then accept a greater amount of air and produce a stiffer result.

Stale whites should not be used. After they have been kept for more than a few days, the whites start to decompose and become watery, the exact opposite of what is required to achieve a good 'snow' or foam.

There are four ways in which the 'snow' can be improved:

- Allowing some of the water to evaporate (as above).

- Adding a little acid in the form of a few drops of lemon juice or a pinch of cream of tartar before starting to whisk the whites. This has the effect of 'toughening' the albumen, thus allowing it to hold more air than usual.

- Adding a pinch of salt before whisking. This has the same effect as the previous one.

- Adding about 1 oz (25 g) of fine caster sugar to each 4 egg whites in a sweet mixture. This creates a syrup which provides a denser solution capable of absorbing a greater amount of air.

The greatest mistake in whisking egg whites is the introduction of grease of any sort. This can be from many sources such as the fingers, the utensils (copper bowls are often suggested for whisking egg whites because the surface is so fine that it is easier to remove all traces of grease) or the tiniest amount of yolk. This affects the elasticity of the albumen, and therefore its ability to absorb air and hold it. Whites which are affected by grease will not whisk up into a snow, the albumen collapsing as the air is whisked in.

Cream should also be whisked carefully as beyond a certain stage the fats will begin to emulsify to form butter. This can be seen at an early stage by the gradual appearance of a grainy look. The thicker the cream (i.e. the greater the fat content) the quicker this will happen.

Beating

This is a slower action than whisking because it applies usually to a thicker or semi-liquid mixture. It is again a method of introducing air and has the added value of mixing ingredients at the same time. Beating is carried out usually with a spoon, which is held so that it cuts down into the mixture, introducing air, and in the upward stroke mixes the

ingredients. The action is elliptical rather than circular, from side to side of the mixing bowl. In effect the action lifts the mixture over the spoon, aerating on the downward stroke and mixing on the upward. The thinner the mixture the faster can be the action.

Folding in

This usually refers to a method where a dry ingredient is added to a light aerated mixture, as for example when sugar is folded into the whisked whites for a meringue mix. The action is designed to introduce the dry ingredient without breaking down the effects of aeration and should be swift but very gentle and not prolonged. The dry

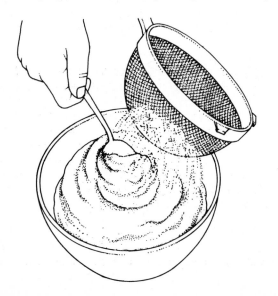

ingredient is usually added to the light mixture rather than the other way round. The action is to cut through the dry ingredients to the bottom of the mixing bowl and then lift the light mixture to the top, thus mixing the two. When two or three mixtures are to be folded in, as in a mousse, the heavier item is folded in first. Thus in a mousse the whipped cream is folded into the basic mixture. The whisked egg whites are folded in last to keep the mixture as light as possible.

Blending

Blending is a method of mixing ingredients smoothly without the introduction of air. The result should be free of lumps and an even dispersion of the various components, as this usually precedes the addition of the blended ingredients to others.

Stocks

Stock is a flavoured liquid used as a basic ingredient in the making of soups, stews, sauces and many other dishes. A good stock should be well flavoured but not overpowering. It should be made from raw bones, poultry and game carcasses, giblets, meat off-cuts (e.g. bacon rinds) with the added flavouring of vegetables and herbs. In the case of fish stock, the bones and trimmings are used, but never the guts, as these give a very unpleasant flavour. A well-made stock is not a liquid formed from just any kitchen debris. It is a carefully balanced liquid with a clear and definite flavour. Stocks are always brought to the boil from cold and boiled for a long period (with the exception of fish stock) so that all the flavour is extracted from the ingredients, especially the bones. Seasonings are not generally added as the stock may need to be reduced and this may concentrate the seasoning to an unacceptable level. The starchy vegetables (e.g. potatoes) are not used as they break up in the long cooking process, clouding and thickening the stock. The most usual vegetables for flavouring are onion, carrot and celery. Leek is also an acceptable vegetable and a little turnip, although the latter can cause a bitterness in the stock. Stocks can generally be stored in a refrigerator for a few days and will freeze very successfully. Before use, they should be well boiled to stop any risk of contamination.

There is a myth that good cooks keep a stock pot constantly in use into which all kitchen debris is placed. Such a process can be unpleasant and dangerous as old food, starches in potatoes, bread, rice or pasta, and green vegetables can quickly sour the stock. It is sensible, however, to collect meat and vegetable trimmings and bones and to make them into stock while fresh. Poultry and game carcasses and ham bones may also be used. These stocks may then be strained and stored in the refrigerator or freezer and reboiled before use.

A stock cube may be used if a small quantity of stock is required and no fresh stock is available. The flavour is rather strong and the finished dish should be seasoned carefully to allow for the saltiness of most stock cubes.

Light stock

A good general-purpose stock can be made from any raw bones, poultry or game carcasses with the addition of vegetables to give a better flavour and a bouquet garni of herbs (thyme, parsley and bay leaf). Wash the bones in cold water. Trim the vegetables of skins (where necessary) and blemishes. The vegetables do not need to be chopped very small as the long cooking will extract the flavour, whatever the size. Tie the herbs for the bouquet garni securely. Place all the ingredients in a large pan and cover with cold water. Bring to the boil and remove the scum as it rises, since it will cause clouding and possibly a bitter flavour if not removed. Lower the heat so that the liquid is just simmering for 3-4 hours. Cool and remove any fat from the surface when it becomes hard. Strain and store in a cold place.

Brown stock

This well-flavoured stock is for richer and darker dishes. The ingredients have to be browned first. For each 2 pt (1.2 litre) allow 1 lb (450 g) shin beef, a veal bone (preferably a knuckle), vegetables and a bouquet garni. Cube the meat, fry it with the bone over a fairly high heat until both are well browned. Remove from the frying pan and place in the stock pan. Fry the whole, trimmed vegetables to draw out some of the flavour and to brown slightly, then place in the stock pan. Swill the frying pan with some water to remove the sediment from the meat and vegetables and add to the stock pan. Add the bouquet garni and cover the ingredients with cold water. Bring to the boil, remove the scum, and simmer for 4-6 hours. Remove the fat when cold. Strain and store in a cold place.

Giblet stock

This is used generally for game and poultry dishes, when the giblets from the bird are used. The neck and heart are usually used for the giblet stock, the liver being retained for other uses. These are boiled with vegetables and a bouquet garni for 1-2 hours, depending on the quantity. Strain and use for making gravy or for other dishes.

White stock

White stock is made from poultry bones, veal or lamb bones, and usually with a small amount of one of the poor cuts of the meat. No browning takes place and the bones are well washed in cold water to remove any excess blood. They are simmered with vegetables and a small bouquet garni (as the taste of the stock is more delicate) for 3-4 hours.

Fish stock

This is a very delicate stock and is made from the bones and trimmings of the fish (and may include a cod's head). These are placed in a pan with a little finely chopped onion or shallot, a few parsley stalks, peppercorns and a small piece of bay leaf. Just cover with cold water and bring to the boil. This should be boiled for 20 minutes only, to prevent disintegration and the trimmings from breaking up and making a cloudy stock. Not too much water should be used as the stock is very thin and delicate. Once the stock has been strained carefully it may be reduced to condense the flavour.

Reduction

Liquid may be boiled, without a lid on the pan, to drive off excess water, to reduce the quantity, and concentrate the flavour of the liquid. This is sometimes done to partially caramelise the solids, as in the case of juices left in the pan after roasting meat, when gravy is being made. Reduction should take place in a thick-bottomed pan, which should be watched very carefully as it is very easy to spoil the liquid by burning on the base of the pan.

Wines and spirits

The flavour of wines and spirits may be intensified in sauces, meat dishes and some sweet dishes. The wine or spirit is boiled rapidly with some of the dry ingredients, before the main liquid is added. If this is not done the flavours may be weak and the amount of liquid too great. This also drives off the alcohol, retaining the concentrated flavour of the liquid. Reduction has to take place before the other liquid is added, as it is impossible to reduce only the wine or spirit after that stage.

Vinegar

The flavour of vinegar in some dishes such as sweet and sour sauce must be intensified. The vinegar is boiled rapidly, usually with a few crushed peppercorns, before other ingredients are added. Remember that when vinegar is boiled rapidly it gives off acrid fumes which cause great discomfort to the eyes and throat.

Pan juices

Reduction is sometimes used to concentrate the flavour of a sauce in which meat has been cooked, such as a casserole. In this case, the meat and other solid ingredients must be removed from the pan, and the remaining juices boiled down to the required consistency and flavour.

Sauces

To concentrate the flavour of a sauce, it is boiled rapidly to reduce the quantity. This only applies to sauces that are thin enough to react well to prolonged boiling, without either spoiling the texture, or making them too thick. Sauces which have had egg yolk added should never be boiled as this will curdle the yolk; though the flavour may not be changed the appearance is not attractive.

Stocks and soups

To concentrate the flavour of stocks and soups, the liquid is boiled until the required strength of flavour is reached.

Marinading and Tenderising

Marinading is a method for tenderising and adding flavour to meat, game and fish. The meat is placed in the marinade and kept cool until the meat is tenderised. Tenderising is a physical or chemical reaction which results in the partial breakdown of the tough fibre of the meat.

Preparing the food

A marinade is a pickle, brine, souse or a mixture of wine and vinegar, flavourings and oil. It can also be a dry mixture of salt and flavourings applied directly to the surface of the meat.

Use a container in which the meat will fit easily. This may be of enamel, glass, ovenglass or china, earthenware, stainless steel or tinned metal. This is to make sure that the acid in the marinade does not react with metal and produce a flavour which will taint the meat. Place about half the dry ingredients in the bottom of the container. Each recipe will vary, but generally a marinade will consist of a mixture of chopped raw vegetables, a variety of herbs and spices. The balance of these will affect the final flavour of the meat. Rub the meat lightly with pepper and salt, and place on top of the dry ingredients. Place the remaining dry ingredients over the meat. Pour on the liquid, trying not to disturb the dry ingredients. Cover the meat, preferably with something through which there can be a small movement of air, such as butter muslin. This prevents drying out and evaporation and excludes dust and flies. The meat should be left for the time specified in the recipe. It should be turned regularly so that all the surfaces remain damp, and that the whole piece is equally affected by the marinade. The time required to marinade varies considerably. It depends on the size of the solid pieces; for example, pieces of meat which are to be used for stews need only be marinaded for a maximum of 3 hours, whereas a very large piece may be left for days. If meat is to be marinaded for more than 24 hours, it is advisable to keep it in the refrigerator. In this case also, the vegetables included in the marinade should be cooked before being added, in order to stop spoilage through deterioration and tainting of the marinade.

To cook marinaded meat, drain off the liquid, but do not throw it away, as in most recipes it is used as either part of the cooking liquor in the sauce. Always make sure that the surface of the meat is well dried before cooking, as a damp surface will stop the meat from browning.

Making a marinade

While it is possible to experiment with the balance of ingredients in a marinade, it is best to refer to a recipe to begin with. Always remember that the lower the quality of the meat to be marinaded, the more acid should be included in the form of vinegar, wine or spirits. This acts on the collagen in meat fibres and helps to break it down, thus making the meat more tender before cooking.

The vegetables can include carrots, onion, leek and celery. Use the latter sparingly as it has an overpowering flavour. Herbs may include whole or powdered bay leaf, parsley (only the stalks need be included), rosemary, juniper berries, thyme or sage. Spices may include peppercorns and cloves and sometimes nutmeg or mace. Garlic may be included with a marinade for lamb or beef, but is not usually used in a game or pork marinade.

Dry marinade

Pork can be marinaded in a dry marinade. This involves rubbing the surface of the pork with salt, pepper and ground herbs (bay, thyme, sage or a combination of these). The meat should be covered and turned several times during the marinading process. This should last for about 2 hours for a small piece (e.g. a chop) and up to 24 hours for a large piece. Before the meat is cooked, the marinade is scraped off so that the flavour of the cooked meat is not too powerful. The surface of the meat must be well dried so that it will brown.

Souses and pickles

Souses and pickles are generally used in fish cookery and for some vegetables. The preparation is the same as for marinading although the ingredients are heated.

Masceration

Fruit that is placed in wine or spirits and sugar for a length of time is usually described as 'mascerated'.

Tenderising by physical means

Some meat is tenderised by physical means. This method is used on thinly cut pieces of meat such as steaks. A steak hammer or heavy wooden spoon is

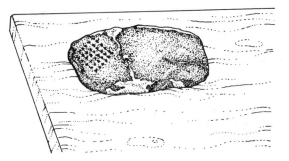

used to beat the meat, causing the tough fibres to be broken and making the meat more tender. This process extends the size of the meat while it is raw, but in the cooking process it will resume its original shape more or less. Hanging meat is a form of tenderising and is dealt with separately (see page 53).

Emulsifying

This is a method by which two usually unmixable ingredients are brought together in the form of droplets of one in the other. They would separate unless stirred together continually or stabilised by an agent such as egg yolk. French dressing is an example of an emulsion without a stabiliser, which therefore needs to be stirred or shaken before serving. There are two main cooking techniques in which an emulsion is used, both producing an emulsified sauce by a hot or a cold method. These are the basic hollandaise and mayonnaise sauces. While they have a reputation of being difficult sauces to make, in fact given simple rules and a little patience they are quite easy.

Hot emulsion

Hollandaise sauce Traditionally the pure hollandaise consists solely of yolks, butter, water and seasoning. This has sometimes been thought too insipid, and a reduction of vinegar or white wine (see page 47) is added at the beginning. Equally a little lemon juice added just before serving can enliven the sauce. The lemon juice should not be added before this as if the sauce is to be kept for any length of time at all, the acid will act on the protein in the yolk causing it to harden and can result in the sauce being curdled. If a hot emulsion sauce has to be kept for any length of time, add a few drops of cold water and whisk in. This will prevent the sauce from cooking too much and spoiling while it is kept. The bowl in which it was made should be placed over a warm pan of water, which should not be allowed to get so hot that it starts cooking the emulsion. Hand heat is quite adequate. Whisk the sauce regularly to ensure that separation does not occur. Hot emulsified sauces can be made in advance and allowed to cool. They can be stored in the refrigerator, but not frozen, for 2-3 days. The emulsion can be reheated very slowly by whisking over heated water.

The proportion of 1 egg yolk, to 1 tablespoon of water to 2 oz (50 g) butter will produce a balanced sauce (it will make 4 tablespoons) which is thick but still of a consistency to be poured. Have ready the required proportions of clarified butter. This is made by heating the butter until it is quite melted. The foam should be removed from the top and after the butter has been allowed to cool a little of the liquid fat should be separated from the milky sediment in the bottom of the pan by carefully pouring it off into another vessel. Beat together the required proportion of water and egg yolks until they begin to become fluffy and pale. The seasoning can be added at this stage. Place the bowl over a pan of hot water, making sure that the bowl is not immersed in the water as the mixture should never become more than body temperature (i.e. warm to the touch) or curdling can occur. Continue beating the egg and water mixture until it becomes thick enough to leave a mark when the whisk is moved through it. By this time it should be quite smooth, fluffy and pale. Remove the pan from the heat and begin to add the slighly warm clarified butter, initially a couple of drops at a time, always whisking with vigour. As the emulsion begins to thicken the butter can be added more swiftly. The sauce should continue to thicken until all the butter has been absorbed. At this stage, the emulsion should form a thin coating on the back of a spoon.

If the sauce at any time appears to be thickening too quickly add a few drops of cold water to slow down the cooking process and lower the heat source. *If the sauce appears to be too thick* add a few drops of water to thin it. *If the sauce is too thin* continue cooking as long as the thickening process continues, being very careful about the amount of heat applied as it is at this stage particularly that curdling can occur. If the sauce is still too thin, it is probable that the wrong proportion of ingredients has been used. In this case it is easiest to begin again by beating a single egg yolk with water and adding the already heated mixture.

A hot emulsified sauce will curdle if the butter is added too quickly initially and if the emulsion becomes too hot. The curdling of the sauce can be rectified only if the emulsion has not become much too hot, in which case the egg will have cooked and formed granular pieces in the sauce and under no circumstances can be brought back.

If the emulsion curdles there are three main methods of reviving the sauce:

- As soon as the emulsion begins to curdle, beat in some crushed ice very quickly. If the sauce is cooled very quickly, the heat of the emulsion may be brought down fast enough for the butter to continue to be brought into emulsion with the egg yolk.

- If the above method does not work, beat the mixture very slowly into a clean bowl in which has been placed a tablespoon of very cold water.

- If the second method does not work, the final method is to start again. Whisk together an egg yolk and a tablespoon of water until it is fluffy and pale and then add the previous mixture a drop at a time until the mixture begins to thicken.

This is an example of a hot emulsified sauce, of which the Sabayon, or Zabaglione, and the French white butter sauce and béarnaise sauce are perhaps the best known. The basic principles of making a hot emulsion are:

- The stabilising agent should be well mixed with the liquid in the recipe. In the case of egg, this should be· whisked until thick and pale, when it will more easily absorb the oil or fat which is to be added. This mixture should be whisked over water to heat it before the oil is added.

- The oil or fat being added should be warm, but no hotter than the stabilising agent and liquid. If liquid fat or oil is added, this should be warm and added to the mixture when it is off the heat. In cases where the oil or fat is cold when added, this should be done over the heat, making sure that each addition of oil or fat is thoroughly absorbed before the next is added.

- The oil or fat should be added very carefully and slowly initially. It can be added more quickly as the emulsion begins to thicken.

- Never overheat the emulsion as this will lead to separation or curdling. It should be noted that separation can occur because the emulsion is not well enough heated and therefore the emulsion has not formed properly. In this case a little more heat should be very gently applied.

- Acid, in the form of vinegar or lemon juice should not be added until just before serving as this may cause the emulsion to curdle. This does not apply where a reduction is used at the outset of the making of the emulsion, although this type of recipe is inclined to separate more easily in the initial stages.

A hot emulsified sauce can be made in a blender in much the same way. The stabiliser and water or other liquid should be beaten as previously in the blender at a medium speed. The heated oil or fat can then be added, slowly at first and more quickly as the sauce thickens. The important part of this process is the beating of the stabiliser and liquid before the oil or fat is added as this will ensure that the oil or fat is easily absorbed into the emulsion.

Cold emulsion

Mayonnaise A cold emulsion can be made well in advance and stored in a cold place in an airtight container, with a little oil floated over the top to stop a skin forming. The basic proportion for a mayonnaise is 2 egg yolks to $\frac{1}{2}$ pt (300 ml) oil with seasoning and a little vinegar, wine or lemon juice which seasons and thins. If the sauce is to be thinned to a great extent this should be done with water, milk or cream. The latter two will make the sauce deteriorate if kept and it is sensible to thin only as much as is required at any one time. If olive oil is used, it is strong enough to give the mayonnaise its traditional flavour. Other oils can be used, but lack the flavour, which can be added in the form of wine, vinegar or lemon juice and mustard but these should be added with care as the sauce is supposed to have a delicate flavour.

When making a cold emulsion it is easier if all the ingredients are of the same temperature, preferably room temperature. If the oil is at all cloudy, it should be allowed to reach room temperature, at which point the cloudiness should disappear. Place the required number of yolks in a bowl and add a pinch of salt. Beat together until the yolks begin to become pale, which is helped by the addition of the salt. Begin to beat in the oil a few drops at a time. As the emulsion begins to thicken, the oil can be added more quickly. The emulsion should be beaten swiftly throughout the process. If the oil appears to be mixing more slowly and has the appearance of curdling at the edges, it may be that the maximum amount of oil has been absorbed, or it may mean that the emulsion is not being beaten enough. Both these can obviously be rectified.

The emulsion may curdle for other reasons, such as the wrong temperature of one of the ingredients, adding the oil too quickly; or not beating the egg enough at the beginning. There are two basic ways in which this may be rectified:

- Beat in a tablespoon of warm water quickly. This will bring all the ingredients to the same temperature. If this was the problem the warmth will bring the emulsion back.

- If this is not the cause, the only answer is to return to the beginning. Beat another egg yolk and pinch of salt in a clean bowl and slowly add the curdled mixture. Sometimes curdling can be caused by old egg yolks, as these will not take as much oil into emulsion nor emulsify so easily as a fresh yolk.

Browning

A recipe often requires food to be browned and this may be for the sake of appearance, or for the important sealing in of juices.

Stews
In the initial stages of making a stew, meat is browned to seal it so that juices do not escape, and to give the liquid a good colour. This is caused partly by caramelisation of the juices on the outside of the meat, brought about by the action of searing in the pan. Meat that is not treated in this way will lose its taste to the broth in which it is cooking. Vegetables are also usually browned to add to the flavour and colour, especially in the case of onions.

Braises and roasts
When braising and roasting, browning is again used for sealing purposes and to improve the appearance of the finished dish. Generally the joint is fried very quickly, at a high heat, on all sides, and is sealed. Alternatively, the joint may be placed in a very hot oven (400-450°F/200-230°C/gas mark 6-8) initially and then the temperature lowered for the rest of the cooking time. This method is sometimes used for small poultry.

Grills
Heat is applied quickly to food being grilled to seal in the juices as usually no other liquid is served with food cooked by this method, which relies on the juices retained inside. The heat may be lowered to finish cooking the food.

Browning liquid
Brown food colouring may be added to sauces and gravies to give added colour and flavour; this may be bought commercially or can be made by boiling sugar to a high degree of caramelisation. When it has reached that stage, a little boiling water is added to liquefy the sugar which is then called 'blackjack'. This can be stored in an airtight bottle and used when required. Browning should always be used sparingly as the addition of too much can cause overflavouring and sometimes bitterness.

Applied heat
Any food cooked in the oven or on top of the stove may require the taking on of a brown colour. This is usually done by the application of high heat for a limited period of time by using a grill, by raising oven heat or by removing protective covering. It may also be achieved by leaving the food at the temperature at which it has cooked long enough

for a brown colour to appear, as in potato-topped hot-pots. If this method is used, check that the additional time will not dry the food.

Roasting
Browning of roast meats is enhanced by basting during cooking (see page 72).

Coating Food with Crumbs

Food coated with crumbs, using egg as an adhesive, gives a crisp coating and pleasing appearance when cooked.

Making the crumbs
Either commercial or home-made crumbs may be used. To make fresh crumbs use either brown or white bread which is stale. For fine crumbs, some brown breads are unsuitable because of the inclusion of whole or part grains. Brown bread can also be more difficult for making crumbs because of the higher moisture content. Remove the crusts from the bread and taking small pieces of the interior, rub them lightly between the palms, allowing the fine crumbs to fall between the fingers. If preferred, rub the pieces through a fine wire sieve. An electric blender or food processor can be used instead and crusts can then be included if not too hard.

Fresh breadcrumbs can be stored in an airtight container or a plastic bag in the refrigerator for several days before going mouldy.

Dried breadcrumbs are made from pieces of stale bread which have been baked in the oven until hard and golden. They can then be crushed with a rolling pin or put through an electric blender. Dried breadcrumbs can be kept for several weeks in an airtight container. Unused crumbs, if not wet, can be returned to the bulk of the crumbs.

Coating the food
The food to be coated should be firm and dry on the outer surface. Coat with a light dusting of flour so that a dry surface is produced to which the egg and crumbs will stick. Dip the floured food into beaten egg, which can be either just yolks or the whole beaten egg. Remove the excess egg by allowing the food to drip for a moment, or by pulling it gently through the closed hand, which is more effective. Now dip the food into the breadcrumbs, and coat completely. Shake gently to remove any loose crumbs. Press the crumbs that have adhered gently into the egg base, which will ensure that the coating is not disturbed during cooking. Do not coat food far in advance of cooking as the moisture in the egg will make the breadcrumbs soggy. It may even lead to the coating curling off the item when cooked because of the build-up of moisture between the surface of the item and the coating.

The process is far easier if each part of the method is carried out separately. Coat all the items with flour, then egg and finally crumbs. This will ensure that the egg will not become mixed with the crumbs making the process more difficult, and it also stops the fingers becoming coated with layers of egg and crumbs.

Coating ham with crumbs
After the ham or bacon joint has been cooked and cooled, remove the outer skin to reveal the soft fat underneath. Dried or commercial crumbs are then pressed firmly onto this surface which is left uppermost for serving. Cooked meat loaves may also be coated with dried or commercial crumbs.

Coating Food with Batter

Food is covered with batter to provide a crisp coating which helps in sealing the item against the direct effects of heat in the cooking method, and the loss of juice.

Making the batter
For coating most foods there are three different batters which may be made either sweet or savoury. The difference between them is the type of raising agent: it may be baking powder, egg or yeast.

The usual basic proportion for a thick coating batter is 4 oz (100 g) plain flour to $\frac{1}{4}$ pt (150 ml) liquid, either milk or water or a mixture, and including the egg. The flour and liquid is beaten until smooth and creamy and then the raising agent beaten in. If baking powder is used, the mixture should be used almost immediately as the moisture activates the chemicals in the powder. Egg and yeast mixes are allowed to 'develop', for at least 30 minutes. In the egg mixture this means that the gluten is allowed to develop so that its elasticity helps to retain the gases which are produced during cooking. Yeast mixtures also need time to become active.

Batters should always be well beaten as it is at this point that aeration occurs, which ensures a good, light, crisp batter when cooked.

It is important that the right consistency is achieved in the batter for successful coating. If it is too thin the batter will float off the item during cooking, especially if deep-fried. If too thick, the batter will not cook properly, giving a crisp brown outside, but an undercooked, stodgy inside. This may also affect the cooking of the food itself, which may be undercooked.

There are two methods by which a batter can be tested for the right consistency. When brought out of the mixture, the back of a wooden spoon should be coated with a layer of batter in which the mark of a finger drawn through will be retained. Alternatively, if the batter is allowed to fall from a spoon, it should form a curving ribbon which is broad at the top and tapers towards the bottom.

Coating the food
Foods which are to be coated with batter need to be firm and have a dry surface. It helps to give a light dusting of flour to ensure that the batter sticks to the surface of the item. After dipping in a piece of food, allow the excess to drip off, or this will float off the surface of the item, especially when deep-fried. Coated items should be cooked immediately.

Food that has been coated with batter and fried should be well drained on a rack or kitchen paper so that excess fat is not absorbed by the batter, making it soggy.

After frying
Food coated in batter should be prepared and cooked just before eating, so that the batter remains very crisp. Food which has been coated in a sweet batter is usually rolled or dredged in sugar or cinnamon sugar when cooked.

Hanging

Meat, poultry and game are made more tender and flavours are developed by the flesh being left for a period of time after killing so that chemical changes begin to occur. Hanging should be carried out in dry, airy conditions, the meat or bird never being allowed to stand in its own juices, as this will cause it to deteriorate too quickly. During hanging the meat should be watched carefully to make sure that it is not infested by flies or other insects, and so that putrefaction does not set in. Birds with damaged flesh from poor shots should be watched particularly carefully.

Beef
The cuts which are to be used in quick cooking processes must be hung. The forequarter, which has most of the longer-cooking joints, may be used soon after slaughter. The hindquarter is hung for up to 4 weeks to develop flavour and tenderness. This is caused by a weak fermentation of lactic acid in this muscular tissue, which helps to break down the tough connective tissues, making the meat more tender. Meat which has been hung should be dull red in colour and should retain an indentation from the fingers when it is handled. Really well hung beef should have a dark ring around the outside of the meat when a cross section is cut. This is not a sign that the meat is 'off'.

Lamb
To develop the taste and tenderness of lamb, the meat should be hung as a carcass for about a week. The flesh should become a dark or dull red colour. If the meat has a pinkish tinge to it, it is too fresh and will be tough, no matter how it is cooked. Lamb which is bought too fresh can be hung in the home by placing it in a cool place with a loose cover of gauze or butter muslin over it for up to 5 days.

Pork
This is rarely hung, as generally the high fat content almost guarantees tenderness. Pork may, however, be marinaded, which has the same effect as hanging, as well as adding extra flavour. If this is done in brine or salt, bacon and ham is produced.

Poultry
The flavour and tenderness is improved if the bird is hung by the neck for 2-3 days after it has been plucked, but with the entrails still in.

Game
Game is hung by the neck in a dry and airy place, outside if possible, with a slight movement of air to allow the bird to mature for a good period of time without becoming 'bad'. The birds should not be plucked and drawn before hanging. To prevent flies attacking the bird, dust the feathers generously with pepper.

Pheasant will be tasteless and very dry if not hung. (Hanging is done just after shooting.) The birds may be hung for up to 3 weeks in cold weather, and as little as 3 days in warm weather. For average taste, hanging for 7-10 days in cold weather will be sufficient. When buying from a dealer, enquire for how long it has been hung. If the bird is too 'high' for cooking, pluck it and wash it in water to which a little salt and vinegar have been added. Rinse and dry the bird thoroughly after this treatment. The pheasant can be judged ready if the tail feathers can be easily pulled out. Grouse needs to be hung for at least 3 days, though if possible for 5-6 days to develop fully the taste and tenderness, but this will depend on the weather. Test as for pheasant. Pigeons do not need to be hung for more than 7 days and in most cases overnight is enough. Snipe may or may not be hung depending on taste, but as it is eaten with the entrails it should not be hung for more than 2 days in warm weather. Woodcock will be very rubbery in texture if not hung, and needs 1-2 days in warm weather for this effect to be overcome. Venison may need 2-4 weeks hanging depending on the type of deer and the size and age of the carcass. The meat when properly hung should have a strong gamey odour and a very dark colour to the flesh.

Dressing

Dressing refers to the plucking, drawing and trussing of poultry or game for sale and for cooking. Some of the small game birds (such as snipe and woodcock) are not drawn but cooked with the entrails in place.

Plucking

All feathers and hairs from game must be removed before cooking. In the case of poultry the bird should be plucked as soon after killing as possible while the bird is still warm, as the follicles at the base of the feathers are still open and this makes plucking easier.

Game is hung before plucking. Because of the mess caused by the feathers being plucked, it is easiest to pluck directly into a bag, or at least on to a large piece of paper in which the feathers can be enclosed immediately.

For the beginner, it is probably easier to pluck the bird while sitting down with the bag between the legs. Hold the legs of the bird in one hand, with the head hanging downwards into the bag. With the other hand, begin to remove the feathers from near the head, working backwards towards the tail end. This is done by taking a few feathers at a time

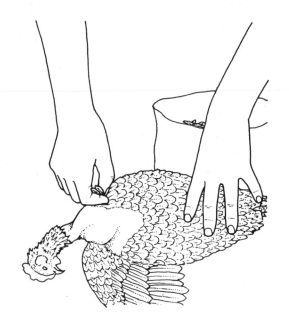

between the thumb and forefingers, and pulling sharply in the direction of the head. Work up the length of the body, removing as much of the down or under-feathers as possible. Taking hold of the tip of one of the wings, remove the feathers from the wing and then repeat for the other. The flight or large feathers on the edge of the wing will require more effort to remove, made easier by using pliers.

When as many of the feathers have been removed as possible, the remaining down and hairs are removed over a naked flame. A gas flame, taper or candle can be used. Holding the bird by the head and the tail or 'pope's nose' turn it quickly through the flame so that the hair and down is singed but without the skin being burned.

If the bird has been allowed to go cold before plucking, it is helpful to hang the bird by the feet from a strong hook to make plucking easier. A well-tried method of making plucking easier, particularly in the case of a cold bird, is to plunge the bird into near-boiling water very briefly. This has the effect of loosening the feathers slightly. Once the feathers have been removed, dry the skin of the bird very carefully.

In an effort to accelerate the process, it is tempting to try to remove too many feathers at one time. This can easily lead to the skin being torn, and the juices from the bird may be lost during cooking, thus spoiling the dish. Trying to pull the feathers out in the wrong direction (i.e. the direction in which they grow rather than against the growth) will also lead to the skin being torn. It will also make the plucking harder than necessary.

Drawing

Once the bird has been plucked, remove the head by cutting through the neck about 2 in (5 cm) from the head of the bird. If a large amount of stuffing is to be used make the cut slightly further away from the body. Slit the skin on the neck still attached to the bird from the first cut to the body on the upper part of the neck (i.e. *not* on the side of the breast). Cut off the skinned neck as close to the body as possible.

Cut off the feet by cutting through the first joint of the leg just below the place where the leg meat forms. This is made easier by cutting through the scale on the front of the leg first whilst the leg is straight, and then by bending the leg until the joint and sinews are exposed. These should be cut straight through at the centre of the joint.

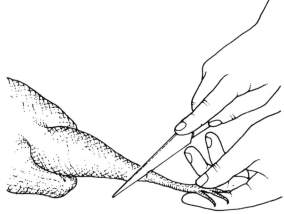

Loosen the windpipe and gullet at the base of the neck, by cutting a small slit to one side and then running the fingers round them. This will allow the windpipe and gullet to be removed from the cavity with the rest of the entrails. Cut round the vent at the tail end, making a hole only just large enough for the fingers to be inserted. In the case of goose and duck, this cut is traditionally made from the vent to the backbone and makes drawing easier.

Insert the fingers as far as possible into the cavity between the entrails and the cavity wall. Move the fingers to left and right in a swivel motion to release the entrails from the connective tissue of the cavity wall. It is very important at this stage, and until the entrails are removed, that the gall bladder is not ruptured as the contents are bitter and will taint the bird, and particularly the liver to which it is attached. Curve the fingers gently over the entrails until the windpipe and gullet are between the first two fingers of the hand and pull gently from the bird. The entrails should come out easily and in one piece. Again at this stage be very careful not to split the gall bladder.

Reserve the giblets (i.e. the heart, gizzard, liver and neck) and dispose of the remainder as they will become bad quickly and are of no use for stocks or flavouring. It is best if these are wrapped in newspaper and burned. They should always be removed from the kitchen as soon as possible, especially in warm weather.

In the case of goose, duck and turkey, when the feet or paddles are removed, a better, less tough result will be attained if the tendons are removed by pulling. This is done when the tendons have been exposed after the first cut on the leg joint. Goose tendons are particularly tough, and should be removed individually by placing each one over a rounded implement and pulling.

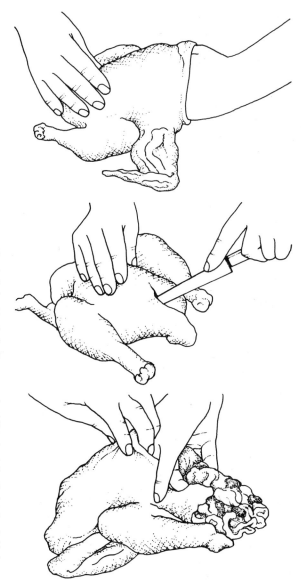

Trussing

A bird is trussed to keep it in good shape, so that it looks attractive on the table and carving is made easier.

A trussing needle, large darning needle or skewer, and fine string or strong cotton are needed for trussing. Fold the tip of the wing underneath the section of the wing closest to the body so that it is held between this section and the body. Fold the neck skin under the body so that it is held in position by the tips of the wings. Pass the trussing needle just behind the base of the wing on one side, through the body, coming out at the equivalent position on the other side. Turn the bird on to its breast. Bring the string over the folded wings, and catch the tips of the wings and the neck skin, with the string actually going through both. Pull the string moderately tight, cut the string and tie a knot.

With the bird on its back and breast uppermost, make a cut in the skin above the vent, and push the tail or 'pope's nose' through, to hold it in position. Press the legs into the sides of the bird underneath

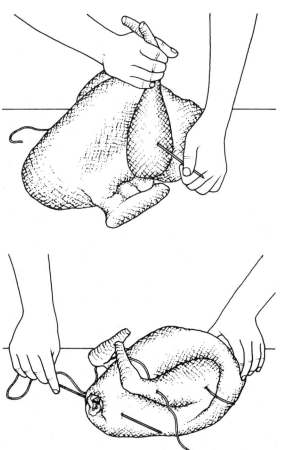

the bulk of the breast, to raise the breast and make a more compact bird. To hold the legs in place, thread the string through the 'pope's nose' and round the two legs and back through the 'pope's nose'. Cut the string and tie tightly in place. These trussing strings should be removed before the bird is served.

If a skewer is being used, it should take the place of the first incisions of the trussing needle and the string should be used to perform the rest of the task.

Small game birds do not need the wings trussed into place, but the legs should be tied lightly. In the case of snipe, the head is kept on the bird. The head is stripped of its skin, bent back, and the beak used to skewer the legs in place.

Boning, Filleting and Jointing

It is extremely useful to practise these techniques at home as some shop owners have little time or willingness to prepare their wares properly. In the country you may also be faced with a freshly caught fish or animal.

Boning and filleting fish

A very sharp, pointed flexible knife is needed for this job. Lay the fish down on a flat surface, preferably a wooden board as this will hold the fish better. Run the point of the knife around the fish between the fins and the main body, cutting the skin and flesh down to the bones but being careful not to cut through the bones, as this will make the process more difficult. Run the point along either side of the backbone, releasing the flesh. With the tail towards you, run the knife under the flesh at the head and near the backbone until it reaches the lateral bones. With the knife blade resting on the lateral bones, make sweeping strokes the length of the fish, removing the flesh from the lateral bones. Having removed the first fillet, turn the fish and remove the second. The other two are removed by turning the fish over and repeating the process.

Boning round fish

With the belly of the fish downwards, cut along the length of the fish to one side of the backbone. Cut downwards from this cut with the blade of the knife resting on the lateral bones, working from the head end to the tail in a diagonal. Turn the fish and repeat for the other side.

Boning herring and mackerel

Place the fish belly side down, with the gutted

cavity separated so that the interior is resting against the board. Press lightly but with some firmness down the length of the backbone, which will have the effect of releasing the bones from the flesh. Turn the fish over and ease out the backbone by running the fingers gently behind the bones between them and the flesh. This may not remove all the bones, but these can be removed separately. The fish can then be split down its length into two fillets.

Boning chicken

Boning must be carried out on a completely thawed bird, as otherwise the flesh will stick unnecessarily to the bones. Remove the pinions (i.e. the tips of the wings). Turn the bird on to its breast and cut through the flesh the length of the backbone. Cut back from here towards the leg and wing joints closest to the body. Keep the knife blade close to the bones so that no flesh is left on the carcass unnecessarily. Cut through the joints that lie next to the carcass without cutting through the main flesh of the bird. Cut the flesh from the rest of the carcass (i.e. the breast), being very careful over the breastbone as the skin and flesh are very thin and delicate. At this point, the main part of the flesh and the wings and legs with their bones in should be left, with the whole of the main part of the carcass removed. Holding the joint of the wing carefully cut the flesh back towards where the pinion would have been. This will cause the flesh of the wing to be turned inside out. Remove the bone completely. Repeat for the other wing. The legs will have two bones inside, the thigh and drumstick. The bone of the thigh is removed first as for the wing. When the second bone is reached break the

joint and cut the tendons. Separate the bones and continue to strip the bone in the drumstick. When both the bones are removed the flesh should be completely inside out.

Jointing chicken

Chickens are usually jointed into four pieces, though these can be divided further. The joints retain their bones for most recipes. With the vent towards you, pull the legs away from the body. Cut the skin which holds the leg to the body. Pull the leg away from the body, outwards and backwards towards you. As the leg reaches about right angles with the body, the joint should stop the leg moving further. At this point give a sharp backward tug which should break the joint. It may be necessary to use a knife to cut through part of the joint and the tendons. Continue pulling the joint towards you and it will pull completely off the bird, taking all the flesh behind the leg with it. In a large bird this can be helped with the use of a knife. This piece forms one joint, but can be divided into two by

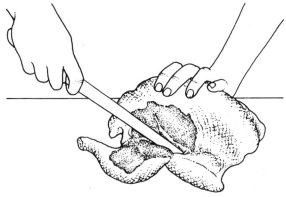

cutting through the joint between the thigh and drumstick.

With the neck end towards you, ascertain the position of the wing joint next to the body of the bird. Cut a straight line through the lower part of the breast from the vent end towards the wing joint. When the joint is reached, cut down through it. Pull the whole joint away from the body. It should consist of the wing and the lower part of the breast. This is not usually divided.

To remove the breast pieces, cut down from the breastbone at the neck end, pull the flesh back towards the vent end, if necessary, loosening the flesh from the carcass with a knife, though generally this should not be necessary. The breast pieces can be divided into two by making a diagonal cut across the length of the piece. This leaves the carcass almost completely free of flesh.

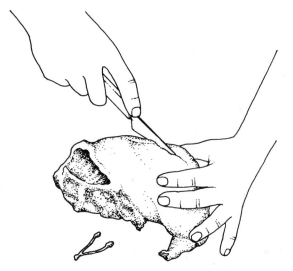

Boning meat

The most important aspect of boning meat is having a short, stiff-bladed and very sharp boning knife. This makes the job easier and much safer.

To bone a chop or steak

Starting from the bone appearing on the outer edge of the meat, scrape very close along the length of the bone removing the flesh carefully so as not to damage the shape of the meat and cause undue juice loss during cooking. If there is a small piece of tenderloin below the main part of the meat, on the other side of the bone, remove it and if the chop or steak is large enough, tie it back in place. If the main part of the meat is not large enough, place the tenderloin close to the main part of the meat during cooking to prevent it becoming overcooked and dry.

To bone a leg

Starting from the broad or tail end, cut the remainder of the pelvic girdle away if it is present. The meat should be cut in short, sharp strokes with the knife blade as close to the bone as possible, but being sure that the soft bone covering is not removed from the bone, and that any tendons and gristle are left attached to the bone. Sever the joint between this bone and the knuckle of the main leg bone. Cut back along the length of this bone, pulling the meat away with one hand and cutting away from it with the other, until the next joint is reached. The knuckle joint now has to be parted from the last bone in the leg which is traditionally left in place. This can be done by making a small slit in the skin at the knee joint and cutting through the tendons and gristle, in which case the hole needs to be sewn up. The joint can also be parted by a patient pulling and cutting action, which will eventually loosen the joint. This should leave a complete leg with the small bone in place and a large 'pocket' which is ready to be stuffed.

To bone a shoulder

In many ways this is more difficult than boning a leg because of the shape of the bones in the shoulder. One side is almost flat and the other has a sort of 'fin' which is at right angles to the main direction of the bone. With the flat of the shoulder on a board, the cut end facing, and the narrow or shoulder part of the joint to the right, make a cut down the right-hand edge until the bone is reached. Taking the top of the bone, which is basically flat, scrape the flesh away as carefully as possible, until the 'fin' is reached. Work the flesh away from this part of the bone and continue along the flat until the whole of the top side of the bone is exposed. Do not cut right through the flesh on the outer side of the bone as this will divide the shoulder flesh into two, making rolling or stuffing more difficult. Turn the shoulder over and remove the flesh from the other side and carefully remove the bone by cutting around the flesh on the outer edge and by severing the knuckle or ball-and-socket joint. The joint can now be rolled. If it is to be stuffed, place the stuffing in the centre and join the two flaps of meat in their original shape and stitch together with thin string or use skewers for cooking. These stitches should be removed before serving.

Chining

This refers to the sawing of the bones between the backbone and the ribs of cuts such as rib of beef and loins of lamb and pork. This makes boning and carving easier when the meat has been cooked.

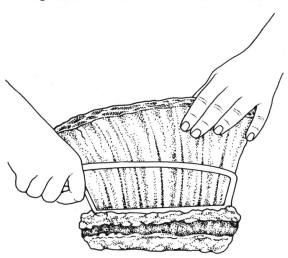

Stuffing Meat and Poultry

Stuffing is placed inside meat or poultry to give flavour and contrast to the dish and to extend servings. The stuffing is made in such a way that it will absorb some of the fat and flavour of the meat or poultry.

Stuffing should be firm, but not too dry. If a stuffing is too soft through the addition of too much liquid or egg, it will ooze out of the meat or poultry, will not absorb the juices and will spoil the final appearance of the dish. Stuffing expands during cooking and may ooze out of position, so it is important not to overstuff food. In balancing the ingredients of stuffing, flavourings which will overpower the flavour of the meat or poultry should be avoided.

When meat is stuffed, extra time should be allowed for cooking on top of that for the actual weight of the meat itself. Allow 15-20 minutes per 1 lb (450 g) of stuffing.

A whole boned joint of meat (e.g. leg or shoulder of lamb)

Lay the boned piece of meat on a flat surface with the skin side underneath. Season the upper surface lightly with pepper and salt. Spread the stuffing over this surface and stuff into the small 'pockets' left from boning the meat. This will help hold the stuffing in position. Do not over-stuff the joint, and only take the stuffing to within 1 in (2.5 cm) of the edge of the piece. This is to stop the stuffing from oozing out during the cooking process. Roll the meat into a neat roll, tucking in any small loose pieces of the joint, so that these are not burned during cooking. Tie loops of string round the rolled joint at about 1 in (2.5 cm) intervals to hold the meat in shape and keep the stuffing in place. Remove the strings when carving. Sometimes it is easier to remove only those where the meat is actually to be carved, leaving the rest to hold the shape of the remainder of the joint.

A flat piece of meat (e.g. breast of lamb or loin of pork)

The procedure is as above, except that generally the amount of stuffing is smaller and more thinly spread as the meat is rolled around itself as well as round the stuffing. It is most important that the stuffing is not taken too near the edges of the meat as in these cases there are no 'pockets' to hold the stuffing in place.

Chicken

Make sure that the flap of skin at the neck end is loose and take care to keep it whole, or the stuffing will ooze out of any tears.

Push the stuffing firmly between this flap and the body of the bird, creating a well-shaped curve from the breastbone downwards, allowing plenty of excess neck skin for closing. Pull the flap of skin tightly over the stuffing and secure it underneath the bird by skewering in place or sewing the flap of skin to the area between the wings. Make sure that there are no gaps through which the stuffing can escape when it expands through the absorption of juices in cooking.

Chicken is traditionally stuffed with parsley and thyme stuffing, but there are many alternatives including the chicken liver, bacon, sausagemeat or fruit.

Turkey

Turkeys are often stuffed both at the neck and in the cavity with two different types of stuffing. Traditionally the neck end is stuffed with chestnut stuffing, and the cavity with sausagemeat.

The neck end should be stuffed as for chicken, but because of the large area of skin to be secured underneath the bird, the flap is better sewn down. This can be done with fine string, or linen thread, or a double cotton thread. If the cavity is stuffed, never fill it completely so that space is left for the circulation of hot air which will aid the even cooking of the bird. The cavity does not need to be sealed.

Duck

Traditionally only older or larger birds are stuffed. For a young bird an apple or a peeled orange in the cavity will add flavour. The stuffing is usually placed in the cavity from the tail end as it is then easier to remove. Leave room for the circulation of hot air during cooking. Duck is traditionally stuffed with sage and onion stuffing, but fruit or dried fruit added to a basic breadcrumb stuffing goes well with duck flesh.

Breast of poultry, or game, chops, steak or other small pieces of meat

Taking the longest side of the piece of meat, make an incision the length of the meat to within $\frac{1}{2}$ in (1.25 cm) of either end. Cut a slit in the meat to make a pocket, leaving a thin slice of bacon or pork along the opening and tie it in place with loops of fine string, holding the bacon or pork in place and the opening closed. Remove the string before serving.

Thawing

Many frozen foods must be raised to a temperature of 35-40°F/1-5°C at which no ice crystals remain in the product and thus the product is ready for use. It is important to thaw these items correctly to avoid the risk of contamination.

Meat

The time required to thaw meat will vary according to its size. It is advisable to thaw meat in the refrigerator because of the risk of degeneration and contamination. If it is not possible to use a refrigerator, leave the meat covered in a cool place, where there is a slight draught and where the temperature does not rise above 60°F/16°C. The time taken for meat to thaw in room temperature is usually two to three times quicker than in refrigerated conditions. Thawed meat that is not going to be used immediately should be stored in the coolest part of the refrigerator, covered, and used within 4 days at the most. Offal and minced meat are more perishable and should be used immediately. Lamb and beef should be thawed in their wrappings so that the meat has a chance of re-absorbing the juices that ooze out of the meat during the process. In the refrigerator, allow approximately 5 hours per 1 lb (450 g) and at room temperature 2 hours per 1 lb (450 g). Pork and veal should be removed from their wrappings and allowed to thaw for 5 hours per 1 lb (450 g) in the refrigerator. Veal may be thawed for 2 hours per 1 lb (450 g) at room temperature. Pork should never be thawed at room temperature because of the added risk of contamination in this meat.

Offal should be uncovered and thawed in a refrigerator, but never at room temperature, due to the contamination risk. This also applies to made-up meat products such as sausages.

Dishes containing meat, such as stews, can be heated gently from the frozen state either on top of the stove or in the oven. They may also be thawed in the refrigerator and then heated, which will cut down on heating time and prevent scorched food.

A general rule of thumb to follow is that the smaller the piece of meat the longer by comparison the thawing time. Thus a 1 in (2.5 cm) steak will require at least 8 hours in refrigerated conditions, and 3-4 hours at room temperature; minced meat needs 10-12 hours in the refrigerator and $1-1\frac{1}{2}$ hours at room temperature per 1 lb (450 g).

Poultry and game
Poultry and game should always be thawed with the covering removed but thawing is basically the same as for meat. Both should be thawed in refrigerated conditions due to the risk of contamination.
Chicken under 4 lb (2 kg) allow 12-16 hours
Chicken over 4 lb (2 kg) allow $1-1\frac{1}{2}$ days
Duck 3-5 lb (1.5-2.5 kg) allow $1-1\frac{1}{2}$ days
Goose 4-14 lb (2-7 kg) allow 1-2 days
Turkey:
- If several days are available for thawing, leave the turkey in its insulated bag or box in a cool place or still in its plastic bag in the refrigerator. Check about 48 hours before it is to be used that it is becoming soft. If it is not, remove the plastic bag and return to the refrigerator.
- If two days are available, place the turkey in a cool place in its plastic bag. There should be a slight draught and the temperature should not rise above 60°F/15°C.

- If only a full day is available leave the turkey in its bag in a warm place.
- If the turkey is needed urgently in less than 12 hours, keep the bird immersed in warm water in the bag. Change the water regularly.

Fish
Fish that is to be coated with breadcrumbs or batter should be completely thawed before coating, as the crumbs or batter will not stick to a frozen surface. Most fish should be thawed in its wrapping, except smoked and kippered fish. Fish may be thawed either in the refrigerator or at room temperature, the length of time required depending on the size and thickness of the fish and on the density of the packing. Whole fish, fillets and cutlets require from 6-10 hours per 1 lb (450 g) in the refrigerator, and 3-5 hours at room temperature. Smoked fish needs 5 hours in the refrigerator and $2-2\frac{1}{2}$ hours at room temperature per 1 lb (450 g). Such small items as shrimps require 6-8 hours in the refrigerator and at least 2 hours at room temperature for a commercially packed 4 oz (100 g) package.

Once fish has been thawed *never* refreeze it due to the great contamination risk when it is re-thawed. Always use thawed fish as soon as possible after thawing because of the fast deterioration rate and the risk of contamination. Many fish items packed commercially can be cooked from frozen and it is important to read the package carefully.

Vegetables
The majority of vegetables can be cooked straight from the freezer. The exceptions are:

Broccoli and asparagus which should be thawed enough to separate the pieces to allow for even cooking.

Corn-on-the-cob should be completely thawed, so that the cob becomes hot right the way through in the cooking process.

Beetroot should be completely thawed and left covered in a warm place for 2-3 hours to allow the flavour to develop.

Mushrooms should be allowed to thaw completely, in their container, but with the air able to get to them, for 2-3 hours.

Fruit
Fruit that is to be used for cooking purposes or for preserves can be used directly from the freezer without thawing. Purées and pulp fruit should be thawed overnight in refrigerated conditions to allow the full flavour of the fruit to develop. Fruit

that is to be eaten raw should be thawed slowly in the refrigerator so that the shape and condition of the fruit is as good as possible. If the fruit is thawed at room temperature the texture may be softer than if thawed in the refrigerator. Very soft fruits need 6-7 hours to thaw in the refrigerator and 2-3 hours at room temperature per 1 lb (450 g). This includes strawberries, raspberries and black currants. The other soft fruits need 7-8 hours in the refrigerator and 3-4 hours at room temperature. Crisp fruits need 7-8 hours in the refrigerator and $3\frac{1}{2}$-4 hours at room temperature. Purées need 6-8 hours in the refrigerator and 2-4 hours at room temperature per 1 lb (450 g).

Baked goods
Cakes should be thawed in their wrappings to retain the moisture content. An exception to this is cakes which are iced, in which case the wrapping should be removed from the icing as it will stick to the wrapper. The length of time required for thawing will vary according to the size of the cake but in general 1-2 hours at room temperature should be sufficient.

Biscuits should be thawed out of wrappings so that they do not absorb any moisture and become soggy. Individual biscuits should take only 30 minutes to thaw.

Cooked pastry dishes to be eaten cold should be thawed in the refrigerator allowing 4-6 hours depending on the size. They should be eaten as soon as possible because of the risk of contamination from the filling, particularly in the case of meat. Uncooked pastry needs to be completely thawed before use (except in the case of made-up items which can be cooked from frozen) and will take 3-4 hours per 1 lb (450 g) at room temperature.

Bread should be thawed in a bag so that the outside does not form a dry crust and the moisture content remains high. To achieve a crisp crust on pre-cooked bread products place the thawed item in a hot oven for 5-10 minutes.

For the best results with uncooked dough, it should be thawed in the refrigerator to allow the yeast time to become active again. Uncooked dough can be left to thaw overnight, but can be thawed in 5-6 hours for a 1 lb (450 g) loaf at room temperature.

Prepared foods
Many prepared foods can be used straight from the freezer. In the case of stews, purées and soups these should be heated over a low heat so that moisture content is kept stable. They may be thawed in the refrigerator before heating, which cuts heating time; foods which do not require reheating, such as mousses, should be thawed in the refrigerator.

Pies and pastries can be cooked straight from the freezer, but if to be eaten cold they should be thawed in the refrigerator (see above).

Dairy goods
Eggs, whole, yolks or whites, should be completely thawed before use. This will take 18-20 hours in refrigerated conditions and 1-$1\frac{1}{2}$ hours at room temperature per $\frac{1}{2}$ pt (300 ml). Thawed eggs should not be kept for more than 2 days due to the great risk of contamination and resultant food poisoning.

Cream should be thawed with the container open and will take 10-12 hours in the refrigerator and 4-5 hours at room temperature per $\frac{1}{2}$ pt (300 ml).

Butter thaws comparatively quickly, taking about 2 hours in the refrigerator and about 30 minutes at room temperature per $\frac{1}{2}$ lb (225 g).

Cheese is best thawed slowly in the refrigerator to stop the development of a rubbery texture. Allow 8 hours per $\frac{1}{4}$ lb (100 g) in the refrigerator.

Short cuts
These apply to foods that are packed in a waterproof wrapping. If frozen food is required in a hurry, it may be immersed in warm water which is changed often. If time allows, the result is better if allowed to thaw in cold water which is left running over the wrapping. Thawing which is speeded up in this way may result in fish and meat having a slightly tougher flesh.

If the wrapper is damaged, water may seep into the food. In meat and fish this will lead to a leaking of the juices into the water, which will result in a deterioration of the flavour. In the case of damaged wrapping, it is best to rewrap the product in a waterproof container.

Although it is possible to speed up the thawing process by placing the food in a very warm place, the outside may thaw properly while the inside, particularly of a large piece, will not be thawed. If the food is then cooked for the normal time, there is a possibility of food poisoning occuring, because the frozen part of the product will be undercooked and prone to the activity of micro-organisms.

Health risks
Under the conditions of freezing most enzyme activity and that of micro-organisms ceases. Some activity continues, which is why all frozen foods have a limited life in the freezer. Commercial product dates should be noted, and home-frozen

products should be given a date. Below temperatures of 40°F/4°C activity of the micro-organisms that produce poisonous products ceases.

In thawing, the bacterial content of food becomes very important. As the food becomes warmer, the bacteria begin to multiply rapidly. It is thus advisable to thaw in the refrigerator at all times, if at all possible, as the lower the temperature of the product the lower the activity of the bacteria. This also results in more even thawing.

Generally, thawed foods deteriorate in the same way as fresh foods, but do so at a faster rate and should therefore be regarded as more perishable. This is particularly so for fruit and vegetables where there has been damage to the tissues due to blanching. Bacteria attack these softened fruits more quickly than those that are undamaged.

All foods which are heated in their frozen state, straight from the freezer, should be heated very thoroughly to stop all activity of micro-organisms.

Boiling

Food may be cooked by immersion in boiling liquid (212°F/100°C). The rate of boiling may be judged according to the speed at which the water bubbles, governed by the amount of heat applied. The most gentle form of boiling is simmering.

Root vegetables

The vegetables should be peeled if this is required and cut into even-sized pieces so that they all cook within the same time. Root vegetables (except new potatoes) are placed in cold water and brought to the boil. This helps to enhance the flavour and will help to remove the acid taste of some raw vegetables. There is no advantage in boiling vegetables rapidly as this can break them or make them too soft. Old potatoes in particular should be brought to the boil from cold and simmered very gently so that they do not break up. In some cases, old potatoes develop a slight discolouration during cooking which is not harmful but unattractive. The addition of a little lemon juice or vinegar during cooking will prevent this. New potatoes should be placed in boiling water so that as much vitamin C as possible is retained. A sprig of mint in the water enhances their flavour. To check if root vegetables are cooked, pierce carefully with a skewer or the point of a sharp knife. The point should enter the vegetable easily. Boiled vegetables should be well drained, tossed in a knob of butter and garnished with a small amount of finely chopped parsley unless they are being served with a sauce.

Green vegetables

All green vegetables should be placed in boiling water to assist in the retention of water-soluble vitamins and to set the colour. Traditionally green vegetables have been boiled in plenty of water with the lid off the pan but more recently it has been accepted that they are better boiled in as little water as possible with the lid on. This means that the vegetables are partially steamed and that a greater proportion of the vitamins are retained, as the process takes a shorter time. Green vegetables are best served slightly crisp, as the colour and flavour are better and a greater percentage of vitamins is retained. Overcooked green vegetables quickly become soggy, loose flavour and colour and a greater percentage of the vitamins.

Fish

Boiling fish breaks up the delicate structure of the flesh and fish is therefore generally better poached.

Meat

Beef In general the tougher pieces of beef are boiled and also salt beef. Other cuts may be boiled but the process is particularly used to tenderise the tough joints. Salt joints should be soaked in clear, cold water before boiling to remove excess salt which will take about 2 hours for very mildly salted pieces. A heavily salted joint should be soaked overnight so ask the butcher for his recommendation. Incorrect boiling when cooking meat can lead to a dry and tasteless joint. The meat should be placed into already boiling water, and then brought back to the boil as quickly as possible. This causes the albumen in the meat to coagulate and prevents the juices from escaping into the cooking liquid. The flavour is also better retained if very little water is used, although it should cover the meat compeltely, so use a pan which is only just larger than the joint. Flavourings are usually added to the liquid such as carrots, onions and herbs to enhance the flavour and these can be used as accompaniments for the meat when served.

For 1 lb (450 g) meat allow 45 minutes from the time the water returns to the boil. For 1-2 lb (450 g-1 kg) allow 1-1$\frac{1}{2}$ hours and for joints over this weight allow 30 minutes per 1 lb (450 g). After the meat has returned to the boil, turn down the heat until the water is only just simmering. This will ensure the tenderness of the meat, for if it is boiled at speed the protein will toughen, giving the whole joint an unattractive toughness and grey colour.

Salt meat is boiled in the same way but is brought to the boil from cold. In the case of very salt meat, the water from the first boiling should be strained off, and fresh water brought to the boil again with the meat in it. This allows the salt to dissolve, which occurs more easily in cold water.

The more usual joints of beef used for boiling are brisket, silverside, topside and any of the salted joints. All joints should be well dressed and flat pieces such as brisket rolled before tying at regular intervals. This will ensure that the meat does not disintegrate during the cooking process and is easier to carve. All meat that is to be eaten cold should be thoroughly cooled in the cooking liquid to ensure that the joint does not become dry.

Other meats Cook as beef. The usual joints of lamb and mutton used for boiling are the leg and the boned and rolled breast which may or may not be stuffed. Pork is usually boiled only if it is salt. The delicate texture and flavour of unsalted pork joints makes these unsuitable generally for boiling.

Bacon joints These should be soaked in cold, clear water for at least 1-3 hours depending on the size and saltiness of the joint. As with other salted meats, a bacon joint should be placed in cold water and brought to the boil slowly, and then simmered for the remaining cooking period. Vegetables and herbs can be added to the water for added flavour and so can cider or beer (to replace half the water). The joint should be placed with the skin downwards in the water to protect the flesh from the heat on the bottom of the pan. Scum should be removed so that it does not taint either meat or cooking liquid.

If the joint is to be eaten hot, it should be removed from the pan and the outer skin removed. At this point the joint may be glazed. The soft fat is scored with a sharp knife, traditionally in a diamond-shaped pattern. This is then brushed with sugar (brown gives a better colour) or honey, which may have some lemon in it. Also traditionally the centre of each diamond is decorated with a clove which is removed before serving. The meat is then placed in a very hot oven (400-450°F/200-300°C/gas mark 6-8) for about 15-20 minutes, or until the glaze has melted and become brown and bubbly. If the joint is to be eaten cold, it should be allowed to cool in the cooking liquid. The skin should be removed when the joint is cold. Traditionally the soft fat is then coated in breadcrumbs.

Tongue This is cooked as other salt meats, the tough outer skin being removed while hot if it is to be eaten hot and cold if it is to be eaten cold.

Accompaniments for salt meat
Generally boiled meat is rather more insipid than meats which have been roasted, stewed or grilled. It is advisable to serve them with well-flavoured vegetables and a sharp sauce such as mustard, horse-radish, caper or one with a tomato base. Boiled meat is also often accompanied by capers and gherkins, to give a sharp contrast.

Eggs
It is a bit of a misnomer to refer to 'boiled' eggs as they should in fact be simmered to prevent toughness. If boiled too quickly, the protein will toughen and the flavour of the yolk will be spoiled. To help prevent the egg cracking during cooking it is advisable to use eggs at room temperature, not straight from the refrigerator. Should an egg crack during cooking, add a little salt or vinegar to the water, which will help the albumen to congeal more quickly. Place the eggs in a pan well-covered with cold water, and bring to the boil as quickly as possible. Once boiling, begin to time the cooking period, and turn down the heat so that the water just simmers. The time required for cooking eggs will vary with size and freshness, as it will take longer for the white to set when an egg is large and fresh. A general guide is to allow 3 minutes for a large, soft-boiled egg and 2-2$\frac{1}{2}$ minutes for a small, soft-boiled egg. Hard-boiled eggs need 6-8 minutes, depending on size. If boiled for too long, the hard-boiled egg will develop an unattractive black ring around the yolk, although this is not inedible. If the hard-boiled egg is to be eaten cold, place under running water immediately the cooking time is completed to stop the cooking process and cool the egg as quickly as possible.

Pasta
This must be boiled in plenty of fast-boiling salted water to prevent it sticking together and sticking to the pan. Pasta should not be boiled from cold as this will cause disintegration. Generally pasta needs only a short cooking time (10-15 minutes) and should be *al dente*, that is slightly resistant to the teeth when bitten. It should not, however, be hard in the centre.

Rice
Most long-grain white rice will absorb double its volume in water during cooking, so for each measure of rice use one and a half measures of water. The water for boiling should be well salted. Bring the salted water to the boil and add the rice. Return to the boil, stirring a couple of times to ensure that no rice sticks to the base of the pan. Turn down to a simmer and cook until the rice is tender. Rice should never be overcooked as this

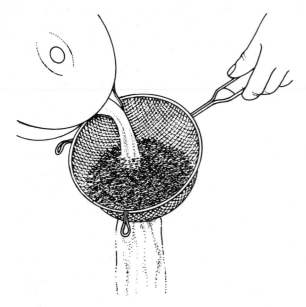

will produce a soggy, solid result which is not pleasant to eat. To ensure that the rice is really light when served, strain through a colander and then pour boiling water over the rice to remove any starch particles that adhere to the outside of the cooked grains and are responsible for the grains sticking together.

Brown rice takes longer to cook than other types, requiring 35-40 minutes, and needs two measures of water to one of rice. Pre-cooked and instant types of rice will take a much shorter time, and the instructions on the packet should be carefully followed.

Poaching and Simmering

Food is poached in a liquid which is kept as close to boiling point as possible and there should be no perceptible movement in the water. Simmering is a cooking method where the water is just at boiling point, but barely moving.

Poaching
The food being cooked should be completely covered by the water, which ensures even cooking. There should be not only enough water to cover the food but also to allow free circulation of the liquid. Foods that are to be poached are usually of a delicate nature and therefore need careful handling. A broad-based perforated utensil such as a fish slice or perforated spoon should be used to remove cooked food from the water. The liquid, which can be water, stock, wine, sugar syrup or other liquid should be brought to the boil first, the item added

and then allowed to poach below boiling point. If boiled, delicate foods will break up in the turbulent water.

Oven poaching
'Poaching' is sometimes used as a term to describe cooking items such as fruit or fish in the oven. In this case, the food is placed in a dish with a little liquid and covered (in the case of fish with a buttered paper) and placed in the oven at a low temperature (275-325°F/140-160°C/gas mark 1-3). The juice in these cases is very often used as the basis for an accompanying sauce.

Eggs
Bring the water to the boil with a little vinegar, which will help the albumen to coagulate quickly. It is best to poach only very fresh eggs, as these will retain their shape well. Old eggs have a weaker albumen which will tend to float away from the white when placed in the water. The water should be brought off the boil and placed on the heat source in such a way as to allow a little movement of the water at one side. The eggs should be broken into this area, as the turbulence of the water will turn the eggs over, creating a well-shaped finished product. The pan should then be removed from the heat, and the food allowed to poach until done. Eggs can be partially poached in this way and used later in another dish. They should be removed when the white is set enough to handle without damaging the egg and placed in cold water, in which they will keep for up to 2 days. They should be thoroughly reheated and cooked in water just below boiling point, or in the oven.

Fish
Fish is poached differently, depending on size and cut. Small pieces, cutlets and fillets should be placed straight into hot water, which should be returned to the boil and then allowed to cool to poaching temperature. Whole fish should be placed into cold water and brought to the boil quickly. When boiling point has been reached, the pan should be taken off the heat and the fish allowed to cook in the cooling liquid. This will ensure that the fish is not broken up and overcooked. This is particularly important for large fish such as salmon which can become very dry if overcooked.

Simmering
This is a form of very gentle boiling. In fact very few foods are boiled hard, and most are simmered to prevent the break-up of the item and the

excessive loss of nutrients. Generally the water is brought to a good boil and then allowed to cool to a very slight boil in which the water is barely moving. Meat dishes cooked on top of the stove in a liquid, such as stews, are simmered so that the protein does not become unduly hardened. The method is used to help break down the connective tissues in the meat which would otherwise cause it to be tough. Fast boiling causes these tissues to contract quickly, which results in the meat becoming tough. Simmering is often carried out without a lid on the pan, as the pressure caused by steam under the lid means that the liquid will boil at a slightly higher temperature, which is more difficult to control.

Steaming

Food may be cooked through the direct or indirect heat of steam. This is a moist method of cooking. The great advantage of steaming is that because the food does not come into direct contact with water, water-soluble vitamins (vitamin C for example) and minerals are retained. This method also ensures that the majority of foodstuffs do not break up during cooking. Steaming does not require a flavoured cooking liquid or fat, retains an individual flavour and the food is not hardened by the action of direct heat on the proteins.

The food to be cooked must not come into contact with the boiling water that is producing the steam. Steamers have a base in which the water is boiled, and perforated containers fit above this to keep the food separate. The perforated food containers allow the steam condensed on the food to drain

away. It is also possible to buy a perforated metal basket on three legs which is placed in a pan containing some water. The pan in which it is being done must have a close-fitting lid to enclose the steam. Alternatively, some foods such as fish can be steamed by being placed on a covered plate over a pan of boiling water. Only small items are cooked by steam; large items would take a long time to cook.

Items to be steamed should be placed on perforated trays to allow the condensed steam to disperse. If being cooked like a pudding in a basin, this should be well covered so that steam does not make the food soggy. Meat or fish should be covered so that juices are not lost. In the majority of cases the water is brought to the boil before the items to be steamed are added.

Care should be taken not to allow the water to boil dry during the cooking time. If extra water has to be added, this should be boiling, so that the cooking process is not stopped while the water returns to the boil.

Oversteamed foodstuffs can become pappy and gain an unpleasantly developed flavour and odour and it is therefore advisable to time steaming carefully.

Parboiling

Food may be partly boiled and then finished a different way, such as roasting.

The food for parboiling is prepared in the usual way. Most vegetables are placed in boiling water, the exception being potatoes, which are brought to the boil from cold. The food is then cooked at a simmer for 10-15 minutes, strained, and the cooking process continued by other means.

For roast potatoes, the best results can be obtained by parboiling them for 10 minutes before roasting. This will result in a good, crisp, well-coloured outside to the potatoes. The process also applies to other roast vegetables. It cuts down the cooking time required for roasting by about one-third. Vegetables that are to be braised (except the very leafy ones), particularly onions, benefit from parboiling.

Advance cooking
It is quite possible to cook vegetables in advance by using this method which is useful when entertaining. The vegetables should be prepared in the usual way and plunged into a large quantity of boiling water (this applies to new but not old potatoes). This is to ensure that the water returns to the boil as quickly as possible. The vegetables

should be cooked to within 3-5 minutes of the time at which they should normally be considered cooked. The more fragile the vegetable the shorter the time. When this point has been reached, remove the vegetables quickly and plunge into very cold water. This is to stop the cooking process. If it is not done, or done ineffectively, the cooking process will continue, causing discolouration, overcooking and in some cases the development of a pungent flavour (this is particularly the case with members of the cabbage family). Drain thoroughly when cold. Just before the vegetables are required, plunge them into boiling water and finish the cooking process.

Blanching

Vegetables for freezing must be blanched by plunging into boiling water. Fruits and nuts may also be blanched to facilitate peeling. The item blanched is immediately cooled to stop the cooking process.

Vegetables for freezing

Before freezing, most vegetables are blanched to kill enzymes and to preserve colour, flavour and texture. This is done by plunging them into boiling water, the length of time depending on the vegetable. They are then refreshed, that is cooled immediately to stop the cooking process. The vegetables should be prepared in the form in which they are frozen, as later handling will defeat much of what has been achieved by blanching.

Eight pints of boiling water are used for each 1 lb (450 g) vegetables. The water should be changed regularly, after every six or seven blanchings. Allow the water to boil, and then plunge the vegetables into the water in a wire basket, or other container through which the water can circulate freely. Cook and bring back to the boil as fast as possible. Timing should start from the moment that the water returns to the boil.

After boiling for the required time, the vegetables should be removed from the water and plunged very quickly in to very cold, preferably iced, water. This is to stop the cooking process and to fix the colours of certain vegetables, most notably the green ones. The cooling process will take as long as the initial blanching.

Blanching can be carried out by the steaming method. This is done over steam in a pan in which a wire basket can be placed and which can be closed with a tight-fitting lid, so that the steam can act on the food. A small amount of water should be boiled in the bottom of a pan in which has been placed a trivet or grid which rises above the water. On this is placed the wire basket in which the vegetables are placed for blanching. This form of blanching takes half as much time again as the boiling method. It is unsuitable for the very leafy vegetables because they collapse in the steam, thus not allowing the steam to move around all the vegetables.

Blanching times

These apply to an 'average-sized' vegetable where this may be applicable (e.g. in the case of Brussels sprouts) and thus time allowances should be made if the vegetable is either very small or large. Times apply to boiling method.

Asparagus (depending on size of spear)	2-4 minutes
Artichokes (depending on size of choke)	5-7 minutes
Broad beans	$1\frac{1}{2}$ minutes
Broccoli (depending on size of head)	3-5 minutes
Brussels sprouts	3-4 minutes
Cabbage (shredded), red or white	$1\frac{1}{2}$ minutes
Carrots (prepared or small whole)	3 minutes
Cauliflower sprigs	3 minutes
Celery (1 in/2.5 cm lengths)	2 minutes
Corn on the cob	5-8 minutes
French beans (whole)	3 minutes
French beans (sliced)	2 minutes
Runner beans (sliced)	2 minutes
Parsnip (diced)	2 minutes
Peas	1 minute
Spinach	$1\frac{1}{2}$ minutes
Turnips (diced)	$2\frac{1}{2}$ minutes

The importance of blanching for the freezer

Vegetables are blanched for a variety of reasons:

- The destruction of most of the enzymes, which would otherwise continue to cause colour change, further softening of the tissues and further loss of nutrients.

- The destruction of up to 99 per cent of microorganisms (though in the home this may only be as high as 80 per cent) which may otherwise cause further deterioration of the food.

- The extraction of a large part of the air trapped in the vegetables. This to a certain extent causes a shrinking in the bulk of the vegetables.

- Wilting is slowed, thus ensuring that texture of food is not too much changed when thawed.

- The green colour in many vegetables is stabilised and enhanced.

The process can result in the loss of 10-20 per cent of sugars, salt and protein, some of the vitamins B_1 and B_2 and up to one-third of vitamin C.

Fruit and nuts

Blanching can also be used to assist in the removal of skins from fruit and nuts, such as peaches, tomatoes and almonds. This is done by plunging the item into boiling water for 10-15 seconds and then cooling immediately. The skin should then peel off easily without damage to the flesh.

Stewing

Stewing is a method of cooking tougher and lower-quality foods in liquid in the oven or on top of the stove to make them tender. With the addition of various flavourings they are made more tasty than when boiled.

The words associated with this method of cooking include *ragoût, casserole, poêlage* and the traditional French names for specific types such as *carbonnade. Fricassées, curries* and *jugged dishes* are also classified as stews. *Ragoût* refers to a dish in which the meat is cut into dice and is cooked in a seasoned sauce or broth. This may be brown as in Goulash, white as in a *blanquette* made with white meats, and boiled such as in Irish Stew. *Casserole* refers to the dish in which the stew is cooked, so that any stew cooked in such a vessel is referred to as a *casserole. Poêlage* refers to a method in which the items are placed in a tight-lidded pan, with vegetables and sufficient butter to baste the meat, in a fairly hot oven. The lid is removed after two-thirds of the cooking time to allow the ingredients to brown. The juices are often removed and added to other ingredients to produce a rich sauce.

Stewing is excellent for cooking tougher cuts of meat, as the long, slow cooking breaks down connective tissue and water-soluble gelatine, thus improving the tenderness of the meat. The gelatine, if present in high enough quantities, will thicken and enrich the gravy. This is why either belly of pork with its skin or pork skin alone is added to some stews as these are high in gelatine. The more usual cuts of meat for stewing are flank, blade, chuck, skirt, leg and shin of beef; breast, scrag end and neck of lamb and mutton; hand, belly and spare rib of pork; and neck, breast, knuckle and hock of veal. Game which is too old for roasting is often cooked by a stewing method.

Vegetables are added to a stew to give more flavour and these are usually root vegetables. Older and larger vegetables can be used, as these need long, slow cooking and will not break up.

Herbs and spices will give additional flavour. The liquid used should be a well-flavoured stock or a stock cube may be dissolved in the correct amount of fluid.

Brown stews

Trim the meat of all fat and gristle and cut into the required size pieces. This will vary with the recipe, but generally 1 in (2.5 cm) cubes are suitable. Toss the meat in flour and seasoning until it is well covered. This will help in sealing the meat and thickening the gravy. Heat a small amount of fat, oil, dripping, butter or an oil-and-butter mixture, in the stewpan or heat-proof casserole. If a pan which cannot be heated on the top of the stove is to be used, heat the fat in a separate pan to which liquid can be added without spoiling the surface. This should preferably have a heavy bottom, as high heat has to be applied and the meat may easily burn in a thin-bottomed pan.

Fry the vegetables in the fat, which should be hot enough to brown them quickly. This process will also help to extract some of the flavour. Remove the vegetables from the pan and fry the meat at a searing heat. The fat should be hot enough to give off a slight blue haze. The meat should be browned quickly to seal in the juices and to give it colour. This has to be done quickly so that the internal temperature of the meat does not change, as the action of the heat could cause toughening. The browning of the meat also creates a little caramel on the outside of the meat which will add to the flavour of the stew.

Replace the vegetables and add the stock and flavourings (herbs and spices) at a lower heat. If a different pan has been used for frying, swill it out with the stock to remove the sediment. Simmer slowly, either on top of the stove or in the oven at 325°F/160°C/gas mark 3 until the meat is tender. This is usually a minimum of $1\frac{1}{2}$ hours, but may be extended for the tougher cuts of meat. A stew should never be cooked at a high temperature as this will make the meat tough. The stew can be partly cooked a day or two in advance and stored in the refrigerator, but should be thoroughly reheated and the cooking finished before serving. This can be a good method of concentrating the flavour as the stew 'matures' after the initial cooking.

White stews

These are made in a slightly different way. Sweat the vegetables (see page 69) until nearly soft and fry the meat only until a pale golden colour and sealed, over a lower heat than for a brown stew. Flavourings can vary considerably and use may be made of tomato purée, herbs, bacon pieces, salt pork, mushrooms and peppers as well as different liquids such as beer, cider, wine or spirits. The more delicate additions (such as mushrooms) require only a short time before the end of the cooking period. Cream is sometimes added, but this is done at the end of the cooking time. The stew should not then be boiled as the cream will curdle.

Stewed fruit

Prepare the fruit by peeling, stoning or topping and tailing. Fruit such as apples and pears should be cored and quartered, unless otherwise stated in the recipe. Stoned fruits such as plums and apricots can be halved and the stones removed. The kernels can be taken from the stones and used as a flavouring for the fruit.

Never use more liquid than is necessary in stewing fruit, as it will easily become pulpy. The soft fruits particularly require very little water. Boil the water and sugar first to obtain a thin syrup before adding the fruit as this will ensure that the fruit keeps its shape. The amount of sugar required will vary with the type of fruit, its ripeness and one's personal taste.

Always simmer fruit, rather than boil it, to give the whole fruit time to cook and stop it breaking up in the liquid. The crisp fruits, if cooked too quickly, may burst open yet remain uncooked inside.

Fruit can be stewed in the oven by adding less water than is required for cooking on top of the stove and placing a tight-fitting lid on the container. Fruit cooked in this way will only need 20-30 minutes at 350°F/180°C/gas mark 4.

The flavour of stewed fruit can be enhanced by additional flavourings added during cooking. Some of the more traditional additions are lemon peel, cloves or cinnamon for apple, and brown sugar will give a richer taste and a darker colour. Wine, cloves or cinnamon are good for pears and the kernels of the fruit for plums or apricots although these can be substituted with a few almonds.

Rhubarb particularly needs very little fluid for cooking. It should be cut into pieces about 1 in (2.5 cm) long and cooked at a low temperature for as little time as possible as it collapses very easily. The addition of a little lemon juice will not only enhance the flavour, but also improve the colour.

Pressure Cooking

This is a method of cooking by 'superheated' steam in a closed pan. The pressure caused by the sealed lid of the pan means that the water boils at a higher temperature and therefore food cooks more quickly. (Always read the manufacturer's instructions for a pressure cooker very carefully as the careless use of pressure cookers can lead to very bad accidents.)

Most items that are boiled or stewed can be cooked by the pressure-cooking method. It has the advantage of retaining the nutrients lost in other cooking methods and also tenderises tough meats quickly. Stews, soups, vegetables and hams and many more foods can be cooked effectively. With the divided containers supplied with many pressure cookers, whole meals can be prepared at the same time.

Only a very small amount of water is needed for the cooking process as none of the steam escapes, therefore making it almost impossible for the pan to boil dry and burn the food. Food should not be packed tightly in the pan as room should be left for a head of steam to build up.

Follow the specific instructions for the particular pan used. As a general rule, it is suggested that the pan should be brought to the boil with the valve open to expel the air, leaving the pan full of steam. The valve is then closed to allow the build-up of pressure. This will vary from pan to pan and for the different foods being cooked. Once the right pressure has been reached, the heat is lowered so that it is only just high enough to keep the pressure at the correct level. Cooking is timed from the moment that the correct pressure is reached.

To stop the cooking and empty the pan, remove the pan from the heat, and allow to cool slightly and then release the remaining pressure by opening the valve. If the rush of steam is very great, the cooker

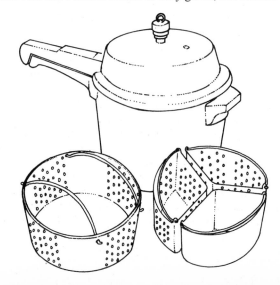

has not cooled enough and therefore should be left a little longer. Finally release the sealed lid.

The timing of pressure-cooked foods is of great improtance as overcooking leads to mushy foods, the break-up of delicate food and in some cases the development of an unpleasant flavour, especially in green vegetables.

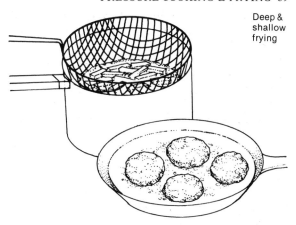

Deep & shallow frying

Shallow-fat Frying

This is a method of frying food in a pan with hot, shallow fat. The control of the temperature of shallow-fat frying is made very much easier if a heavy-bottomed pan is used. This will also cut down the possibility of foods burning. The same fats are used as for deep-fat frying (see below). Butter may also be used and will give a better result if the solids have first been removed by clarifying (see top page 50). The temperature for shallow-fat frying may vary considerably depending upon the food being cooked. Many items are first placed in a very hot fat to seal and brown them and are then finished at a lower temperature.

Most foods can be fried, with the exception of lower grades of meat. This is because the frying process has the effect of toughening the protein in foods. The toughening of the protein also helps to explain why fried foods are rather less digestible than other foods.

Foods which are to be deep fried should be coated to help seal the food, to stop the loss of nutrients and juices and to provide an attractive appearance. Most foods which are shallow fried do not necessarily need this treatment, although it is advisable to coat such items as liver and fish with a dusting of flour to prevent a tough outer skin forming. Foods with a high fat content can be fried without the use of extra fat. This is done by beginning the frying at a low temperature to allow the fats to melt out of the food and provide the frying medium. This applies to such foods as fat bacon and sausages.

If frozen foods are fried and not fully cooked, the centre will remain frozen, or become slightly heated and will form a potential source of food poisoning. Frozen pieces of food should be started on a low heat, increased towards the end of the cooking to give a well-coloured outside.

A slight shimmering on the surface indicates that the fat is hot. Foods that are to be shallow fried should be seasoned before frying. The best side of the food should be fried first and then the food turned over to ensure even cooking. Do not turn food back again, as the good side will pick up any sediment in the bottom of the pan which will spoil the appearance. Drain fried food well to remove any excess fat.

Sauté refers to a method of shallow frying which indicates that tossing the food is part of the process in order to acquire even colouring during cooking. In the case of meats, it indicates also that the sediment produced during the cooking is used in the making of a sauce served with the food. Sautéd food is usually cooked very rapidly.

Meunière is the technical term to describe fish which has been shallow fried, and also usually indicates that the food is fried in clarified butter.

Sweating is a term usually applied to the cooking of vegetables (e.g. for a soup) and refers to a method by which the finely chopped vegetables are fried very gently in shallow fat with a lid on the pan, so that they cook but do not colour.

Deep-fat Frying

This involves the food being completely submerged in hot fat or oil. The pan used for deep-fat frying should be strong and have high, straight sides which will ensure that the fat does not burn too easily and is heated evenly. It will also rise evenly when food is put into the hot fat. A wire basket, or other utensil which will allow the free movement of liquid fat, should be used to remove the items being fried. It should always be at hand in case the fat boils up quickly when food is introduced, so that the food can be taken out quickly and the fat will not boil over the top of the pan. While there should be plenty of fat to cover the food being fried it should not reach the top of the pan. Allow generally at least 3 in (7.5 cm) for expansion of the fat when food is put in.

Choosing the fat

The fat used for deep-fat frying can be either an oil or an animal fat, but should be capable of being heated to a high temperature without burning. Burning can be noticed when a heavy blue smoke appears from the fat. The usual temperature for deep-fat frying varies between 320 and 385°F (160 and 196°C) depending on the item being cooked. The fat should always be clean and strained regularly to remove small, burnt pieces of food. These will otherwise spoil the appearance of food being cooked and will eventually taint the fat.

Testing the heat

The fat is hot enough for frying when it remains still in the pan with no bubbles (which indicate the presence of moisture). There should be no swirling motion (particularly at the bottom) which indicates that the fat is not yet hot. But great care should be taken when heating fat to this level, as it is very near to the point when combustion can occur. The fat should be hot enough to seal the food immediately.

To test if the fat is hot enough, drop a $\frac{1}{2}$in (1.25 cm) cube of bread into the fat. The bread should sink slightly and then bob to the surface within a few seconds with small bubbles appearing around the outer edges. It should brown within a further few seconds and when removed and broken open should be gently coloured right through, and should not be fatty inside. This test can also be done with batter, if it is being used. Do not overload the pan, as this will cause the temperature of the fat to drop rapidly and this will spoil the food allowing fat to enter the centre or the food may break up and lose its juices, which will spoil the fat.

Frying the food

Most food is seasoned and coated before deep-fat frying. Coating can be done with batter, flour, egg, or egg and breadcrumbs. This helps in the sealing of the food and provides a crisp coating once the frying is carried out. The main exception to this is raw potato in the shape of crisps, game chips, and chips which should be carefully dried before frying. This is to ensure that no water is introduced into the fat, causing the temperature to fall and it also stops the fat bubbling up on contact with the liquid. Food that needs to be turned during the cooking process should be handled with care, as it is often fragile. Many items turn themselves over as the bottom section cooks. This is because during the cooking process the water is driven out of the coating, and the bottom section becomes lighter so that the heavier top section will turn towards the bottom. Large, dense items and those that are fried

from frozen should be fried at lower temperatures and for longer than light, unfrozen items. Follow instructions on packets of frozen food. Deep-fried foods should be cooked just before eating as otherwise they will absorb moisture and become soggy and unpalatable.

Potato chips can be blanched before being finally fried by immersion in the hot, deep fat until they are soft but not coloured. They should then be removed and thoroughly drained. This will cut down the time required in the final cooking and give a crisp, golden result.

Safety

The most common kitchen fires are caused by fat bubbling over the top of the pan and catching fire on the heat source. This can occur just as easily on electric rings as on gas. Do not over-fill the pan and never introduce wet objects into the hot fat. Never leave a deep-frying pan while cooking is in process, and turn off heat immediately when finished, removing the pan from the heated area. Old or dirty fat can bubble up rapidly when food is introduced, so discard fat when it begins to react in this way or if it smells stale.

Use a frying basket or other utensil to remove food quickly if the fat bubbles up and rises too near the top of the pan. During deep-fat frying, a certain amount of steam is given off from food, so be careful not to reach across the pan as the steam will scald.

Grilling

Food may be cooked by radiated heat from a grill. This is often preferred to frying because the food is more digestible and less fattening. Authentically the heat source should be below the grill bars or grid but today the heat source is usually above. The source of heat may be electricity, gas or solid fuel such as charcoal.

Grilling is a fast cooking process and therefore is used for foods that will not become tough under these conditions. Lower grades of meat are unsuitable as they are very thick cuts, nor is thick fish as the outside will burn before cooking has started in the centre. Grilled foods are not usually served with a gravy as they are moist in their own juices from the grilling process. Sauces and flavoured butters are more usual accompaniments.

It is well worth keeping the splash trays really clean. A tray or other container of water below the grill will also deflect the heat.

The grill should be heated before cooking begins, as the application of fierce heat to the outside of the food seals it, stopping the loss of juices. In some cases, once this has been achieved, the grill may be turned down to continue the cooking process. The greatest mistake when grilling is not preheating the grill — this defeats the purpose of grilling, which is to seal the juices and flavour into the food. If the heat is not strong enough at first these will escape, giving a tougher and less flavoursome result.

Food which is to be grilled should be brushed with oil or fat, to prevent burning and to provide moisture on the surface of the food on which the heat can act. Food should also be seasoned before grilling, so that the seasoning forms an integral part of the crisp crust which is formed. So that the skin of fish is not damaged by the action of the heat, it is advisable to flour it, then oil and season. This will also help to give a crisp finish to the fish. The distance that the food is placed from the heat source depends on the size of the item, and the required cooking time, and the degree of heat needed. A small, thin item, which needs a very short, very hot treatment should be placed very near the heat source. The basis of grilling is to place the item under a high heat source to seal in the juices and to give a good colour formed by a crisp crust which acts as a seal for the flavours of the food.

Foods being grilled should be turned often to ensure even cooking and to prevent juices escaping from areas that are not completely sealed. Some items which are particularly delicate (e.g. some types of fish) should not be turned more than once, so that both sides are cooked but the flesh not harmed. Do not pierce food during cooking as this will lead to a loss of juices if the item is not completely cooked. Test the degree of readiness by pressing flesh very gently. If underdone the flesh will give easily under the pressure. If cooked, it will become more and more resistant to pressure.

Foods which are to be grilled can be prepared well in advance but should actually be cooked just before serving. If they are left, the internal juices, so carefully preserved during the cooking process, will begin to seep out and spoil the food's flavour and moisture. The crisp outer coating will become soggy.

When using the grilling method, consider the time required to cook different items. For instance, when cooking a mixed grill, allow for the fact that generally sausages will take longer to cook than bacon and so on. Equally, the thickness of items will affect the cooking time quite considerably.

Roasting

Food cooked in the oven and basted with fat is now said to be roasted. Originally the word referred only to meat cooked on a spit — meat cooked in the oven really is baked. Roasting is best suited to high quality, tender foods and the food should be seasoned before being cooked, so that the seasoning is absorbed.

Prior to roasting
It is advisable to roast food lifted off the bottom of the pan, using a grid or trivet. This prevents frying on the bottom which makes the base likely to be tough and overcooked. The roasting process should be started in a hot oven (400°F/200°C/gas mark 6) to seal the food, preventing the loss of juices during cooking. The heat is then lowered for the remaining cooking time. Meats or other foods which do not have a high fat content should be larded or have fat added to them, and should be basted during the cooking process to ensure that the food does not become dry and tough.

Because roasting does not break down the connective tissue in the meat (this is the part which makes the meat tough), only tender joints should be used. The heat should not be too high, as this will cause the connective tissue to contract quickly, making the meat tough. The only exception is very rare beef, where the inside is basically left raw.

The same principle applies to roasting on a spit, which may be placed in front of a fire, over charcoal, under an electric or gas grill or in a specially fitted oven. It is particularly important to baste spitted meats as otherwise they become very dry. The spit should turn at a regular speed to ensure even cooking.

The larger the joint the less time comparatively is allowed per 1 lb (450 g) for cooking. If meat or poultry is stuffed, the cooking time will be extended. The cooking time will also be altered if meat is boned, as the bone acts as a conductor of heat (see page 72).

Beef
The best joints for roasting are the rib, sirloin, topside and silverside. These joints are the most tender and do not require the slower, longer cooking of less tender pieces. When beef is used for roasting, it should be well fleshed and have good 'marbling'. This refers to the tiny threads of fat found in a good quality joint which give a marbled effect to the appearance of the meat. During the cooking process, these will help to develop the taste of the meat and will add to its juiciness and tender-

ness. If there is not fat on the joint, either tie a thin layer around it or lard it. Larding is the insertion of thin strips of fat into the body of the meat, using a larding needle.

Cooking times vary considerably, depending on the degree to which the beef is required to be cooked, either rare, medium or well-done. Time also depends on size and whether meat is on the bone. A general guide is to allow 20 minutes per 1 lb (450 g) of meat and an extra 20 minutes. Allow very slightly less if there is a bone in the meat, and also if the joint weighs over $4\frac{1}{2}$-5 lb (2-2.5 kg). Before cooking the meat should be tied into shape with regularly placed loops of fine string to prevent it from moving out of shape during cooking and to make carving easier.

Melt enough fat or dripping in the bottom of the roasting pan to cover the bottom with a very thin layer. Heat this gently in the oven or on top of the stove until it just begins to smoke. Lightly season the joint, and brown it lightly in the fat, turning so that all sides are just brown and sealed. Place the browned meat on a trivet or grid in a roasting pan and place in the middle of an oven which has been

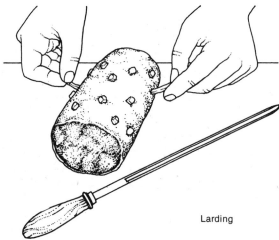

Larding

preheated to 325-350°F/160-180°C/gas mark 3-4 and cook for the required time, basting two or three times with the fat in the pan. Alternatively, preheat the oven to 400-450°F, 200-230°C/gas mark 6-8. Place the seasoned joint on a trivet or grid in the roasting pan with a small amount of fat or dripping spread over and place at the top of the oven for 15-20 minutes. This will effectively colour and seal the meat. Turn the oven down to 325-350°F/160-180°C/gas mark 3-4, and place the meat in the centre of the oven to continue cooking, basting two or three times. When using either of these methods, the meat should not become much browner during the cooking process.

If this happens, then the oven temperature is too high. To test if the meat is done, press the top of the joint. If it is soft and giving to the touch it is underdone. If very resistant it is well done. Alternatively pierce the meat with a skewer. If the juice which runs out is very pink, the meat is underdone. If no juice, or a clear juice, runs out of the meat it is well done. This method should be used with care, particularly if the meat is undercooked, as the juices will continue to ooze out during the rest of the cooking time and may lead to dry meat.

To get the best from the joint when carving it should be allowed to 'rest' on a warm serving dish for 15 minutes after it has been taken from the oven. This will allow the juices to move back into the tissues, making the whole of the joint moist. This is particularly important if part of the joint is to be eaten cold. If carved too soon after removal from the heat a great deal of meat juice will be lost.

Lamb

The shoulder and leg are the most usual joints of lamb to be roasted as well as the 'crown roast' and 'guard of honour' made up from the best end cutlets. Meat for roasting should not be too pink, as this is a sign of a recently killed carcass, which will mean a tough joint. Lamb should have been hung for about a week before use to help tenderise the flesh. The flesh should appear a darkish or dull red. This is usually the case with meat from the butcher, as delivery will generally have allowed enough time for hanging to have taken place.

To prepare the joint for roasting, bone if necessary and tie it in shape if this is called for in a recipe. Remove all loose pieces of fat, but do not pare down the firm fat as this helps to baste the meat while it cooks. Check the ends of bones to make sure there

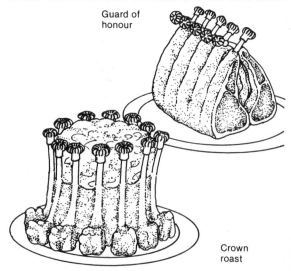

Guard of honour

Crown roast

are no small chips of bone from the butchering, as lamb bones are prone to chipping. As with beef, cooking times will vary enormously, depending on the size and degree of cooking required. It is more usual to find lamb underdone in France, whereas in Britain lamb is more often well done. As a general guide, at an oven temperature of 350°F/180°C/gas mark 4 a joint with bone will need between 15 and 20 minutes per 1 lb (450 g) depending on the degree of cooking required. A boned joint will need 25-30 minutes per 1 lb (450 g).

Preheat the oven to 400-450°F/200-230°C/gas mark 6-8. Melt 2-3 oz (50-75 g) fat, oil or a mixture of oil and butter in the roasting pan. Put the joint on a trivet in the pan and use the hot fat to baste the lamb. Place in the top of the hot oven for 20 minutes and baste every 5 minutes for this time. This will seal the juices in the meat. After 20 minutes, the oven should be turned down to 325-350°F/160-180°C/gas mark 3-4 to continue the cooking. The joint, because of the fatty nature of lamb, need not be basted further. To test for the right degree of cooking, press the flesh of the joint. If still soft the joint will be quite rare; if slightly resistant, medium done and slightly pink; if resistant, the joint will be well done. This can be tested with a skewer. When the joint is pierced the juices which run out will be dark pink if rare, light pink if medium done, and clear if well done. As with any meat, the lamb joint should rest for about 15 minutes before it is carved.

Pork

The leg, loin and hand of pork are considered the joints best suited to roasting. While pork should not be over cooked so that is is dry and unpalatable, it should never be rare. This is because the pig can be infected with a form of worm, which is destroyed only at a certain temperature coinciding with that at which the pork will be cooked right through to the bone.

If crackling is required, the thick outer skin

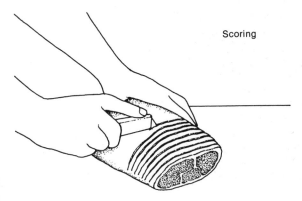

Scoring

should be left on and scored deeply with a very sharp knife. The skin should then be brushed with oil and a good quantity of salt rubbed into the score lines. The skin should not be basted during cooking as this will soften the crackling. In any case pork contains a lot of fat and will not need basting even if the crackling is absent.

Preheat the oven to 400-450°F/200-230°C/gas mark 6-8. Place the joint on a grid or trivet in the roasting pan with the fattiest side of the meat uppermost. The fat that melts from here will baste the rest of the joint. Put in the top of the oven for 15-20 minutes and then lower to the centre of the oven and bring the heat down to 325-350°F/160-180°C/gas mark 3-4 for the remainder of the cooking time. As a general rule below 20 minutes per 1 lb (450 g) for pork with the bone in, and 5 minutes extra per 1 lb for joints which have been boned. As with any meat, the pork joint should rest for about 15 minutes before it is carved.

Chicken

Most young chickens are suitable for roasting, but the sizes and types vary considerably as the does the cooking time. The chicken should be dressed and trussed. If stuffed, the extra weight must be allowed for in timing the cooking and this will be 15-30 minutes depending upon the amount of stuffing. It should be noted that comparatively less time per 1 lb (450 g) is required when cooking a large bird. At a temperature of 325-350°F/160-180°C/ gas mark 3-4, allow:

Poussin	($\frac{3}{4}$-1 lb/350-450 g)	30-40 minutes
Spring chicken	($1\frac{1}{2}$-$2\frac{1}{2}$ lb/675 g-1.2 kg)	40-60 minutes
Roasting chicken	(3 lb/1.5 kg)	1 hour 10 mins — 1 hour 20 mins
	(4 lb/2 kg)	1 hour 15 mins — 1 hour 30 mins
Capon	(5 lb/2.5 kg)	1 hour 30 mins — 1 hour 45 mins

To test if the chicken is done, pierce the fattest part of the thigh. The juices that ooze out should be clear. If it is at all pink the bird is not ready.

There are two equally good methods for roasting chicken, though the second is recommended if the bird is stuffed and is larger.

Method 1 Preheat the oven to 400-450°F/200-230°C/gas mark 6-8. Make certain that the cavity of the bird is clean and dry and insert a small knob of butter and if liked an onion, piece of garlic or a sprig of a fresh herb. Truss the chicken (see page 56), or if small enough, simply fold the wings back on themselves so that the tips are held in place by the first joint of the wing, and hold the drumsticks in place by putting them through a hole in the skin of the vent. Brush the skin with melted butter or spread a little softened butter, particularly on the breast which is most likely to dry during cooking. Place the bird directly in the roasting pan with the breast uppermost. Place at the top of the hot oven for 5 minutes. Turn the bird on to one side of the breast and then after a further 5 minutes turn on to the other side. Return to the upright position for the final 5 minutes.

Lower the heat of the oven to 320°F/160°C/gas mark 3 and place the bird on one side in the centre of the oven. Half the cooking time should be done with the bird on this side, and then the bird should be turned. For the last 15 minutes cooking time, have the bird with breast-side up to allow even colouring. The bird should be basted regularly during cooking to allow a good, crisp brown skin to form, retaining all the flavour and to stop the bird from becoming dry. It will be noticed that the bird is not placed on a trivet. This is because it is turned regularly during cooking, and will therefore not have a chance of becoming greasy or of frying in the juices.

Method 2 This is a more traditional method. Stuff the bird at the neck end and truss (see page 56). Brush the bird with melted butter, especially the breast and stuffed area, and season with salt and pepper. Lay a few slices of thinly cut streaky bacon over the breast and place the bird on a grid or trivet in the roasting tin. Place in a preheated oven (400-450°F/200-230°C/gas mark 6-8) at the top of the oven for 15 minutes. Lower the heat to 325-350°F/160-180°C/gas mark 3-4 and put the bird to the centre of the oven for the remaining cooking time. Baste regularly. Remove the bacon 15 minutes before the end of cooking time to allow the bird to brown.

Duck

Young duckling does not need to be stuffed, but it is usual to stuff an older bird at the tail end, traditionally with sage and onion stuffing. If the breast is very fat, prick it with a very fine point to allow the fat to flow out more easily. Rub the skin with salt. Place the bird on a trivet in a roasting pan in which has been put 3-4 tablespoons of water. The steam created by this in the early stages of cooking will allow the fat to melt out of the bird more easily. Fat is not needed for basting as the duck has enough of its own. Roast at 400°F/200°C/gas mark 6 allowing 20 minutes per 1 lb (450 g). Alternatively, especially for an older bird, place in the hot oven for 20 minutes, and then cook at 325°F/160°C/gas mark 3 for 25 minutes per 1 lb (450 g). After draining off the excess fat, the gravy should be made in the roasting pan to ensure that all the flavour of the roast is included.

Goose

After stuffing (if required) and trussing, rub the skin lightly with salt. Place the bird on a grid or trivet in the roasting pan. Cover the breast with any excess fat which has been taken from the interior of the bird. This can then be covered with strips of streaky bacon if extra protection and flavour is required. Cook the goose throughout at 350-375°F/180-190°C/gas mark 4-5, allowing 20 minutes per 1 lb (450 g) and 20 minutes extra. Remove what remains of the fat and the bacon for the last 15 minutes cooking time to allow the bird to become brown.

Turkey

Traditionally the neck end is stuffed with chestnut stuffing and the cavity with sausagemeat or an alternative stuffing. Spread the bird generously with softened butter or dripping and cover it with thin strips of streaky bacon. Because turkey may be dry, it is advisable to cover the bird completely in foil, removing it 30 minutes before the end of the cooking period to allow the bird to brown. If foil is not used, the bird should be basted regularly to prevent drying.

The best results are obtained from a turkey that is roasted slowly at 325°F/160°C/gas mark 3 allowing 30 minutes per 1 lb (450 g) for a small bird up to 8 lb (4 kg); 20 minutes per 1 lb (450 g) up to 10 lb (5 kg) and 15 minutes thereafter per 1 lb (450 g). Because of the varying build of turkeys, these timings are guides only. The turkey should be basted before it is finally removed from the oven and an allowance should be made for extra cooking time, in case the turkey is not yet cooked. The cooking time will also be affected by the amount of stuffing, and whether both ends of the bird are stuffed, and whether the bird is tightly stuffed or not (there should always be some space left in the cavity for the hot air to circulate). Allow 15 minutes per 1 lb (450 g) extra for the stuffing.

Game

It is only worth roasting good young game since it becomes tougher when older and should them be casseroled or cooked by some other, longer process.

The majority of game birds do not have very much fat, if any, and to obtain a moist bird the breast should be well buttered or spread with very fat bacon or fat pork.

Most game birds are roasted on a trivet in a roasting pan except for very small birds such as woodcock or snipe. These are roasted with their entrails in, and are placed on a piece of fried or toasted bread during roasting, to catch all the juices. Game birds should be roasted at a high temperature, as they should be very tender from hanging. At 425°F/220°C/gas mark 7 a young pheasant will take 30-40 minutes and a larger, older bird 40-60 minutes; a partridge or grouse 30-40 minutes; and woodcock or snipe 20-30 minutes.

Vegetables

Although it is perfectly possible to roast vegetables such as potatoes, parsnips and onions from the raw state, a more delicious result is obtained if they are parboiled (see page 65). This prevents a tough outer skin from forming, and gives a much crisper ouside and better browning. After preparing the vegetables, add them to hot fat in a roasting pan. Season in the pan and spoon hot fat over them. The vegetables should be turned once during cooking to allow both sides to become brown and to be sure of even cooking.

Without parboiling, generally allow 1 hour for the vegetables to cook. With parboiling, allow about 45 minutes. In either case, return to a hotter oven once the meat has been removed to give a browner and crisper finish. Roast vegetables should be well drained to prevent absorption of fat and resulting sogginess.

Baking

This is a method of cooking food in the dry heat of the oven. The degree of dryness can be modified by the steam given off by the food (as in the case of bread) or by the introduction of a source of steam such as a bowl of water.

The baking temperature will vary considerably with the food being baked. Yeast goods require a high temperature to stop further development of the yeast, and to 'set' the gluten. Foods with a high air content for rising, such as a soufflé, need the heat to expand the air and give the food body and height. Other items of a more delicate nature, such as pâtés and baked custards, need a far lower heat so that the protein content is not damaged which makes the food dry or tough.

There are four main types of food which are baked: meat (see Roasting), fish, vegetables and fruit, and flour products (cakes, pastry and yeast products).

Fish

Prepare and clean the fish. Baked fish is often stuffed to give it extra body and flavour, or herbs may be inserted to give extra flavour. Place the fish in a buttered ovenproof dish. Metal dishes are not recommended as they may colour or taint the fish. Brush with melted butter or place small knobs of butter on top. If the fish is not stuffed, a little knob of butter placed inside will help to keep the fish moist. Place uncovered in a preheated oven at 350°F/180°C/gas mark 4, allowing approximately 20 minutes per 1 lb (450 g). Fish should not be heavily seasoned as the flesh has such a delicate flavour.

Vegetables and fruit

Few vegetables are suitable for baking as they become dry very quickly. The most usual vegetable to be baked is the potato which should be scrubbed to remove any earth or other debris. The skin should be pierced to allow the steam to escape and to prevent the potato splitting. Place in a moderate oven and bake until soft. This can be tested by running a sharp knife into the centre of the potato; there should be no resistance. If spiked on a potato baker or skewer the potatoes will cook more evenly as the metal conducts heat. Other vegetables are best baked in their skins to prevent loss of shape (e.g. Jerusalem artichokes), drying and loss of nutrients. They should always be carefully cleaned. Fruit should also, if possible, be baked in their skins (e.g. apples, pears, bananas) and should always be pierced to allow steam to escape. Fruits with stones can be cooked very successfully by the baking method, with the full retention of their flavour. Place the whole fruit in a greased dish, sprinkle with sugar and place in a low oven 300°F/150°C/gas mark 2-3 until tender. The dish can be lightly covered so that a small amount of steam builds up, helping to keep the fruit moist.

Flour products: cakes

The ingredients for baking are very important, and poor quality can lead to disappointing results. Butter is usually considered the best fat for cake baking, but with the advent of good-quality margarines this is not now necessarily true, particularly as certain margarines have been developed specifically for cake baking. Butter is only really justified in baking if it is present to add its particular flavour to a very delicate mix.

There are various grades of flour with differing properties (see page 12) which will affect the outcome of the baking process. Strong or bread flour is generally used for yeast products because of the higher protein and gluten content. It also absorbs a higher percentage of water. These factors are important in giving a good rise to the bread, a fine crumb and a pleasant texture. Most other baked products require a soft flour or baking flour, which has a lower gluten content and will not be so tough when cooked. It also absorbs less liquid generally.

Perhaps the most important factor in flour baking is the raising agent. Commercial baking powder is a balanced mixture of tartaric acid and sodium bicarbonate, which when moistened and heated, releases carbon dioxide which aerates and thus raises the mixture. Baking powder should be kept for as short a time as possible in a well-sealed container as any absorbtion of moisture will lessen the ability to react. Items which are to be aerated by this method should be placed in the oven as quickly as possible as the baking powder begins to react once it is mixed with liquid.

An alternative is to use cream of tartar with bicarbonate of soda in the proportion of 2:1. This mixture reacts slightly more slowly than baking powder and therefore gives a little extra time in the process. Self-raising flours have a raising agent 'built in' which is rather more slow working than either of the powders. Yeast, a fungus, is used because of its ability to grow using the ammonium salts and carbohydrates present in the mixture to which it is added, and produces carbon dioxide as a waste product which aerates the mixture. The best conditions for yeast growth are moist and warm.

Generally, if the balance of the ingredients is correct and the temperature of the oven right, the results of cake baking should be good. As a guide, the following basic proportions are suggested:

One egg will aerate its own weight in flour. Most eggs weigh about 2 oz (50 g). It therefore follows that for every 2 oz (50 g) of flour 1 egg should be used unless other means of aeration are being used. If the flour exceeds this proportion, then baking powder or a substitute should be used as well.

Small, plain cakes can tolerate a greater amount of aeration when they are cooking than large or fruit cakes. This should be allowed for if modifying a plain recipe into one containing fruit, especially heavy fruits such as glacé cherries or large pieces of nut.

Sugar should only ever account for one-fifth of the weight of all the ingredients.

There are four main methods of preparing the ingredients for cake baking:

The flour batter method This requires the making of two batters which are amalgamated. The first is the flour and fat batter which is produced by mixing the flour with the softened fat. The weight of the flour should not exceed that of the fat and any excess flour from the recipe should be folded in carefully when the batters have been mixed. This will produce a lighter cake without toughness as the mixing of the fat with the flour retards the development of the gluten. Next a batter is produced from the eggs and sugar, which should again be of equal weight, any excess sugar being folded in after the two batters are mixed. This batter should be very well beaten to give a high degree of aeration. The two batters are then mixed a little at a time, adding the sponge batter to the flour batter and beating vigorously between each part added so that aeration continues. Any excess flour and sugar is then folded in carefully so that body is not lost, and the baking powder added. The mixture is then ready to be baked. If the mixture has not been well beaten, or the folding in has been done clumsily, aeration will have been lost, and the rise will have to rely heavily on the baking powder which may not be strong enough to give a light result. Though this appears to be a rather complicated method the results are well worth it. The added aeration means a very light cake, which is not at all tough, and it is a method of achieving first-class results with slightly lower quality ingredients.

The sugar batter method This is the more usual method of making a cake mixture. The fat and sugar are beaten together to form a pale creamy-textured mixture which is light and slightly fluffy. The paler the mixture the greater amount of aeration, because the small bubbles of air introduced by the beating allow the light to pass through the fat and sugar mixture, making it appear pale in colour. When starting to beat the two ingredients together, it is advisable to have softened fat, as otherwise much energy is wasted in trying to soften it while beating. The eggs are then beaten into the mixture one at a time to ensure further aeration. If many eggs are added there is a tendency for the mixture to curdle. This is first observable when the mixture begins to slip at the sides of the bowl. If curdling is allowed to continue, aeration will be lost as the mixture can no longer support the air bubbles. Curdling can be prevent- by adding no more than a quarter of the flour to the mixture, but it should be remembered that this will affect the aeration of the mixture to a certain extent. When all the eggs have been beaten in, the flour and other flavourings are added. The flour should be sieved, first to get rid of any lumps, but equally importantly introduce more air into the mixture. The baking powder is also added at this point. These ingredients should be folded in very carefully to prevent the loss of air from the mixture. The whole mixture should now appear pale, light, smooth and creamy, and should drop lightly from the beater. It is now ready for the oven.

The boiling method This method is particularly suitable for sponge mixes which are supposed to be moist and slightly dense, such as Genoese or Madeira. It is quite unsuitable for any mixture which has any fruit in it as the fruit will certainly sink to the bottom of the mixture during cooking.

The eggs and sugar are beaten together until they are really stiff and quite pale. The fat is heated until the liquid in it boils, at which point it is removed from the heat and the flour and baking powder stirred in quickly and vigorously, making sure that they are well blended. The egg and sugar batter is then added to the flour and fat, mixing them until a smooth batter is obtained. The whole mixture should be placed in the oven as quickly as possible as the warmth of the flour mixture will cause the baking powder to begin working and will cause the air bubbles to expand.

The 'all-in' method This produces good results when an electric mixer is available or a strong arm and wooden spoon. All the ingredients are placed together in a bowl, and are then beaten together to produce a smooth batter. Because this may lead to a lack of aeration, extra baking powder may have to be added. The method can lead to a dryer cake and a less fine texture.

There are two other cake-making methods sometimes used. Fruit cakes may be made by the 'rubbing-in' method, with the fat worked into the flour before the liquid ingredients are added. Gingerbreads are often made by the 'melting' method, with syrup and fat heated together before being added to dry ingredients and any other liquid and raising agent.

Cake-making faults

The most common faults in baking result from the oven temperature. Check with an oven thermometer that the thermostat is reading correctly. If the cakes are cooking too quickly on the top, try placing them further down in the oven. If this does not work place a shallow tray of water in the bottom of the oven; this will cause a certain amount of steam and will help to produce a more even temperature throughout the oven.

If cakes are burning on the bottom or becoming dry on the bottom while the top remains less well cooked, place the tin on some sheets of paper on a baking tray — the sheets of paper will stop the heat from reaching the bottom of the cake so quickly.

Cakes can collapse or sink for many reasons. If this happens, check the following possibilities and then check very carefully the ingredients used against those suggested in the recipe. The reason for sinking is nearly always an imbalance of ingredients. Collapsed or sunken cakes can be due to:

- *Too much sugar* This can be identified by the appearance of white sugar spots on the outside crusts of the cake. The sides of the cake will tend to fall inwards, and there will be a definite dip in the top. In many cases, there will also be a soggy centre to the cake.

- *Too much fat* This can be identified by a hard, rather glossy crust and a rather dense texture which, when eaten, tends to stick to the roof of the mouth.

- *Too many eggs* This can tend to lead to a tough crumb and too much rising, causing cracks in the surface followed by the collapse of the cake.

- *Too much baking powder* This will cause the cake to expand too quickly. The mixture will not set fast enough to support the amount of air produced and will collapse.

- *Too little flour* This acts in much the same way as too much fat, as the usual action of the flour is to absorb the fat. If there is not enough flour, not all the fat will be absorbed and result in a hard, glossy crust and a cloying texture.

- *Too much liquid* This can be identified by a great loss of volume, and generally a soggy or hard bottom to the cake.

- *Moving a partly cooked cake* After a certain time in the heat of the oven the mixture becomes very liquid and unstable. When in this condition, even a small amount of movement can cause the mixture to collapes.

Other problems may occur which can be rectified quite easily at the next baking session.

- *If the texture of the cake is very dense* it is probably due to a lack of aeration. This may be from a shortage of baking powder, or from too little beating and clumsy folding-in of the dry ingredients.

- *If the cake is full of rather large holes* it may be due to either too much baking powder or to air pockets introduced when the mixture was transferred from the mixing bowl to the tin.

- *Fruit which sinks to the bottom of the cake* can be caused by several faults. If the mixture is over-aerated by the addition of too much baking powder or too many eggs, the fast-expanding and delicate mixture is unable to support the weight of the fruit. Alternatively, a common fault is using fruit with a large amount of syrup, e.g. glacé cherries. These should always be rinsed in warm water to remove the excess syrup and then dried. Generally too much sugar in the recipe can cause sinking fruit.

Flour products: pastry

There are four main types of pastry that are baked: shortcrust, sweet paste, rough puff, and puff or flaky pastry. Pastry does not have any raising agent to make it light, other than the air that is introduced during the making. This is particularly important in the making of rough puff and puff pastry. With this in mind, the flour for pastry should be sieved, and when rubbing in the fat, the mixture should be lifted from the bowl and rubbed lightly through the tips of the fingers.

The fat in pastry creates what is called the 'shortness' of the product. This refers to a light crumbly texture which almost melts in the mouth when eaten. To achieve this, a combination of fats is used, particularly in shortcrust pastry, of butter or hard margarine with lard. This is because the lard contains no water and when absorbed by the starch in the flour creates a crisp effect. The water content of butter or margarine leads to a softer effect. Within reason, the less the amount of water used in mixing the pastry, the 'shorter' will be the result. Over-handling of the ingredients during mixing can lead to a lack of shortness. This is because the fat becomes oily and melts out of the pastry too quickly during cooking. To counteract this effect, the fat should be quite hard when rubbed in. Also all the utensils used in making and rolling pastry should be cold, and the water added to bind the ingredients should be cold or even iced. Rubbing in should be done with the finger tips so that the fat does not come into contact with the palm of the hand which is warmer than the finger tips.

The flour for sweet and shortcrust pastry should be fine and soft (as opposed to strong) and too high a gluten content will make the pastry tough. The pastry in these cases should be worked as little as possible so that the gluten is activated as little as possible. Rough puff and puff pastry should be made with strong flour because the dough needs to be strong and elastic to support and enclose the amount of air needed to create the desired effect. (For information on flour, see page 12.)

Less salt should be added to shortcrust pastry than to rough puff or puff pastry, as salt acts on the gluten, making it stronger and more elastic. Once the pastry has been made it should be allowed to 'relax'. This allows the pastry to absorb some of the water used in the making, and the gluten to contract back into shape. If pastry is used straight after making, it will almost certainly pull out of shape and in the case of pie coverings and linings will pull away from the sides of the dish. The period of relaxing also allows the pastry to cool and makes it easier to roll out.

Rolling should be done on a board or marble slab very lightly dusted with flour. It should be rolled from the centre outwards, away from the body, in short, light movements. When rolled far enough in one direction it should be turned at right angles, rather than trying to roll at an awkward angle to the body, which may result in stretching of the pastry. If this happens, it will contract during cooking, and leave the edges of the dish in which it is being cooked, or will pull out of shape.

The richer the pastry, the higher the temperature at which it should be cooked. Thus sweet paste, which has egg yolks and sugar added, should be cooked at the highest temperature, followed by puff pastry and rough puff pastry and finally shortcrust. The basic proportions of fat to flour for the four main types of pastry are:

Shortcrust	Half fat to half flour.
Sweet paste	Half fat to half flour plus 3 egg yolks per 8 oz (225 g) flour and an optional 1-2 oz (25-50 g) caster sugar.
Rough puff pastry	Two-thirds fat to one-third flour.
Puff pastry	Three-quarters fat to one-quarter flour (part of which is added to the dough and the remainder layered between the dough with successive turns).

Yeast products

The basis of yeast cookery is to activate the yeast in a suitable medium, which is elastic enough to allow the expansion of air during proving and cooking, to allow the optimum development of the yeast to aerate the product; and to cook the product at a high enough temperature to stop the development of the yeast and to set the gluten so that the product keeps its shape.

Generally 2 oz (50 g) yeast is required to aerate effectively 3 lb (1.5 kg) flour. This proportion will vary with certain recipes such as Savarins and special very light mixtures.

Strong flour should be used in yeast mixtures because of its high gluten content, which is activated by the liquid and handling of the product. It is important as it forms an elastic medium in which the carbon dioxide given off by the yeast is trapped, and it allows these air bubbles to expand without bursting during cooking and causing the collapse of the product. Bread and some other yeast products are kneaded to distribute the yeast evenly throughout the dough. This also helps to activate the gluten and distribute it evenly in the dough. The even distribution of the gluten leads to an even and fine texture in the finished product.

Salt is added to yeast mixtures, not only to enhance the flavour, but also to 'strengthen' the gluten. The salt acts on the gluten, tightening and stabilising it to give a better and firmer rise. Yeast goods should be baked at a high temperature 400-450°F/200-230°C/gas mark 6-8 to stop further development of the yeast. By the time the yeast dough is ready to be cooked, the gluten is soft and very elastic. When the heat is applied the air trapped by the gluten expands, and further expansion is caused by the steam from the liquid in the dough. While time is needed for this expansion to occur it need only be short. What is important is that once the expansion has occurred the gluten should be quickly set to retain its shape. At too low a temperature, while the expansion may occur, the setting will not be quick enough and so the dough will begin to collapse.

Faults in baking with yeast can occur for many reasons, the main one being the wrong oven temperature. Failure of the product to rise or retain its shape during cooking can also be caused by:

- *Too little water in the dough* making it difficult for the gases to expand and not allowing the gluten to develop to any great extent.
- *Too little yeast* so that full aeration does not occur.
- *Too much yeast* causing over-proving and collapse. This can be noticed particularly in yeast goods which appear to have a wrinkly crust. In these cases, the dough has expanded beyond its ability to support the expanding air when heat is applied. The outside crusts set quickly, but the interior collapses. When cooled, the crust will also collapse and become wrinkled. Too much yeast can also give an over-strong yeasty flavour to the goods.
- *Over-proving* will also cause collapse, or in less advanced states give a loose texture with large holes.
- *Under-proving* will result in a solid, tough product, with a rather damp texture.

If yeast products are to be glazed, this should be done while they are still very hot, so that the liquid in the glaze is driven off and not absorbed by the product.

The addition of fat or eggs to a yeast mixture slows down the action of the yeast and will affect the development of the elasticity of the gluten. These ingredients are generally added after the basic dough has been worked a little so that the gluten has had some time to develop.

Braising

Braising is similar to stewing but the meat is cooked in less liquid. The lid of the pan is sometimes removed before the end of the cooking to allow the meat to brown. The liquid may be removed and reduced to make a thicker, richer sauce to be added to the meat. The tougher cuts of meat, poultry and game are the usual foods to be braised.

The pan in which the food is to be braised should only be a little larger than the food so that only a little liquid has to be added. Meat to be braised may be cut into small pieces, but is often cooked in the form of a joint or whole bird.

A small amount of fat should be heated in the bottom of the pan and the meat fried quickly until brown, sealing in the juices and developing the flavour. This will also improve the colour of the finished dish. Remove the meat and put a 'bed of roots' in the base of the pan. This consists of roughly cut vegetables such as onion, carrot and celery, with the addition of herbs.

Replace the meat and cover with the liquid only half-way up the depth of the meat. This may be stock, wine, beer, cider or a mixture of wine and spirits. Place the lid on the pan. This should be very tight fitting so that none of the liquid is lost during cooking, and so that a certain amount of steam builds up in the pan.

Place the pan in the oven at 350°F/180°C/gas mark 4 until the meat is tender. The time will of course vary, depending on the weight of meat and whether the meat is in pieces or whole. Generally allow a minimum of $1\frac{1}{2}$ hours before testing with a skewer which will enter easily when the meat is tender.

If the sauce is to be thickened and additions made after the cooking is finished, remove the meat and strain the liquid into a saucepan. Reduce it to the required thickness and quantity by boiling and make any additions required by the recipe. Serve the sauce separately, or pour over the meat.

Stir Frying

This method of frying tender foods quickly to retain the greatest amount of crispness and flavour is very popular and essential in preparing many dishes.

Stir frying is carried out in a thick-bottomed saucepan, or in a *wok*. The thickness is needed because the heat used is very high, and a thin-bottomed pan will burn the food before it is cooked. *Wok* is the Cantonese name for a large, curved metal frying pan. The bottom is curved because originally it was placed directly on the embers of a fire. Today a wok is usually sold with a ring on which it can stand over an electric or gas ring. The pan is particularly suited for stir frying, because very little oil is needed for the cooking process as it remains in a reservoir in the bottom of the pan. It is also easier to toss and stir the food because of the high, curved sides. The aim of stir-frying is to preserve the individual flavours of the foods being cooked. Vegetables will retain their crispness. The technique is also very economical as the cooking time is so short.

Both meat and vegetables can be stir fried. In both case, the food should be finely cut or shredded across the grain. This is because the stir-frying technique is very fast and food cut across the grain is usually tender. In Chinese cookery, a couple of tablespoons of oil are placed in the pan and heated until a slight blue haze is given off. A little onion, chopped fresh ginger and garlic are fried for about a minute so that the oil is flavoured, though this is not absolutely necessary. The meat or vegetables are then placed in the oil and fried quickly for 3-8 minutes. During the frying process the food should be stirred vigorously to ensure even cooking and to stop burning. Very soft or leafy vegetables will need just 3 minutes; chicken 4-5 minutes and other meats up to 8 minutes. No food should ever be over-cooked as it will become tough or lose its crispness.

If meat and vegetables are to be combined in a dish, meat should be partly cooked first and then removed and the vegetables fried in the juices. The meat is then returned and the ingredients finished together. Just before the end of the cooking time, a little wine, sherry or stock may be added which will give a very delicate sauce when thickened with a little cornflour.

Oven Bricks

An oven brick is a terracotta, unglazed container in which food is cooked by oven heat. It is thought to be a derivation of a cooking technique in which the food was enclosed in wet clay and baked in the embers of an open fire.

Oven bricks are suitable only for those cuts of meat, poultry and game which are tender and would normally be used for roasting and for fish. The food is placed in the container, which should be a very little larger than the item to be cooked. No fat or liquid should be added as the food is cooked in its own juices by a combination of baking and steaming. The steam is created from the liquid within the food, and the container should be well sealed so that steam is not lost and the food become dry. Part of the steam and the fat will be absorbed by the oven brick. The meat or fish should be well seasoned and may be rubbed with a little butter for extra flavour. A few herbs may be added or stuffing can be used.

At an oven temperature of 350-375°F/180-190°C/gas mark 4-5 meat will take the same time to cook as by the roasting method, allowing 20 minutes per 1 lb (450 g) and 20 minutes extra. The length of time

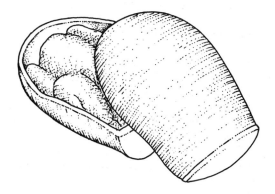

required for fish will vary considerably with its size and the thickness of the oven brick, but as a guide allow 40-45 minutes for a 2 lb (1 kg) fish. This allows time for the heat to penetrate the brick and then act on the fish itself.

Care of oven bricks

The unglazed and porous terracotta absorbs liquid and to a certain extent fat. To prevent tainting of food when the oven brick is next used, the brick should be thoroughly soaked in very hot water to remove the fat and any flavours which have been absorbed. Soapy water should not be used as the detergent will be absorbed by the terracotta and will taint food the next time.

Terracotta will crack very easily if subjected to very rapid changes of temperature. Never place it directly in boiling water when it is cold. Before placing the oven brick in the oven make sure that it has been warmed. Do not place it straight from the oven on to a cold surface as this will cause cracking; never pour cold water into a hot brick.

Sugar Boiling

Sugar and water may be boiled together rapidly to change the condition of the sugar, so that it may be used to form different types of sweetmeats and icings.

It is essential that a heavy-bottomed pan is used for sugar boiling, to prevent any chance of burning. It is advisable to use lump sugar for sugar boiling, as this is the highest grade and has the fewest impurities. Lump sugar is more difficult to dissolve because of the density of the pieces, but this is balanced by the easier and better results. Other sugars may be used, but careful attention should be paid to the removal of scum, otherwise a discoloured end-product may result. It is important to see that all sugar is dissolved before actual boiling point is reached, as after this point it is possible for recrystallisation or 'graining' to occur.

It should be remembered that while 1 pt (600 ml) cold water will absorb about 2½ lb (1.2 kg) sugar, the same amount of water at boiling point will dissolve at least 4 lb (2 kg) sugar. In general the sugar should not be stirred during the boiling process, particularly after the 'feather' stage (see below), as any agitation as this stage can cause the sugar to begin to recrystallise. The sides of the pan should be washed down frequently with a small brush dipped in warm water, as crystals of sugar will otherwise form above the boiling sugar. If they fall down into the solution they will cause crystallisation to occur.

To help stop crystallisation in the case of such mixtures as toffee, a little butter or other fat can be added to the solution. This is done only in recipes which call for the addition of fat as an integral part of the recipe. In cases where this is not so, acid in the form of a pinch of cream of tartar or a little vinegar is added. This reacts with the boiling solution to form invert sugar, of which the important ingredient is glucose. Glucose changes condition at a lower temperature than sugar, and therefore discolours more quickly. Therefore the acid should not be added until the solution has reached 225°F/107°C to delay this reaction. The greater the amount of glucose produced, the earlier the various conditions of the sugar occur and the lower the temperature at which they occur. This is why the temperature of the solution should never be used as the sole guide to the condition of the sugar solution, although it gives a general guide; the finger tests (see below) are much more accurate in showing the actual condition of the sugar, which is more important than temperature.

To stop the discolouration of the solution once the 'feather' stage has been reached, it is necessary to boil the solution as rapidly as possible. The stages after this will occur rapidly, and the solution should be watched carefully. If the sugar solution becomes over-boiled and goes beyond the condition required, but is not discoloured, it is possible to rectify this by thinning the solution with the addition of *boiling* water. This should be added very carefully as the sugar has a tendency to splutter. *Never add cold water to a boiling sugar solution*, as it will erupt in the pan and splutter viciously, causing very bad burns. Be exceptionally careful when handling boiling sugar, as liquid sugar sticks to the skin and can cause some of the worst burns.

Finger tests for boiling sugar

It is possible to carry out these tests with the fingers, without burning, by just touching the surface of the boiling sugar. Some people may not wish to do this, in which case an implement can be used to remove the small amount of sugar solution needed for the tests. It should be remembered, however, that after the feather stage, the introduction of a foreign body to the solution can cause crystallisation. When starting to test, have ready a basin of ice-cold water. The temperatures given below are approximate indications only.

a) *Thread degree* (225°F/107°C) Dip a dry finger on (not into) the surface of the sugar solution. Join the thumb and finger together, then separate them. A fine thread of sugar will form which is fairly elastic if the right degree has been reached.

b) *Pearl degree* (230°F/110°C) Repeat the above and the thread should be stronger and thicker. When the fingers are repeatedly brought together a pearl of sugar should form on the end of the thread when it breaks.

c) *Blow degree* (235°F/112°C) Dip a wire loop about $\frac{1}{2}$ in (1.25 cm) in diameter into the solution, and a film should form across the loop. If blown gently, the film should expand a little and then break.

d) *Feather degree* (240°F/115°C) As above, except that when the sugar is blown a few sugar bubbles will fly from the loop.

e) *Soft ball degree* (245°F/118°C) At this stage have ready the iced water. Dip the finger and thumb on the surface of the sugar, pinching them together and plunge as quickly as possible into the iced water. If the sugar is in the right condition the sugar that adheres to the fingers will work into a small, soft and pliable ball. At this stage, if you find

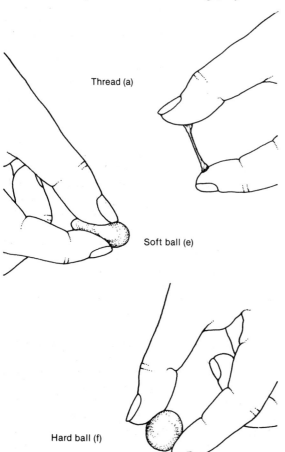

Thread (a)

Soft ball (e)

Hard ball (f)

yourself unable to use the finger method, dip an implement that is perfectly clean and warm into the solution and allow a drop of the solution to fall into the iced water. The test can then be continued as before. Remember that this takes longer than the finger method, and the speed of change of the solution's condition at this stage is quite fast.

f) *Hard ball degree* (250°F/121°C) As above, but though the ball moulds easily it becomes harder. If dropped on a slab it will sound hard, whereas in the previous test it will sound dull. As the temperature increases, this ball will become harder, until it reaches the stage at which it can no longer be moulded.

g) *Soft crack degree* (270-280°F/132-138°C) Continue as before, except that when the sugar is plunged into the water it will form an irregular-shaped piece of transparent sugar. If this is bitten, the exterior should be brittle, but the interior still soft and sticky.

h) *Hard crack degree* (280-310°F/138-154°C) As above, but the piece of sugar should be completely brittle and crunch between the teeth.

i) *Caramel* (312°F/157°C) From this point on, the sugar begins to discolour, turning from amber right through the range to black. It will finally burn. At the early stage of caramel, the process is used for the caramel in sweets, and at the other end of the scale is used for blackjack, which is used for colouring.

The Use of Gelatine

Gelatine is extracted from the skin and hooves of animals and the knuckle bones of veal. It passes into solution in hot water and is transparent. When cooled, the solution forms a jelly the thickness of which is controlled by the amount of gelatine present. Gelatine is used for its setting qualities in both sweet and savoury dishes and also in the form of aspic in savoury dishes.

Gelatine may be bought in either powder (granular) form or in sheets. Normally a sheet of gelatine weighs 2 g and four sheets are approximately equal to $\frac{1}{4}$ oz of powdered gelatine. To be effective, the gelatine has to be dissolved in water which is just off boiling. Overheating of gelatine leads to the degeneration of the protein content.

To use powdered gelatine

Sprinkle $\frac{1}{4}$ oz (8 g) gelatine on approximately $\frac{1}{4}$ pt (150 ml) water or stock depending on whether the recipe is sweet or savoury. Let the gelatine soften for 4-5 minutes, then add it to the rest of the liquid and stir over a low heat until the gelatine has completely dissolved and no granules are left, particularly in the bottom of the pan. For many recipes, the solution is then required to cool before being added to other ingredients.

If there is no additional liquid, soak the gelatine in 2-3 tablespoons water in a cup. Stand the cup in a pan of hot water until the gelatine is syrupy. Cool and use in recipe.

To use sheet or leaf gelatine

Soak the sheets in cold water for about 10 minutes or until they become soft and very flexible. Drain thoroughly, as any liquid included unnecessarily at this stage will add to the liquid in the recipe, and alter the density of the gelatine solution. Stir the leaves or sheets into the liquid from the recipe over a gentle heat until completely dissolved. When available, sheet gelatine is a far easier product to use.

Wines, spirits and other flavourings can be added when the gelatine solution is in the liquid stage, but it should be remembered that additional liquid will alter the setting capacity of the gelatine, and should therefore form part of the amount of liquid specified in the recipe. In the case of flavourings with an alcoholic content, it should be remembered that the alcohol evaporates when heated and lessens the amount of the liquid. This should be taken into consideration when balancing the ingredients of the final solution.

It is well worth testing gelatine solutions when included in a recipe to be sure that they will do their work effectively. There are small differences in the effectiveness of different brands, and age will also affect the quality of the gelatine. Before adding the solution to the rest of the ingredients, take a little of it and place it in a small container before refrigerating for 10-15 minutes. This will allow the jelly to set. It should then be removed from the refrigerator and allowed to gain room temperature, which should take about 5-10 minutes. This is necessary as these are the conditions in which the finished dish will be served, and the jelly may collapse in the warmth while holding its shape in the cold. Test the jelly for the right consistency. If it is hard, add more liquid and test again. If too soft, add more gelatine, remembering to let it soften first, and retest. While this is being done, keep the gelatine solution warm so that it is ready to be used once the tests are finished, but do not allow it to become too hot or evaporation will change the consistency. Although the testing may appear to be a long process, it is

well worth while as a guarantee of good results, expecially when expensive ingredients are being used. Gelatine solution which has set can always be softened again by the application of low heat.

Mistakes with gelatine generally occur through not allowing the raw gelatine to soften sufficiently before dissolving, and through not dissolving it completely. Both these faults can result in solutions that do not set, and to the inclusion in the finished dish of small lumps of gelatine, which have not only an unpleasant texture but also a slightly unpleasant flavour in their concentrated form.

Aspic

This is a solution of gelatine and meat, fish or vegetable stock to make a savoury jelly. It is used in cold dishes, savouries and garnishes.

Aspic can be made in the home quite easily from either calves' feet or cracked veal knuckles in combination with pork skin. These are boiled together to extract the gelatine naturally found in them.

Two *calves' feet* are enough to make 5 pt (2.75 litre) aspic. The calves' feet should be soaked in water for at least 8 hours with regular changes of water. They should then be boiled rapidly for 5-10 minutes and washed in cold water. This is a cleaning and softening process. The feet, 4-8 oz (100-225 g) pork skin and water should then be simmered for 4-5 hours and then the liquid clarified before use (see below).

Veal knuckles should be treated in the same way as calves' feet and then added to the pork rind and simmered in the same way. In both cases, vegetables can be added to the stock for greater flavour. As scum rises to the surface of the stock, it should be removed to help ensure a clear result.

To clarify the stock allow it to cool and then mix in 2 or 3 slightly beaten egg whites. Heat the stock very slowly. The albumen should coagulate from the bottom of the stock upwards bringing with it the sediment and debris in the stock. This is then removed by very carefully straining though a fine meshed sieve or muslin. Aspic can be coloured with commercial food dyes, caramelised meat juices or blackjack.

Aspic may be made with commercially produced gelatine, using stock, bouillon or consommé (home-made or tinned). The proportions for various uses differ slightly. Using $\frac{1}{4}$ oz (8 g) gelatine a jellied soup requires $\frac{3}{4}$ pt (450 ml) liquid; for covering, coating or decoration use $\frac{3}{4}$ pt (450 ml) liquid; for lining moulds $\frac{1}{2}$ pt (300 ml) liquid is needed. Always test the consistency in the same way as with gelatine.

Sauces

A sauce is a form of liquid seasoning, designed to complement and enhance another dish. There are basically three main types of sauce: flour-based, emulsions, and those that are made with the natural juices or sediments of the cooking process which do not have an additiion of flour to thicken them.

Flour-based sauces

These can be divided into three main types:

Béchamel or white sauce made with milk.

Velouté or white sauce made with white stock (chicken, veal or fish).

Brown sauce.

Tomato is added to these in a category of its own.

The base of all these sauces is the *roux*. This is the thickening agent and can spoil the sauce if it is not properly prepared. Equally important in the velouté and brown sauce is the quality of the stock. If this is poor there is nothing which can be done to improve the end result of the sauce (see Stocks, page 46).

The *roux* is basically the same in all cases, but is changed in the extent to which it is allowed to colour. For a béchamel the roux should remain as pale as possible, for a velouté it should also be pale but can take on a slight colour depending on taste. For the brown sauce the roux should be allowed to gain a nut-brown colour and give off a pleasant biscuity smell.

To prepare a roux, use a heavy-bottomed pan as this will prevent needless burning of the sauce which can happen very easily in a thin-bottomed pan. The pan should be one in which a metal whisk can be used and so non-stick pans are not recommended. Nor are aluminium pans, for the chemical action between the pan and any acid in the sauce will cause discolouring and sometimes an unpleasant flavour in the sauce.

The basic proportion of the roux will vary, depending on the use to which the sauce is to be put. For a general-purpose sauce of pouring thickness the proportion of 1 oz (25 g) butter, to 1 oz (25 g) of flour to $\frac{1}{2}$ pt (300 ml) liquid is usual. If different consistencies are required, these proportions may be calculated along the range from $\frac{1}{2}$ oz (15 g) butter to $\frac{1}{2}$ oz (15 g) flour to $\frac{1}{2}$ pt (300 ml) liquid, which is the usual thickness for the base of a soufflé mixture.

Melt the butter (a margarine-butter mix *or* an oil-butter mix or pure margarine can be substituted, though the flavour will be altered) in the thick-bottomed pan. This should be done quite slowly as the solids in the butter can colour easily and spoil the final colour and taste of the sauce. Over the same heat add the flour and stir it into the melted butter until there are no lumps. This blending is important as lumps of flour in the mixture at this stage will be difficult to move when the liquid is added. When the mixture is boiled, these lumps will swell and harden, leading to a thoroughly lumpy sauce. This flour and butter mixture should be allowed to heat until it becomes frothy. It should be stirred continually to prevent it sticking to the bottom of the pan and burning.

At this stage the sauces begin to differ. For béchamel allow the mixture to foam very gently, without taking any colour, for 1 or 2 minutes. This ensures that the ingredients are well mixed and will be well and evenly distributed through the sauce when the liquid is added. It also begins the cooking process by bursting open the flour grains and releasing the starch, which will act as the thickening agent. For velouté the cooking time can be extended slightly depending on whether a slightly nutty flavour is required for the sauce, and a slightly deeper colour. For brown sauce, this cooking process should be continued with very careful stirring until the mixture becomes a deep nutty brown, with a clean, clear, biscuity smell. If that smell begins to become even slightly unpleasant, the cooking has been taken too far.

At this point, the roux should be allowed to stop frothing, but should not cool a great deal. The liquid is then added. This is made much easier if the milk or stock is just off boiling point. This will lessen the cooking time and will help in producing a smooth sauce. The simplest way to add the liquid is to whisk it in. This disperses the roux quickly and efficiently in the liquid and helps to make the sauce smooth and glossy. A metal or a wooden spoon can be used as an alternative, but it should be remembered that a metal spoon should not be used in either non-stick or aluminium pans.

The liquid should be added in a slowly poured stream, over a gentle heat, whisking vigorously all the time, remembering particularly to clear the angle of the pan of any roux, for if this is left it can cause a lumpy sauce at a later stage. If all the roux is not whisked in, the consistency of the sauce will change. Turn up the heat and bring the sauce to the boil, stirring all the time to prevent the sauce from catching and ensuring the even distribution of the roux. Again, at this point the sauces differ in their treatment. A béchamel needs only 3-5 minutes at a minimum to cook the flour although longer (about 15 minutes) is recommended for a well-developed taste. The velouté needs 15-30 minutes at this stage to allow the taste to develop. Brown sauce should have at least 1 hour, although it will be improved over 3-4 hours. During this stage, the sauce should barely simmer, and should be skimmed of any scum that may arise. Seasoning should be added at this point to ensure that it is fully incorporated in the taste of the sauce.

If the sauce is not well boiled and thus reduced, the flavour will be insipid and the starch will not be cooked and will give the sauce a pasty flavour and an unpleasant texture.

Two main problems can occur with the sauce up to this stage, both of which can be rectified. *If the liquid is added too slowly* the heat in the roux will cause the sauce to thicken too quickly, as it has only a small amount of liquid to absorb. This will lead to a lumpy sauce which can be rectified by adding more liquid off the heat and beating vigorously. *If the liquid is added too quickly* it is possible that not all the roux will be beaten in, particularly from the edges of the pan. This again can lead to a lumpy sauce and can be rectified by vigorous beating. *If the basic roux has not been fully blended* and lumps appear when the liquid is added, these should not be boiled as they will harden and not blend with the sauce. In this case, the sauce should be strained to remove the lumps. If they have not been hardened by boiling it is possible to force them through the strainer into the sauce and incorporate them with it. If this is not possible, a small amount of extra roux should be made, or another thickener (see below) added to make the sauce of the right consistency.

The basic flour-based sauce is now ready for addition and flavourings. Vegetables unless very soft (e.g. tomatoes) should be sweated and then added. Wines and spirits, as well as vinegar, should be reduced to concentrate the flavour, and, in the case of the former two, to drive off the alcohol. Butter should be swirled into the sauce over a low heat to retain the buttery flavour and to stop it imparting a greasy texture to the sauce. Cream and egg yolks should be whisked in and the sauce should then not be boiled again as they will curdle. Detailed recipes are given later in the book.

Sauces with a flour base can be kept warm by placing them in a water bath or over water in a pan. The surface should be covered with a buttered paper or a thin layer of butter floated over it, to prevent a skin forming. They can also be kept cold for later use in a tightly covered container in the refrigerator. Béchamel and velouté should be kept only up to 2 days but a brown sauce can be kept for up to a week. Sauces with egg yolk or cream may tend to separate when re-heated, a problem which can be rectified by vigorous beating, forcing through a fine strainer, or by blending electrically. Veloutés and brown sauces can be successfully frozen, but a sauce with milk, cream or eggs is likely to separate when thawed.

Alternative thickenings

Different methods of thickening sauces, using flour, are the use of arrowroot, cornflour or potato flour and beurre manié. Arrowroot and potato flour should be added just before the sauce is finished, as they both degenerate quickly when boiled, allowing the sauce to become thin again. Cornflour can be added at an earlier stage as it does not react in this way. All of them should be mixed with water, milk or stock and thoroughly blended before being added to the sauce which should be boiling when they are added. Pour the mixture into the sauce slowly, whisking all the time to ensure the starch is evenly distributed and prevent lumps forming. All these thickening agents act quickly in the heat, and so the thickness of the sauce can be judged as they are added.

Beurre manié is a mixture of equal portions of flour and butter, kneaded together. Small balls of this are added to the boiling sauce and whisked in quickly. The melting butter distributes the flour evenly through the sauce, but the thickening does not occur instantly as in the previous cases, and so care should be taken not to add too much initially. Five to ten minutes should be allowed for the flour to cook thoroughly.

Sauces from the natural juices or sediment of the cooking process

Very good, tasty sauces can easily be made from the cooking juice left in the pan after meat or fish has been cooked. These should be reduced to concentrate the flavour, and in the case of meat to deepen the colour and produce a small amount of caramel, which will colour and flavour the sauce. Once reduced, the juice should be seasoned, and any additions made, and should be extended with the addition of wine or really good stock, or a mixture of the two. Should a thicker sauce be required, it can be thickened with a little cornflour, arrowroot, or beurre manié. Cream can also be used to thicken such sauces, but it should be thick and added carefully. The sauce should not be boiled afterwards as the cream will curdle.

Successful sauces

Every sauce should be smooth, creamy in texture and of a concentrated flavour to complement the dish with which it is to be served. While the basic sauce can be made to produce these results, it may be enhanced with the use of egg yolk, cream or butter. These should be added carefully so that their consistency and texture and that of the sauce are not spoiled. If any of these are added to sauce that is too hot, they will cause an unattractive greasiness and a grainy texture. Excessive heat in the cases of cream or egg yolk will cause curdling.

Sweet sauces are often made using these methods, though in general the thin sauces are thickened with cornflour so as not to spoil the colour of the syrup. The béchamel sauce is used as the basis of many sweet sauces with the addition of sugar and flavourings. Sauces made with the emulsion technique include true egg custard and the French Sabayon sauce.

Emulsion sauces

These are discussed fully on page 49 (Emulsifying).

Ice-cream Making

True ice-cream is a frozen mixture of cream and flavouring, sometimes extended with the addition of eggs, egg custard or whipped egg white. Ice-cream can be made with or without eggs and there are many variations in its composition. The main basic ingredients are cream or a cream-and-milk mixture with sugar, flavouring and a stabiliser. The stablilser may be egg, gelatine, flour or cornflour which helps to give the ice-cream body and a creamy, smooth texture.

The quality of the ingredients for making ice-cream is very important, to give it a good flavour and texture. Freezing takes away some of the flavour and unless the flavour is full and developed as in fresh, ripe fruit the end result will be insipid.

When selecting a recipe bear in mind that the freezing time will be longer according to the proportion of sugar to the other ingredients. Do not use more sugar than is indicated in a recipe as this can prevent freezing altogether. Frozen and canned fruits can be substituted for fresh fruit, but care should be taken not to introduce an excessive amount of the syrup in which they were stored, as this may change the balance of a recipe. Remember also that the syrup contains sugar and allow for this when calculating the amount of sugar to be added to the mixture. Large pieces of fruit generally freeze with large crystals formed by the high water content. This can be rectified by heating the fruit and sugar to form a syrup, and cooling before adding to the rest of the ingredients.

Ice crystals will be smaller and the ice-cream smoother if the mixture is frozen quickly. Ice-cream should be stored in airtight containers so that it does not become contaminated by smells in the freezer. The stored ice-cream should be kept at a stable temperature. If the temperature fluctuates a good deal, ice crystals will form and re-form, giving the ice-cream a grainy appearance and texture.

Preparing and freezing

The best results in making ice-cream are obtained if all the ingredients are the same temperature when mixed. For example, if whipped cream and an egg custard are in the recipe cool the custard slightly before folding them in together. This will also ensure that the full volume of the whipped cream is retained.

Place the ice-cream mixture in a shallow tray for freezing, as the mixture will freeze more quickly if the container is shallow. Allow the ice-cream to freeze until about $\frac{1}{2}$ in (1.25 cm) is hard round the edges and bottom. Turn the mixture into a cold bowl and beat vigorously. Do not let it become too warm as the volume will begin to fall. Repeat this two or three times at 30-minute intervals to ensure a good volume and a light, smooth ice-cream. The mixture should then be allowed to freeze completely. If a particularly light ice-cream is required whipped egg whites can be folded in after the last beating.

A smoother quality can be achieved by the addition of 1 teaspoon of gelatine for each $\frac{1}{2}$ pt (300 ml) liquid ice-cream mixture. This is added before freezing begins. Additions such as nuts, wine, liqueurs and other ingredients which may be spoiled if added while the mixture is very liquid should be added when the mixture is partially frozen.

Cream and eggs

Cream is easy to beat to the right consistency when chilled to 35-40°F/1.5-4.5°C. It should be whipped until just forming mounds, and it is capable of holding its shape. If it is over-beaten, it will give the ice-cream a slightly butterly flavour and a slightly greasy texture. The cream should not be sweetened until ready to be frozen and should then be folded in carefully to prevent the loss of volume. If sugar is added too soon before freezing, the cream becomes less stable and will lose volume.

Some recipes call for the combination of egg and some other stabilising agent. These other ingredients usually take longer to cook and combine with the liquid and should therefore be well cooked before the egg is added. Care should be taken not to overheat the egg as this will cause it to curdle. If egg whites are to be added, they should be beaten until they are stiff and not dry. They should form a peak which remains standing when the whisk is removed, and should appear moist and glossy. Beaten egg whites should be folded in carefully to retain their volume.

Poor results are obtained from the following causes:

- Using poor quality ingredients, such as over-ripe fruit, old eggs or cream that is not completely fresh.
- Folding whipped ingredients into a warm egg mixture will result in poor volume and a dense texture.
- Not cooling the various components to the same temperature before mixing can lead to loss of volume, to a grainy mix or to uneven freezing, giving an unpleasant texture.
- Freezing too slowly, which allows large crystals to form, giving a rough texture. This may also lead to a loss of volume.
- Storing in tainted containers. Ice-cream is particularly susceptible to picking up other flavours, because of the large proportion of dairy products in its components.
- Fluctuating temperatures during freezing, which cause the development of large crystals and so spoil the texture of the ice-cream.

Serving temperatures

When serving ice-cream it should be removed from the freezer before serving to allow it to soften and the flavour to develop. The more deeply frozen the ice-cream the less the flavour can be tasted. Allow approximately 10 minutes per 1 pt (600 ml) of ice-cream which has been stored at 0°F/−18°C but longer if the temperature has been lower.

Sherbets

A sherbet is made from a frozen milk-and-cream mixture into which is beaten fruit purée or juice after freezing has begun. It is stabilised by the addition of a mixture of egg whites and gelatine, which again is beaten in after freezing has begun. Difficulties can be encountered in freezing sherbet because the sugar content is almost double that of ice-cream. This can be rectified by folding in extra whipped egg whites.

Water ices or sorbets

Water ices or sorbets are closely related. The water ice is frozen fruit juice or purée with the addition of sugar syrup. It should be beaten regularly during freezing to break up any large crystals which may form. A water ice is changed into a sorbet with the addition of a stabiliser such as beaten egg white or gelatine. These are added after freezing has begun. Two to three egg whites or $\frac{1}{4}$ oz (8 g) gelatine are added after freezing has begun to each 1 pt (600 ml) water ice mixture. The gelatine should be dissolved in the syrup of the water ice before freezing.

Garnishes, Accompaniments and Presentation

The garniture as an integral part of the dish is more traditionally French than English. Many of the garnitures in French cookery give their name to the dish. Nantua, for instance, is famous for its shrimps and Crécy grows some of the finest carrots. Sometimes the name of a chef or the patron for whom a dish was created indicates the correct presentation.

Accompaniments are separate items which are presented with the main dish and are usually cooked or prepared in their own right, such as Yorkshire Pudding with roast beef.

Presentation refers to the appearance of the whole dish, with its garniture or accompaniments, and the dish in which it is served.

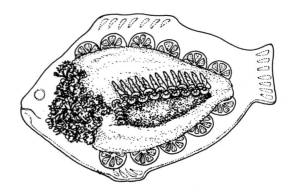

Garnishes

A garnish is not added to a dish simply to make it attractive and appetising, nor should it be added to conceal an otherwise poor dish. The garnish is to add both to appearance and its taste and texture. It may complement or contrast with the dish, and should never overpower its flavour nor swamp its appearance.

Fried and toasted bread Fried bread is used as a

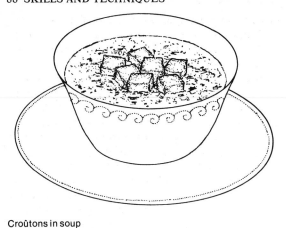

Croûtons in soup

Beef	Horse-radish relish, mustard
Lamb	Mint sauce or jelly, red currant jelly
Mutton	Onion sauce, red currant jelly
Pork	Apple sauce, cranberry sauce
Venison and jugged hare	Red currant jelly, cranberry sauce
Duck	Apple sauce, orange sauce, black cherry sauce
Turkey	Bread sauce, red currant jelly, cranberry sauce
Chicken	Bread sauce with roast bird, and an almost infinite variety of other sauces including wine, cream and mushroom

garnish in two main forms, as croûtons and as heart-shaped pieces and sometimes as triangles. Croûtons are made from $\frac{1}{4}$ in (6 mm) cubes of white bread, fried quickly in clarified butter or oil until light brown and crisp. They are traditionally served with thin meat soups and cold tomato soups, although they are a good addition to many others, supplying a contrast and absorbing any small amount of grease on the top of the soup. They should not be added until the soup is about to be eaten as they quickly become soggy. Heart-shaped, fried bread pieces are usually added as a garnish to rich meat stews and sautés and are placed around the edge of the dish. Triangles of fried bread may be used for some dishes and small supper dishes such as kidneys. Toasted bread is most often used in the bottom of the bowl in which French onion soup is to be placed, and is also used underneath small game birds, to absorb the juices during cooking. Rounds of toast may also be placed under small, thick steaks such as tournedos and may be spread with pâté.

Sauces and relishes Sauces can be hot or cold, and very delicate or strong in flavour, and will either complement or contrast with the dish. Generally, if the main ingredient of the dish is delicate, then the sauce should be delicate as well, although it may provide a contrast as in the addition of cheese sauce to cauliflower. Piquant sauces are usually added as contrast, as for example tartare sauce with fried foods, horse-radish relish with roast beef, and mint sauce with lamb. These also give textural contrast. Some traditional sauces and relishes are listed below.

| Fried fish | Tartare sauce, mayonnaise |
| Baked or poached fish | White sauce, cheese sauce, parsley sauce |

Most meats, other than grilled, are generally served with a gravy made from a good stock and the sediment from the cooking process, or the reduced and/or thickened cooking juices.

Many vegetables are served with a sauce, such as cheese, white or tomato. When using a sauce with vegetables, be certain that the vegetables are well drained as excess liquid will thin the sauce. Pour the sauce over very hot vegetables, and do not use the hot sauce as a method of heating warm vegetables. Serve quickly so that there is no chance of a skin forming on the sauce, which will spoil the appearance. The sauce should be thin enough to coat the vegetables lightly and not so thick that it does not move down gently through the whole dish.

Relishes are not usually placed on the main dish, but are served separately.

Fruit and vegetables It is a mistake to presume that the addition of a cleverly cut tomato and a piece of watercress or parsley truly represents a garnish. This is a poor substitute for something which is well thought out and designed. Fruit and vegetable garnishes can be either cooked or raw. The variety is endless, the best listing being available in Saulnier's *Le Repértoire de la Cuisine* (Leon Jaeggi and Sons Ltd, London).

Cooked garnishes may be puréed, fried (as in the case of game chips, straw potatoes or onion rings), boiled and glazed, roast, etc. The amount presented as a garnish should be small, but enough for each portion to have an adequate amount. Purées should be well-coloured and of a good consistency. In most cases a purée should hold its shape when placed on the dish, but should not be so thick as to have an unpleasant texture. Fried garnishes should be cooked just before serving and placed on the dish in such a way that they do not absorb any liquid.

If vegetables are to appear with the dish in an almost whole state, they should preferably be small and very young. If these are not available, then larger vegetables should be shaped and pared down to give an attractive appearance and also so that they are not mistaken for the main vegetable in the course. There are traditional methods of arranging the cooked garnishes on the serving dishes, but today this is very much more a matter of taste. Remember never to cover the main constituent of the dish, as this can seem to be a disguise and can make serving more difficult. Always bear in mind the colours of the dish itself and the garnish so that they harmonise.

It is important to remember that the garnish is to be eaten, that it is to make the food more attractive and that it is an integral part of dish and should be treated as such. Cooked fruit garnishes should be considered in the same way as cooked vegetables whether added to a sweet or savoury dish.

Raw vegetable or fruit garnishes should be quite small and easily eaten. All raw garnishes should be well washed, and some of the salad garnishes are enhanced by being dipped into a French dressing. Some cooks believe in shaping raw garnishes into the most marvellous shapes and while this may be considered attractive, it is unnecessary on a well prepared and simply garnished dish. Small sprigs of parsley or watercress should be used, or finely chopped herbs lightly sprinkled over the top of vegetables and some meat and fish dishes. This is just as attractive as more complex designs and takes a great deal less time. Most vegetables and fruits should be skinned and reduced in size before being used for garnish, so that they are obviously supposed to be eaten and enjoyed, but are not a meal in themselves. Never over-garnish a dish but let the main part of the dish speak for itself, and the garnish enhance what is being said.

Cream and butters Cream can be used as a garnish either whipped or unwhipped. The former is more often used to garnish sweet dishes, and is whipped on its own or with caster sugar to give Chantilly Cream. Whipped cream is usually piped on the dish in a pattern, or in shell or rosette shapes. When garnishing with cream, the size and richness of the dish should be borne in mind, as well as the balance of the main part of the dish to the cream. Over-decoration with cream can give a dish an over-sweet, filling appearance, and may not complement the dish itself.

Unwhipped cream is often added to savoury dishes such as cream soups, some cream sauces and the top of some stews. The cream should be added with care, and usually a small swirl in the centre of the dish is sufficient. Add the cream just before serving so that it remains on the surface and does not amalgamate with the rest of the dish. Unwhipped cream served with a sweet dish is usually considered to be an accompaniment rather than a garnish.

Butter or flavoured butters are often used with dishes which would otherwise perhaps be rather dry. Plain boiled vegetables and baked potatoes are enhanced by the addition of a knob of butter just before serving. A knob of butter swirled into a béchamel-based sauce just before serving gives a richer flavour and a glossier appearance. Flavoured butters, such as garlic, anchovy or herb are usually served in the form of small rounds on dry cooked meats and fish, such as those that have been grilled. The butter should be added just before serving so that it still retains its shape. Melted butters may also be used as garnishes such as meunière (a nut brown butter with the addition of a little lemon juice) and are generally added to grilled and shallow-fried fish.

Anchovies, olives and shellfish These are all used as garnishes and should be palatable and easily eaten. Anchovy fillets should be steeped in milk for a short period to remove the excessive saltiness sometimes present. Olives and any other stoned fruit should be stoned and possible halved. Shellfish is usually shelled or peeled before being used as a garnish.

Glazes These can be sweet or savoury and are generally applied to dishes which are to be eaten cold. The glaze gives a smooth, well-coloured finish to the dish and helps to keep the food moist. Savoury glazes are usually based on gelatine or aspic for white fish and meat, a béchamel set with gelatine is generally used for red meat and certain meat mixes, and aspic is used which has been enriched with a concentrated meat juice, and coloured with blackjack. Some meats require a lighter glaze, in which case a light aspic is used with the addition of wine. Sweet glazes are usually made with a reduced fruit juice or liquid, or with a juice jellied with gelatine. Thinned jams and marmalade can also be used.

Gratins A finished dish may be enhanced by browning the surface of the dish. Correctly, this is carried out by strewing the surface of the food with fine breadcrumbs and placing under a hot grill until brown. The breadcrumbs should absorb some of the liquid from the dish, particularly fat, and thus become very crisp. The term has also come to mean the browning of a layer of cheese on a dish. In this case, grated or thinly cut slices of cheese are put on top of the dish which is put under the grill until the cheese has melted and is bubbling and brown.

Accompaniments

Accompaniments like garnishes are many and varied. They are to enhance the dish, and to provide variety in texture and taste, and in some cases have been introduced for a specific purpose. Yorkshire Pudding, for instance, was initially introduced as a first course to be eaten with the gravy from the roast beef, and to provide a filler so that less meat was eaten. Pease Pudding was served with boiled bacon, as the boiling broth around the meat was a perfect medium for cooking the dried peas. Other accompaniments are served to give a sharpness to the dish as in the case of lemon with fried foods, smoked salmon or oysters. Melba Toast, buttered bread and rusks are usually served as a medium for carrying food such as pâté to the mouth or as a foil to a liquid such as soup.

Presentation

This is as important as the garnishing and accompaniments of a dish. If a meal is presented in an unattractive fashion in ugly dishes the food will appear less appetising. Food should not be piled into a dish that is too small, which makes serving difficult; nor should it float about in the middle of a dish which is too large. Allow enough room in the dish for portions to be clearly laid out, or for a gentle mound of vegetables. In the case of a dish that needs to be carved there must be room for the carver to dismember the joint or bird without having to juggle with the food.

If hot food is being served, be sure that the dish is also hot. This will help to preserve the food hot during serving, although serving dishes should not be so hot that they are difficult to handle. Any splashes on the serving dish should be removed. In the case of serving utensils which have been used for cooking in the oven or top of the stove where food has been burned on, the splash can be removed quite easily with a damp cloth. The serving dishes, particularly glassware, should be shiny and clean to give an appearance of freshness and care. Dishes that are cracked ought not to be used, not only because they are unattractive but because the cracks can harbour bacteria.

The type of dish in which the food is to be served is important for keeping the food hot or cold. Glass, silver and stainless steel are particularly good for dishes which are cold. Glass and silverware are not so suitable for dishes which have to be heated or kept hot as damage can occur. Silverware should not be used for dishes containing egg in any form as they will quickly discolour the silver. Copper serving dishes are becoming more usual now and are attractive because of the colour and shine. However, they should not be used for acid dishes as these will cause a reaction with the copper, discolouring both dish and food and in some cases causing an unpleasant taste in the food. Terracotta and earthenware are also often used but care should be taken as both will crack easily with great changes in heat. Never place an earthenware or terracotta dish directly on the heat of an electric or gas ring and never pour hot liquid into a cold dish and vice versa. This is equally true for most china, and instructions should be carefully read when new china is purchased, to be sure that it is ovenproof if this is required.

Basic Recipes and Variations

The recipes in this section are basic kitchen tools. They have been constructed to give a cook the confidence to move on to more complicated dishes. It is important to remember that every dish is based on one or more simple techniques, and even an apparently complicated recipe may be analysed and broken down into component parts which have already been mastered. Carefully made sauces, good pastry, light stuffings and well-prepared meat, poultry, fish, fruit and vegetables are essential to good cooking, and once the simple techniques have been mastered, no recipe is beyond the skills of even the novice.

Just one word of warning. Do follow a recipe carefully the first time you use it, before trying to improvise or change ingredients. Collect all the raw materials and equipment you need first, then measure the ingredients carefully. Follow the method step-by-step, and use the specified containers and oven temperatures. Time the cooking carefully and follow any instructions for finishing the dish before serving. When you have once followed the basic recipe with success, you may use it over and over again with your own variations of flavouring or substituted ingredients, but always follow the basic principles of careful measuring, thorough preparation and accurate timing.

Soups

Soup is a pleasant beginning to a meal, but may also form a complete lunch or supper. There are many types of soup, but they should all be served with similar care. Soup must either be piping hot or very cold, and should be free from grease. Soup must be carefully seasoned and very attractive in appearance with a distinctive colour and neatly prepared, appropriate garnishes.

Well-flavoured stock is the basis of many soups (see page 46) and clear soups such as consommé and broth must be made with stock which has a clean fresh flavour. Consommé is made from beef or chicken stock or a mixture and should be transparently clear whether served hot or jellied. Broth is also clear soup, but with the addition of vegetables, and sometimes a cereal such as barley. Thick soups may be prepared with a roux thickening of butter and flour, or milk, or cream which gives a smooth velvety cream consistency. Soups may also be thickened with vegetables such as potatoes, root vegetables, fresh or dried peas, beans or lentils.

SOUP GARNISHES

Bacon
Grill or fry lean bacon rashers until very crisp. Crumble into small pieces and sprinkle on top. This is particularly good with pea or bean soups.

Cheese
Use very hard, dry cheese and grate it finely. Parmesan is ideal, but really hard Cheddar is good too.

Cream
Whip double cream into soft peaks and put a large spoonful on each bowl of soup just before serving.

This is particularly good with tomato or beetroot soup. Commercial soured cream can also be used as a soup topping and is thick enough without whipping.

Croûtons

These small cubes of bread may be fried or toasted. For fried croûtons, cut bread in small cubes and fry in oil until golden. Drain well before putting onto soup. Alternatively, toast slices of bread and cut into small squares before serving.

Herbs

Chop herbs finely and sprinkle on soup. Basil, mint, tarragon, chives and parsley are all ideal for vegetable soups.

Pasta

Short lengths of macaroni or spaghetti or spaghetti shapes can be used as a garnish, also adding a little bulk to a recipe. Cook the pasta first for 10 minutes in boiling water before draining and adding to the soup to finish cooking without breaking up. About 2 oz (50 g) pasta is enough for 4 servings of soup.

CONSOMMÉ   *Serves 4*

2 pt (1.2 litre) beef stock
4 oz (100 g) lean beef
2 eggs
2 tomatoes
Salt and pepper
2 tbsp sherry

The liquid may be a mixture of beef and chicken stock if liked. Heat the stock and remove every trace of fat with kitchen paper. Put into a clean and fat-free pan with the beef cut into very small pieces. Break the eggs ad remove the yolks (these may be used for other dishes). Put the whites and the shells into the liquid. Skin and seed the tomatoes and add the flesh to the soup. Add seasoning. Simmer for 45 minutes with a lid on the pan just tilted to allow some steam to escape. Pour through a piece of scalded cloth, reheat and stir in the sherry just before serving.

Garnishes

Consommé may be garnished with small pieces of cooked vegetables (e.g. carrots, turnips, peas). Root vegetables should be cut into tiny dice or shaped like peas. Fine shreds of vegetables may be used, or a few tiny sprigs of herbs such as tarragon and chervil.

Chilled consommé

Consommé may be chilled and served in cups. The basic soup should be set lightly and may then be broken with a fork, or spooned into the cups. If the mixture is not quite firm enough for your taste, a little gelatine may be used to stiffen it.

CHICKEN BROTH   *Serves 4*

2-3 lb (1-1.5 kg) chicken
3 pt (1.8 litre) water
2 oz (50 g) bacon
1 small carrot
1 small turnip
1 small onion
1 bay leaf
Sprig of parsley
Sprig of thyme
Salt and pepper
1 oz (25 g) pearl barley

Joint the chicken and put into the water. Add the chopped bacon. Peel the carrot and turnip and add peelings to the pan, but reserve the vegetables. Add the chopped onion, herbs and seasonings. Tie the barley into a piece of muslin and add. Simmer for 3 hours with the lid on. Strain off the liquid into a clean pan. Reserve the barley. Chop a little of the chicken breast and add to the strained liquid (the remaining chicken may be used for another dish). Dice the carrot and turnip neatly and add to the pan. Bring to the boil and then simmer for 15-20 minutes. Remove the barley from the muslin, add to the soup and reheat for 5 minutes.

VEGETABLE SOUP   *Serves 4*

1 medium onion
12 oz (350 g) carrots
2 tomatoes
2 medium leeks
2 medium potatoes
2 oz (50 g) butter
1½ pt (900 ml) water
Salt and pepper
1 oz (25 g) pasta shapes
1 oz (25 g) finely grated cheese.

Chop the onion finely. Grate the carrots coarsely. Skin the tomatoes, remove seeds and chop the flesh. Slice the white parts of the leeks and dice the potatoes. Melt the butter and cook the onion until soft but not browned. Stir in the other vegetables and 2 tablespoons water, and simmer for 5 minutes. Add the remaining water, bring to the boil, season and simmer gently for 25 minutes. Add the pasta and continue simmering for 10 minutes. Serve in bowls and sprinkle each serving with grated cheese.

CREAM OF CHICKEN SOUP   *Serves 4*

1½ oz (40 g) butter
1½ oz (40 g) plain flour
2 pt (1.2 litre) chicken stock
6 oz (150 g) cooked chicken
Salt and pepper
¼ pt (150 ml) single cream
Chopped parsley

If fresh chicken stock is not available, water and chicken stock cubes may be used, but careful attention must be paid to seasoning so that the soup does not become too salty. Melt the butter, stir in the flour and cook for 1 minute until the mixture becomes straw-coloured. Take off the heat and stir in the stock gradually. Return to the heat and bring to the boil, stirring well. Simmer for 5 minutes. Add very finely chopped chicken and continue simmering for 5 minutes. Season to taste. Just before serving, stir in the cream and heat gently, but do not boil. Serve sprinkled with parsley.

Cream of mushroom soup

Omit chicken. Use only 1 oz (25 g) butter, with the flour, and use the remaining ½ oz (15 g) to cook 4 oz (100 g) finely chopped mushrooms for 4 minutes. Add the mushrooms and their juices to the soup before adding the cream.

Cream of haddock soup

Poach smoked haddock (see page 113), and use the cooking liquid instead of chicken stock. Serve the haddock as a separate dish, but add 4 rounded tablespoons flaked fish to the soup.

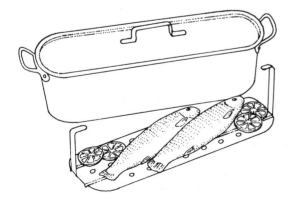

WATERCRESS SOUP   *Serves 4*

2 oz (50 g) butter
1 medium onion
8 oz (225 g) potatoes
½ pt (300 ml) chicken stock
1½ pt (900 ml) milk
1 large bunch of watercress
Salt and pepper
Pinch of ground nutmeg
½ tsp cornflour
2 tsp water
2 tbsp double cream

Melt the butter and cook the finely chopped onion until soft but not browned. Add chopped potatoes and stock. Bring to the boil and then simmer for 15 minutes. Add the milk and continue simmering for 10 minutes. Reserve 12 watercress leaves for a garnish. Add the remaining leaves to the soup and simmer for 10 minutes. Blend to a purée or put through a sieve. Reheat and season to taste with salt, pepper and nutmeg. Mix the cornflour and water and stir into the soup. Bring to the boil again and then take off the heat. Stir in the cream and serve garnished with reserved leaves.

LEEK AND POTATO SOUP   *Serves 4*

3 large leeks
1 medium onion
8 oz (225 g) potatoes
2 oz (50 g) butter
2 pt (1.2 litre) chicken stock
Salt and pepper
Chopped parsley

Clean the leeks very thoroughly and slice the white parts thinly, discarding the green leaves. Chop the onion finely and slice the potatoes. Melt the butter and cook the leeks and onion over low heat, stirring well, until soft and golden. Add the potatoes, stock and seasoning and bring to the boil. Lower the heat and simmer for 30 minutes. Stir in the parsley just before serving. This is a good basis for a winter soup, and may be blended until smooth if preferred. Milk, or a little cream, may also be added.

Creme vichyssoise

Follow the basic recipe, omitting the parsley. Purée the soup in a blender, or put it through a sieve and chill thoroughly. Stir in ¼ pt (150 ml) single cream just before serving and garnish with chopped chives.

TOMATO SOUP   *Serves 4*

1 lb (450 g) tomatoes
1 pt (600 ml) beef stock
1 small onion
1 bay leaf
Sprig of parsley
Sprig of thyme
$1\frac{1}{2}$ oz (40 g) butter
$1\frac{1}{2}$ oz (40 g) flour
$\frac{1}{4}$ pt (150 ml) milk
Salt and pepper

Chop the tomatoes without peeling them. Put them into a pan with the stock, chopped onion and herbs. Simmer for 1 hour and put the mixture through a sieve. Melt the butter and work in the flour. Cook for 1 minute and stir in the tomato mixture. Stir over low heat until the mixture comes to the boil. Stir in the milk, sugar, salt and pepper and reheat gently. For a special occasion, the soup may be served with a garnish of whipped cream and finely chopped parsley.

LENTIL SOUP   *Serves 4*

1 medium onion
2 rashers streaky bacon
2 medium carrots
4 oz (100 g) lentils, soaked
$1\frac{1}{2}$ pt (900 ml) beef stock
$\frac{1}{2}$ oz (15 g) cornflour
$\frac{1}{4}$ pt (150 ml) milk
Salt and pepper
Chopped parsley

The lentils should be soaked in cold water for 2 hours before cooking. Chop the onion and the bacon and heat gently together so that the bacon fat runs and the onion cooks until soft and golden. Add sliced carrots and cook for 2 minutes. Add the drained lentils and the stock. Bring to the boil, cover and simmer for 1 hour. Blend or sieve the soup and return to the pan. Mix the cornflour and milk and stir into the soup. Add seasoning and simmer for 5 minutes, stirring well. Serve in bowls, garnishing with parsley.

See also Broad Bean Soup, page 117; Beetroot Soup, page 119; Sprout Soup, page 120; Celery Soup, page 122; Spinach Soup, page 127.

Omelettes

Omelettes are very simple to make if fresh eggs are available, and an omelette pan is always kept carefully for use. An omelette pan should be thick and flat with a rounded join between base and sides, and made of iron or aluminium. For a small omelette (using 2-3 eggs), use a 7 in (17.5 cm) pan; for a 4-egg omelette, use a $8\frac{1}{2}$-9 in (22 cm) pan. To prepare a new pan, cover the bottom with salad oil and leave for 12 hours, then heat the pan, pour off the oil, and wipe the pan well with a dry cloth. After use, wipe the pan with kitchen paper, then with a damp cloth dipped in salt. Avoid washing the pan, as scouring will roughen the surface, and do not use an omelette pan for anything but omelettes and pancakes, as other foods often leave small remains which stick and are hard to remove.

An omelette should not be kept waiting for its filling, so it is important to prepare this first, and to have a hot plate ready to receive the completed dish. An omelette is at its best when eaten fresh, and ideally individual ones should be prepared and eaten at once. For larger families, it may be necessary to make one large omelette (an 8-egg one will need a 10 in (25 cm) pan) and divide it into portions, but this never looks very attractive.

THREE-EGG OMELETTE   *Serves 2*

3 eggs
Salt and pepper
$\frac{1}{2}$ oz (15 g) butter
Flavouring or filling

Some fillings, such as herbs and cheese, may be added to the omelette mixture; others are put on the omelette just before it is folded. Before cooking the eggs, make sure that herbs are chopped, cheese is grated, or the filling is prepared. Break the eggs into a bowl. Season with salt and pepper, and mix the eggs with a metal fork until they are lightly mixed but not beaten. Put the butter into the pan and heat slowly so that the butter sizzles but does not brown. Pour the eggs quickly into the pan, and use the fork to keep drawing some of the mixture to the middle from the sides of the pan. In $1\frac{1}{2}$ minutes the omelette will be softly cooked, but not runny. It is important not to overcook the eggs since they continue to become firm while the omelette is served. Take the pan from the heat and using a palette knife, fold the omelette half over *away* from the handle. Tip the pan gently over the hot plate and the omelette will fold again and slip forward onto the plate.

Cheese

Grate 2 oz (50 g) hard cheese finely and add to the eggs, saving a little for sprinkling on the cooked omelette.

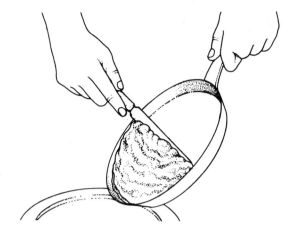

Herbs

Chop 1 tablespoon parsley and a few stems of chives very finely and add to the eggs.

Kidney

Cut 2 lambs' kidneys into small pieces with 1 small onion or shallot. Melt 1 oz (25 g) butter in a separate pan and cook kidney and onion until soft. Put onto the centre of the omelette just before folding and serving.

Mushroom

Chop finely or slice thinly 3 oz (75 g) mushrooms and soften in $\frac{1}{2}$ oz (15 g) butter. Put onto the centre of the omelette just before folding and serving.

BAKED OMELETTE   *Serves 2*

This type of omelette may be made with chopped herbs, cheese or ham added to the beaten eggs, but as the egg mixture is a little drier when baked, the omelette is nicest with a creamed filling of mushrooms, prawns, kidneys, chicken, asparagus, etc. The chopped main ingredient should be lightly cooked in a little butter and then folded into a little creamy sauce. For this, use a basic white sauce (see page 129) and stir in a little cream just before filling the omelette.

4 eggs
$\frac{1}{4}$ pt (150 ml) creamy milk
Salt and pepper
Flavouring or filling

Mix together the eggs and milk with a fork just enough to break up the eggs thoroughly, but do not beat. Season with salt and pepper. Butter an omelette pan or shallow ovenware dish and pour in the eggs. Bake at 350°F/180°C/gas mark 4 for 15 minutes until the top is golden. Put filling on half the omelette, fold over and serve at once.

SOUFFLÉ OMELETTE   *Serves 2-3*

This is served as a sweet omelette, filled with jam, or with fresh fruit which has been sliced and then left to stand in a little liqueur and sugar to taste.

4 eggs
2 eggshells of water
1 oz (25 g) butter
Filling
A little icing sugar

Separate the eggs and put the yolks into a small bowl. Add the water and beat with a wooden spoon until the mixture is creamy. Whisk the egg whites to stiff peaks and gently fold into the yolks. Heat butter and pour in the egg mixture. Cook over low heat until the underside is golden brown, but do not move the eggs as in a plain omelette. Spread the filling on half the cooked omelette and fold over, and lift onto a hot serving dish. For a professional finish, heat the grill while cooking the omelette. Slip the omelette onto a fireproof serving dish and sprinkle thickly with sieved icing sugar. Mark crosswise lines to form diamonds on the sugar, using a skewer. Put under the hot grill for a few seconds, so that the sugar starts to colour, and serve at once.

SPANISH OMELETTE   *Serves 2-3*

This variation on the traditional omelette provides a filling meal, and may be made from a combination of fresh and leftover ingredients. In addition to the basic items, a little chopped green pepper, mushroom or chicken liver, or a few cooked peas may be added. The omelette is delicious hot or cold, and may be used to fill a split crusty French loaf to make a substantial picnic meal.

6 oz (150 g) potatoes
1 medium onion
2 oz (50 g) bacon or ham
3 tbsp olive oil
Salt and pepper
4 eggs

Peel the potatoes and cut them in thin slices or in small dice. Chop the onion and bacon or ham. Heat the olive oil in the omelette pan and cook the potatoes, onion and bacon or ham over medium heat until soft and golden. Drain off surplus oil. Sprinkle the ingredients in the pan with salt and pepper. Break up the eggs with a fork and pour into the pan. Cook until firmly set, moving the mixture slightly with a fork as it cooks. Do not fold, but cut into wedges like a cake.

Soufflés

There is no mystery about creating a perfect soufflé, as the basic preparation is very simple. The secret lies in attention to detail in the matter of oven temperatures and timing, weight and balance of ingredients, and the size of the dish used. Soufflés should not be kept waiting as they collapse quickly, so it is better not to attempt one unless you know exactly when it will be eaten. The basic mixture can, however, be prepared in advance, and needs only finishing with egg whites just before baking time. Although it seems to be a luxury, the soufflé is cheap to prepare, consisting basically of eggs and the flavouring ingredient, which may often be a leftover from a previous meal.

The soufflé may be savoury or sweet, and basically consists of a thick white sauce, flavouring and eggs. A sweet soufflé needs sugar in addition. A 3-egg soufflé will serve 4 people, and need 4-6 oz (100-150 g) savoury flavouring; a sweet soufflé will need 2 oz (50 g) sugar and about 4 tablespoons purée if to be fruit-flavoured.

To make the soufflé you will need a thick saucepan, an egg whisk, and a straight-sided soufflé dish. For a 3-egg soufflé, use a 2 pt (1 litre) dish; four individual dishes may be used and then cooking time must be adjusted (see recipe). The classic dish has fluted sides and is deep enough to contain the rising soufflé. If the dish is too shallow, fold a piece of greaseproof paper or foil two or three times to the depth of the dish plus 3 in (7.5 cm) to give strength. Brush with oil and attach round the outside of the dish with a paper clip and string to form a collar 2-3 in (5-7.5 cm) above the rim.

When ready for eating, a soufflé should be well risen, firm to the touch and a good colour, fluffy and lightly set. If it is undercooked, the centre will remain runny; if it is overcooked, the soufflé will become like a cake with a tough, dry texture.

Before preparing the soufflé, get the dish ready. Grease the inside of the dish with oil. For a savoury soufflé, coat the oiled surface with a sprinkling of dry breadcrumbs or grated cheese; use caster sugar for a sweet one. If you want to prepare a soufflé for more people than specified do not try to bake a double mixture in one dish, but bake two soufflés instead or it will be very difficult to assess the correct baking time, and the outside will be baked hard while the interior of the soufflé will be very runny.

Assemble all the ingredients before starting preparation, and be sure that the flavouring ingredients are ready. Cook meat, fish or vegetables and then chop very finely or make into a purée. Use firm, dry cheese and grate it finely. Be sure to season strongly with freshly milled pepper and sea salt to give a good flavour when cooked. For a sweet soufflé, chop or purée the flavouring ingredients, and remembers that a tablespoon of liqueur will heighten the flavour of a sweet soufflé which can otherwise be bland.

BASIC SOUFFLÉ　　　*Serves 4*

3 oz (75 g) butter
2 oz (50 g) plain flour
$\frac{1}{2}$ pt (300 ml) milk
3 eggs
Flavouring ingredients

Preheat the oven at 375°F/190°C/gas mark 5. Melt the butter in a thick saucepan over low heat. Stir in the sifted flour and slowly add the milk, blending it in smoothly (this will be easier if the milk is just warm). Bring to the boil, stirring carefully, and cook for 3 minutes. This thick white sauce is known as the panada. Add any prepared flavouring. Separate the eggs and beat the yolks lightly. Stir the yolks into the mixture, then remove from the heat. At this point, the mixture may be left for some hours until baking time, but should be gently reheated before the final stage.

Just before baking time, beat the egg whites until stiff peaks form. Fold very gently into the sauce. Fill the prepared dish with the mixture. Using a palette knife, run a line 1 in (2.5 cm) deep all round the mixture about $\frac{1}{2}$ in (1.25 cm) from the edge of the dish. This will ensure a puffy 'cauliflower' top when cooked. For a crisp crust, the soufflé can be put straight into the oven; if a soft, even surface is preferred, stand the dish in a pan of hot, but not boiling water. Bake for exactly 45 minutes (15 minutes for individual dishes). If necessary, remove the paper collar by running a knife quickly inside it.

Apple
Add 4 tablespoons thick apple purée, 1 teaspoon lemon juice and 2 oz (50 g) caster sugar.

Asparagus
Add 6 oz (150 g) finely chopped canned or cooked fresh asparagus, with salt and pepper.

Cheese
Add 4 oz (100 g) finely grated Cheddar cheese, salt, pepper, $\frac{1}{2}$ teaspoon mustard powder and sprinkle the top of the soufflé with Parmesan cheese.

Chocolate
Melt 2 oz (50 g) plain chocolate in the milk with 2 oz (50 g) caster sugar before making the sauce. Add $\frac{1}{2}$ teaspoon vanilla or almond essence with the egg yolks.

Crab
Add 4-6 oz (100-150 g) flaked crabmeat, salt, pepper and a pinch of mustard powder. Sprinkle the top lightly with Parmesan cheese.

Fish
Add 4-6 oz (100-150 g) cooked, flaked fish, salt and pepper. Smoked haddock and kipper are very good flavours.

Ham
Add 4-6 oz (100-150 g) finely chopped cooked ham, salt, pepper and a pinch of mustard powder.

Lemon
Add 2 oz (50 g) caster sugar, the finely grated rind of 1 lemon and the juice of $\frac{1}{2}$ lemon to the sauce.

Mushroom
Add 6 oz (150 g) finely chopped mushrooms lightly cooked in butter and seasoned with salt and pepper.

Raspberry
Add 8 oz (225 g) raspberries, 1 teaspoon lemon juice and 2 oz (50 g) caster sugar.

Batters and Pancakes

A batter is a creamy mixture of eggs, milk and flour which may be baked, fried or steamed. A thin batter is used for pancakes, and for baked and steamed puddings. A coating batter, which contains less milk, is for covering savoury and sweet foods which are then deep-fried. Plain flour should always be used as the eggs act as the raising agent.

BASIC BATTERS

Thin batter   Makes $\frac{1}{2}$ pt
$4\frac{1}{2}$ oz (115 g) plain flour
$\frac{1}{4}$ tsp salt
2 eggs
$\frac{1}{2}$ pt (300 ml) milk

Coating batter   Makes $\frac{1}{4}$ pt
$4\frac{1}{2}$ oz (115 g) plain flour
$\frac{1}{4}$ tsp salt
2 eggs
$\frac{1}{4}$ pt (150 ml) milk

For both recipes, sieve the flour and salt into a bowl. Make a well in the centre and drop in the beaten eggs. Gradually add half the milk, drawing the flour into the centre. Beat thoroughly until the mixture is smooth and bubbly. Cover the bowl and leave in a cool place for at least 30 minutes. Stir in the remaining milk just before cooking (see following recipes).

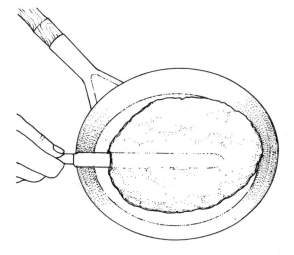

PANCAKES   *Makes 8*

$\frac{1}{2}$ pt thin batter
2 oz (50 g) lard

Using an 8 in (20 cm) pan, you should get 8 pancakes from this amount of batter. Heat a tiny piece of fat in the pan until it is very hot. Pour in about 2 tablespoons batter and tilt the pan quickly so that the batter covers the bottom of the pan evenly and thinly. Cook quickly until the pancake is golden brown underneath. Turn with a palette knife and lightly brown the other side. Fold in three lengthwise, or into quarters and put on a plate over a pan of hot water, and cover with another plate. This will keep the pancakes hot until all the batter is finished. Serve with lemon juice and sugar, jam or fruit filling, or with a savoury filling. Savoury-filled pancakes may be arranged in a heatproof dish, covered with cheese sauce, sprinkled with cheese, and quickly browned under the grill, for a substantial dish.

YORKSHIRE PUDDING   *Serves 4-6*

$\frac{1}{2}$ pt thin batter
2 oz (50 g) dripping

If possible, use fat which has run from the joint while roasting. Beef dripping has the best flavour. Preheat the oven at 400°F/200°C/gas mark 6. Put the dripping into a roasting tin approximately 7 × 11 in (17.5 × 27.5 cm). Put into the oven for 5 minutes until the fat is smoking hot. Pour in the batter and bake for 35 minutes until the pudding is puffy, crisp and golden.

TOAD IN THE HOLE   *Serves 4*

$\frac{1}{2}$ pt thin batter
4 large sausages or pork or lamb chops
2 oz (50 g) lard

Grill the sausages or chops until cooked through but not browned. Preheat the oven at 400°F/200°C/gas mark 6. Put the lard into an ovenware dish and heat in the oven for 5 minutes until smoking hot. Put in the sausages or chops and pour over the batter. Bake for 35 minutes until the batter is puffy, crisp and golden.

BAKED FRUIT BATTER   *Serves 4*

$\frac{1}{2}$ pt thin batter
8 oz (225 g) fresh fruit
2 oz (50 g) butter
A little caster sugar

Apples, plums or cherries are very good in this dish. Peel apples and slice thinly (if liked, leave to soak for 30 minutes in a little brandy or Calvados). Plums should be halved and stoned; cherries need stoning. Preheat the oven at 400°F/200°C/gas mark 6. Put the butter in an ovenware dish and heat in the oven for 2 minutes until it is hot but not browned. Pour in the batter. Bake for 40 minutes until the top is crisp and golden. Sprinkle with caster sugar before serving.

STEAMED BATTER PUDDING   *Serves 4*

$\frac{1}{2}$ pt thin batter
2 tbsp caster sugar

Stir the sugar into the batter and pour into a greased 1 pt (600 ml) pudding basin. Cover with greased greaseproof paper and a piece of foil tied with string. Steam for 1 hour. Turn out on a warm serving dish and serve with golden syrup or jam, or with fruit and cream.

FRUIT FRITTERS

$\frac{1}{4}$ pt coating batter
8 oz (225 g) eating apples *or* 3 bananas *or* 8 oz (225 g) canned pineapple rings
Deep fat for frying
A little caster sugar

Prepare the fruit just before the fritters are to be made. Peel the apples and cut into $\frac{1}{4}$ in (6 mm) thick rings. Peel bananas, cut in half lengthwise, and cut each piece in half. Drain pineapple rings. Heat the fat until a faint blue haze appears on the surface. Lift the fruit with a skewer, dip into the batter and drain well, then lower carefully into the fat, removing the skewer by twisting it. Fry until the fritters are golden brown and crisp, then lift out and toss in caster sugar before serving at once.

Savoury fritters
Small pieces of cooked vegetables (e.g. cauliflower sprigs), brains, or seafood may be dipped into the batter and fried, and served with a tartare sauce or tomato sauce.

Pâtés and Terrines

A really good pâté is a deliciously flavoured mixture of meat and seasonings with a clearly defined texture. It should either be thick and smooth or slightly chunky but juicy.

There is often confusion between the words 'pâté' and 'terrine'. Briefly, pâté is the actual meat

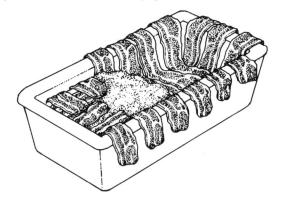

mixture, and terrine is the covered dish in which it is slowly cooked (in early days, this was a thick pastry crust which was discarded). The terms are often interchanged, but when the meat mixture is called a 'terrine' it usually indicates a coarse-textured pâté, often a mixture of minced and cubed or sliced meat arranged in layers, and most suitable for serving in slices with salads or hot potatoes. Whatever you call it, make it with good fresh ingredients, carefully seasoned, and prepare it two or three days ahead so that the flavours blend and mature.

Pâté should have a high proportion of fat, usually fresh pork fat, but it can be fat green bacon or lard. Smoked bacon can be used with highly flavoured game; but it does lend a rather robust flavour to the dish and is best not used where a delicate pâté is needed. Without fat, a pâté can be dry, crumbly and dull. Sometimes breadcrumbs are added to give texture, and eggs may be used to bind the mixture and make it easier to slice. The uncooked mixture should be moist and indeed even sloppy before being cooked, and if it seems stiff and dry, it may be moistened with a little stock, some cream or a little wine.

Careful seasoning is vital to a good pâté. Salt and pepper are obvious additions, but a pinch of ground mace or nutmeg helps to bring out the other flavours. The Danes like to add a little anchovy (either the pounded salt fish or a few drops of essence) to enhance the flavour of liver. A pinch of cloves is liked by some, and so is crushed garlic and/or a good sprinkling of fresh mixed herbs.

The finished mixture should be cooked in a deep glazed earthenware dish, but may be prepared in an enamelled iron dish or in oven-glass. There should be a lid with a hole in it, to allow steam to escape. A loaf tin may be used in emergency, with a covering of foil, but when the pâté has cooled and firmed up, it may leave a stain on a metal container of this type. The container is best placed in a roasting tin half filled with hot water, and the pâté cooked in a low-to-moderate oven. In this way, the mixture is cooked through evenly without hard over-cooked patches. To tell if a pâté is cooked, stick in a skewer. The juices should run clear, without any blood, and the fat should be transparent, without a pinkish tinge. The pâté will shrink in cooking.

Pâté should cut in firm neat pieces, so it is important to finish it correctly after cooking. Put a flat board or dish on the cooked pâté, and weight it evenly with scale weights or tins of food until cold and set. This will press out air bubbles and give a closer texture. The top of the pâté may be finished with aspic, melted butter or lard, but aspic should be used only if the dish is to be used up in one or two meals. If a pâté is completely sealed with fat, it will keep refrigerated for about 10 days, but is best not stored this way if it has a high bread content or a lot of jellied juices surrounding the meat. Pâté may of course be frozen, but is best kept no longer than 2 months, like other cooked meat dishes.

SIMPLE PÂTÉ   *Serves 10-12*

12 oz (350 g) pig's liver
1 lb (450 g) belly pork
Salt, pepper and nutmeg
1 medium onion
1 oz (25 g) butter
1 egg
1 oz (25 g) plain flour
1 bay leaf

Mince the liver and pork together or chop them very finely. Season to taste. Chop the onion very finely and soften in the butter until tender. Stir into the meat with the egg beaten with flour. Put the bay leaf in the bottom of the container and put in the meat mixture. Cover and put into a baking tin of hot water. Bake at 350°F/180°C/gas mark 4 for $1\frac{1}{2}$ hours. Cool under a weight until the next day. If liked, the container may be lined with thin strips of streaky bacon or pork fat before putting in the meat.

PORK AND SAUSAGE PÂTÉ   *Serves 4-6*

8 oz (225 g) pig's liver
4 oz (100 g) lean bacon
8 oz (225 g) pork sausagemeat
1 oz (25 g) white breadcrumbs
4 oz (100 g) mushrooms
$\frac{1}{4}$ tsp sage
2 tsp tomato chutney
Salt and pepper

A very homely pâté which is easy to make and very good with salad or in sandwiches. Mince the liver and bacon and mix with the sausagemeat and breadcrumbs. Add finely chopped mushrooms and other ingredients and mix well together. Press into a container, cover and put the container in a roasting tin of hot water. Bake at 325°F/160°C/gas mark 3 for 1½ hours. Cool under weights for 24 hours.

HARE PÂTÉ   *Serves 8*

Joints of hare
2 medium onions
1 bay leaf
Bunch of mixed herbs
1 lb (450 g) fat bacon
Salt and pepper
4 bacon rashers
$\frac{1}{2}$ pt (300 ml) red wine
A squeeze of lemon juice

A hare is a large animal, so it is useful to convert at least part of it into a completely different dish which may be used some days later, or of course frozen. A couple of legs should produce enough meat for this pâté. Put the hare, sliced onions, bay leaf, herbs, cubed fat bacon and a little salt and pepper into a covered pan and cook very slowly in a low oven until the meat will just leave the bones. Take the meat from the hare bones and put through the mincer with the fat bacon and any juices in the container. Season again to taste. Flatten the bacon rashers with a knife and line a container. Put the minced meat in and pour in the red wine. Add the lemon juice. Cover and put the container in a baking tin of hot water. Cook at 325°F/160°C/gas mark 3 for 2 hours. Cool under weights for 24 hours. A little port or brandy may be added to the mixture (with the seasoning) or a spoonful of red current jelly, which will add colour and flavour.

CHICKEN LIVER PÂTÉ   *Serves 4*

8 oz (225 g) chicken livers
3 oz (75 g) fat bacon
1 small onion
1 oz (25 g) butter
2 garlic cloves
1 egg
Salt and pepper

Cut the chicken livers, bacon and onion in small pieces. Cook bacon and onions in a little butter until onion is just soft. Add livers and cook gently for 10 minutes. Put into a blender with peeled garlic cloves, egg and seasoning and blend until smooth. Put into an ovenware container so that the mixture comes just to the top. Cover with a piece of greaseproof paper and then foil, or a lid, and stand the dish in a roasting tin of water. Cook at 325°F/160°C/gas mark 3 for 40 minutes. Cool under a weight for 24 hours. Cover with a little melted clarified butter.

SEAFOOD PÂTÉ   *Serves 4-6*

8 oz (225 g) shelled prawns
4 oz (100 g) butter
8 oz (225 g) white fish (haddock, cod or whiting)
$\frac{1}{2}$ tsp anchovy essence
Pinch of ground mace
Pinch of cayenne pepper

Chop the prawns into small pieces. Soften the butter, but do not melt it. Simmer the fish in a little water for 10 minutes, and then remove any skin or bones. Put the fish into a blender with all the butter and half the prawns. Add the essence and spices and blend until smooth. Fold in the remaining prawns and press into a serving dish. Cool completely and cover with a little melted clarified butter.

KIPPER PÂTÉ   *Serves 4*

8 oz (225 g) kipper fillets
1 oz (25 g) melted butter
Juice of $\frac{1}{2}$ lemon
1 garlic clove
1 tbsp brandy
A few drops of Tabasco sauce
2 tbsp single cream

Poach the kipper fillets until tender and remove any skin and any bones. Flake the flesh and put into a blender with the butter, lemon juice, chopped garlic, brandy and Tabasco sauce. Blend until smooth. Add cream and blend just long enough to incorporate it. Press into a serving dish and cover with a little melted clarified butter.

Beef

When choosing beef, look for a fresh, slightly moist appearance. The lean of roasting joints should be smooth and velvety in texture. Coarse lean is generally an indication that the meat is suitable only for braising and stewing, and beef that is very coarse will almost certainly be tough. The lean should be surrounded by a layer of creamy-white fat. The colour of the fat may vary, but the important thing is that the fat is firm and dry. Marbling or flecking of fat in the meat is an aid to successful cooking as the flecks of fat melt into the lean, and help to keep the meat's flavour and succulence.

ECONOMICAL CUTS

Top rump (also called thick flank, bed of beef or first cutting) is a lean cut which makes a roasting joint, but must be cooked slowly as in pot-roasting. The meat may be sliced for frying or braising.

Brisket may be kept on the bone, or boned and rolled, and requires slow, moist cooking, such as pot-roasting so that it does not shrink. Very good salted for eating hot or as pressed beef.

Silverside is very lean and is the best cut for salting to boil with carrots (in Scotland, the joint is roasted).

Shin is excellent for making soup, jellied stock and brawn, or it may be stewed or made into beef tea.

Neck and clod are full of flavour and excellent for hot-pots and stews as the juices make rich gravy.

Flank may be pot-roasted on the bone, or cut up for stews and hot-pots and needs slow, moist cooking. It may be salted if liked.

Chuck and blade form a large, fairly lean cut. The meat is boned and sold as chuck steak for braising, stewing, puddings and pies.

Skirt is a thin, lean stewing meat which comes from inside the ribs and flank. It may be rolled round stuffing and pot-roasted slowly.

Leg may be used like shin, and is good in soup.

BETTER CUTS

Sirloin is tender and delicious and may be roasted in the piece or grilled as steaks. The *fillet* is found on the inside of the sirloin bone and may be roasted with the sirloin. If the sirloin is boned and rolled for roasting, the fillet can be used separately for roasting in one piece (delicious when served very rare), or put into a pastry case, or sliced for very tender steaks.

Rump steak makes excellent steaks with full flavour, although not as tender as fillet. The lean should be velvety, close-grained and bright red in colour, with a moderate amount of fat.

Ribs may be cooked on the bone, or boned and rolled for roasting. The rib joints should have a layer of firm dry fat, and marbling in the lean.

Fore ribs are a traditional roasting joint. *Wing ribs* may be roast or cut into grilling and frying steaks. *Back ribs and top ribs* are ideal for pot-roasting.

Topside is a lean cut, which needs a piece of fat

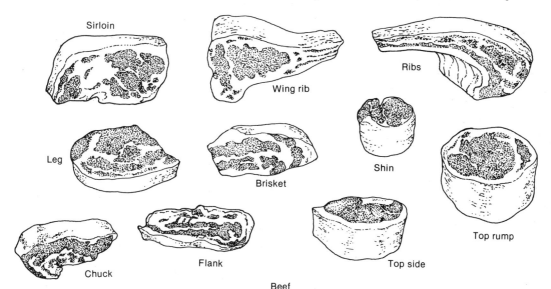

Beef

tied over the joint when roasting slowly (keep it well basted and serve slightly underdone). It is very good for pot-roasting.

SCOTTISH CUTS

In Scotland topside and silverside may be called rump, buttock or round steak. Rump steak is sometimes called pope's eye; leg and shin are hough; and chuck and blade are sold as shoulder.

ACCOMPANIMENTS

Beef dishes may be enhanced by herbs and spices. Garlic and celery seed give a good flavour to casseroles, and so does a bay leaf. Steaks can be made more tender for grilling if they are soaked in a mixture of oil and vinegar or lemon juice with a sprinkle of thyme and garlic. Add red wine to a beef stew for a rich flavour, allowing a large wineglass for 2 lb (1 kg) meat, or use ale or cider instead of water or stock. The traditional accompaniment to beef is horse-radish sauce, but for a change try mustard or onion sauce.

ROASTING BEEF

Lean joints should be cooked very slowly to retain their succulence and flavour. Preheat the oven to 375°F/190°C/gas mark 5 and put 3 tablespoons dripping into a tin. Heat in the oven and then put the meat into the tin and baste well. Allow 20 minutes for each 1 lb (450 g) and 20 minutes over, and keep well basted. For a crisper roast, sear the cut surface of the meat in the hot fat and then pour over a tumbler of water and cook at 350°F/180°C/gas mark 4 for 20 minutes per 1 lb (450 g) and 20 minutes over. Season beef after cooking, and leave to 'rest' for 15 minutes before carving. *For pot-roasting* seal the joint in a little hot fat and place in a casserole with root vegetables all round. Add about $\frac{1}{4}$ pt (150 ml) stock, season and cover tightly and cook on low heat.

BEEF IN ALE   *Serves 4*

$1\frac{1}{2}$ lb (675 g) stewing steak
1 large onion
$1\frac{1}{2}$ oz (40 g) butter
$\frac{3}{4}$ pt (450 ml) brown ale
2 tsp made mustard
2 tsp malt vinegar
1 tsp salt
1 bay leaf
A pinch of thyme
2 oz (50 g) white breadcrumbs

Cut the steak into 1 in (2.5 cm) cubes. Chop the onion finely and cook in butter until soft and golden. Add the steak and fry until brown all over. Stir in all the remaining ingredients except the breadcrumbs. Put into a casserole dish, cover and cook at 350°F/180°C/gas mark 4 for $1\frac{3}{4}$ hours. Cool and store in the refrigerator overnight. Next day, turn into a saucepan and bring to the boil. Cover and simmer for 30 minutes, stirring occasionally. Stir in the breadcrumbs just before serving.

STUFFED BRISKET   *Serves 6*

1 oz (25 g) butter
4 oz (100 g) button mushrooms
2 oz (50 g) cooked ham
2 oz (50 g) fresh white breadcrumbs
1 tsp mixed·herbs
Salt and pepper
1 egg
3 lb (1.5 kg) boned brisket
2 oz (50 g) dripping

Melt the butter and cook the chopped mushrooms for 5 minutes. Stir in the chopped ham, breadcrumbs, herbs and seasonings and enough egg to bind. Spread the stuffing on the meat, roll up and secure with string in several places. Put into a roasting tin with the dripping. Roast at 300°F/150°C/gas mark 2 for $3\frac{1}{2}$ hours. Serve with gravy made from the pan juices (see page 85).

JUGGED BEEF   *Serves 4*

$1\frac{1}{2}$ lb (675 g) shin beef
2 oz (50 g) seasoned flour
6 lean bacon rashers
2 onions
4 cloves
Grated rind of 1 lemon
A sprig of parsley
A sprig of thyme
1 bay leaf
6 small mushrooms
$\frac{3}{4}$ pt (450 ml) beef stock

Cut the meat into 2 in (5 cm) cubes and roll the pieces in the seasoned flour. Chop the bacon and fry in its own fat until golden. Add the meat and brown lightly. Stick the cloves into the onions. Add the onions to the beef and bacon, with the lemon rind, herbs, mushrooms and stock. Cover and simmer on top of the stove for 3 hours. If preferred, cook in a casserole dish at 300°F/150°C/gas mark 2. Season half way through cooking, but remember that the bacon will already have added salt to the dish. Remove herbs and onions before serving.

PROVENCAL BEEF CASSEROLE   *Serves 4*

$1\frac{1}{2}$ lb (675 g) chuck steak
1 tsp olive oil
1 carrot
1 onion
3 large ripe tomatoes
4 oz (100 g) mushrooms
$\frac{1}{2}$ pt (300 ml) beef stock
12 pitted black olives
1 garlic clove
$\frac{1}{2}$ tsp salt
A pinch of basil
1 bay leaf

Cut the steak into cubes and brown in hot oil. Lift out the meat and place in a casserole dish. Peel the carrot and onion, and cut across in thin slices. Cook them in the oil until soft and golden. Drain and add to the meat. Peel the tomatoes. Add the whole tomatoes, mushrooms and stock to the meat. Stir in the olives, crushed garlic and seasonings. Cover and cook at 325°F/160°C/gas mark 3 for 2 hours. Remove the bay leaf before serving.

HUNGARIAN GOULASH   *Serves 4*

$1\frac{1}{2}$ lb (675 g) chuck steak
2 oz (50 g) dripping
2 medium onions
1 garlic clove
2 tsp paprika
$\frac{1}{2}$ tsp cayenne pepper
1 tbsp plain flour
1 pt (600 ml) beef stock
2 tbsp tomato purée
Salt and pepper
$\frac{1}{4}$ pt (150 ml) natural yogurt

Cut the steak into cubes and brown on all sides in hot dripping. Lift out the meat and keep on one side. Slice the onions and crush the garlic. Fry in the dripping until soft and golden and stir in the paprika, cayenne pepper and flour. Cook for 1 minute. Return the meat to the casserole dish and add the stock, purée, salt and pepper. Cover and simmer for 2 hours. Just before serving, stir in the yogurt. Serve with rice or boiled potatoes.

Lamb

Leg may be prepared simply as one large joint, but this may be too large for the family and is worth dividing into two joints. *Half leg shank end* is the tenderest part of the lamb, and makes a nice small joint if roasted and served slightly pink. *Half leg fillet end* is not quite so juicy, but may be roasted, or pot-roasted with vegetables. The old way of cooking was to simmer the leg until tender and serve it with caper sauce, made from white sauce liberally spiked with capers and you could try this with one of the smaller joints for a change. Don't forget that a slice of leg cut across the bone makes a beautiful 'steak', so you can reduce the size of your leg joints by cutting off one or two of these slices and cooking them separately.

Shoulder is another excellent roasting joint, but may be cut into two joints. A boned shoulder is excellent if stuffed and firmly sewn again into shape or tied. Cubed shoulder is the meat to use for lamb pies or kebabs.

Loin is versatile and may be prepared as joints of any length you choose. *A double loin or saddle* is a spectacular party joint and may be worth having for a special occasion. The loin may also be cut into chops and chump chops are the very meaty ones

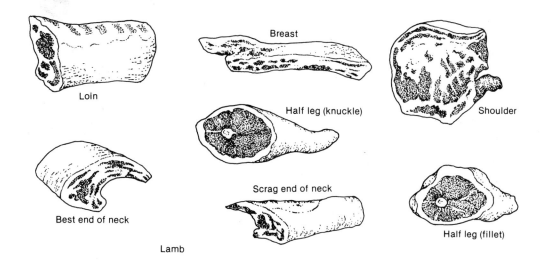

Loin

Breast

Shoulder

Half leg (knuckle)

Best end of neck

Scrag end of neck

Half leg (fillet)

Lamb

cut from where the loin joins the leg.

Breast can be useful, although many people find the meat fatty. Either have it boned, ready for stuffing and rolling; or cut into bite-sized pieces which can be used in stews or fried to serve with sauce.

Neck can be divided into a number of portions, of varying quality and use. *Best end of neck* may be used as a nice small joint, either on the bone, or boned and rolled. The rolled joint may also be cut across into neat little rounds which are very good grilled, fried or roasted with sauce. This piece of meat may also be made into *cutlets* which are small chops trimmed of excess fat and with just a small 'eye' of meat. *Middle neck* is very good for casseroles, curries and an old-fashioned Irish Stew or hot-pot. *Scrag neck* is best used for pies or casseroles since it is rather fat and gristly, although the flavour is good.

ROASTING LAMB

Roast at 350°F/180°C/gas mark 4 for 30 minutes per 1 lb (450 g), to give a tender juicy joint which is full of flavour. If you like the meat a little pink, allow only 25 minutes to 1 lb (450 g). If you enjoy roast lamb, try basting a joint with a little fruit juice (orange, apple or pineapple are good) or with red or white wine. Try tucking a sprig of fresh rosemary and a couple of split garlic cloves into the joint before roasting. For a flavoured skin, spread a little mint or red current jelly on top, or some honey or marmalade, or a crust of breadcrumbs, melted butter and fresh herbs. If you like sauces, you can serve mint sauce, but cranberry sauce, red current jelly, mint jelly, onion sauce or caper sauce are just as delicious.

BOILED LAMB AND MELTED BUTTER   *Serves 6-8*

1 leg of lamb
1 large onion
1 carrot
1 turnip
A bunch of mixed herbs
6 peppercorns
A pinch of ground mace
Salt
4 oz (100 g) butter

Put the meat into a saucepan and cover with boiling water. Boil for 5 minutes and then add the vegetables, herbs and seasoning. Lower the heat and simmer, allowing 20 minutes per 1 lb (450 g)

and 20 minutes over. Remove any scum from time to time, but keep the meat covered during cooking. Add the salt only about 30 minutes before serving. To serve, drain the meat and put on a warm serving dish. Chop the vegetables and put round the meat and pour on 4 oz (100 g) melted butter. If liked, the cooking liquid may be made into white sauce with plenty of chopped parsley or capers which can be served with the meat.

LAMB IN THE ROUND   *Serves 6*

1 boned shoulder of lamb
6 medium onions
Rosemary or parsley
2 oz (50 g) butter

Stuff the meat with half the onions finely chopped and plenty of rosemary or parsley. Skewer and tie into a round cushion shape. Put into a roasting tin with the remaining onions cut in thin slices. Brush with melted butter and roast at 350°F/180°C/gas mark 4 for 20 minutes per 1 lb (450 g) and 30 minutes over. Serve cut in wedges with red currant jelly and gravy. If you like kidneys, put only 1 chopped onion into the shoulder with the herbs and add 3-4 chopped lambs' kidneys.

APRICOT LAMB   *Serves 4-6*

1 medium onion
1 oz (25 g) butter
8 oz (225 g) canned apricots
3 oz (75 g) white breadcrumbs
2 tbsp chopped parsley
2 oz (50 g) currants
Salt and pepper
1 egg
1 small shoulder lamb, boned

Chop the onion finely and cook in the butter until soft and golden. Drain the apricots and chop them roughly. Add apricots to the onion with the breadcrumbs, parsley, currants, salt, pepper and egg, and mix thoroughly. Open the shoulder of lamb and season well with salt and pepper. Put in the stuffing, reshape the meat and secure with skewers. Put in a roasting tin with a little dripping, and roast for 1½-2 hours at 350°F/180°C/gas mark 4 according to the size of the meat. Drain off excess fat and make gravy with the pan juices, a little stock and a little of the juice from the apricots.

LEMON AND GINGER CHOPS   *Serves 6*

6 loin chops
4 tbsp cooking oil
2 tbsp lemon juice
1 tsp ground ginger
1 tbsp soft brown sugar

Put the chops into a shallow dish. Mix the oil, lemon juice, ginger and sugar, and pour over the chops. Leave overnight if possible, but for at least 2 hours, turning the chops once or twice. Grill the chops for 8 minutes each side under medium heat, basting with any leftover mixture. Serve with lemon slices, fried potatoes and a green salad.

ROSEMARY LAMB   *Serves 6*

1 shoulder lamb
6 sprigs rosemary
6 garlic cloves
Salt and pepper
Juice of $\frac{1}{2}$ lemon

Put the lamb into a roasting tin. Put half the rosemary sprigs on top and season the skin with coarsely ground black pepper. Do not peel the garlic but tuck the cloves under the meat. Put into oven at 425°F/330°C/gas mark 7 for 15 minutes, then continue roasting at 375°F/190°C/gas mark 5, allowing 24 minutes per 1 lb (450 g). About 30 minutes before roasting time is complete, pour off surplus fat and remove the rosemary. Add $\frac{1}{4}$ pt (150 ml) water to the pan and the lemon juice. Sprinkle the lamb skin with salt and put on the remaining fresh rosemary. Baste twice while finishing cooking, without disturbing the rosemary. Serve the meat with the pan juices as gravy. This is very good cold as well.

SPRING LAMB   *Serves 4-6*

2 lb (900 g) shoulder lamb, boned and cubed
3 tbsp oil
3 small onions
1 oz (25 g) plain flour
1 pt (600 ml) stock
Salt and pepper
A sprig of rosemary
1 garlic clove
1 bay leaf
1 lb (450 g) new potatoes
8 oz (225 g) new carrots
4 baby turnips
1 lb (450 g) shelled peas

Cut the lamb into neat cubes. Heat the oil and cook the sliced onions until soft and golden. Add the meat and continue cooking until meat is sealed. Work the flour into the pan and add the stock. Stir and simmer until smooth. Season with salt, pepper, rosemary, crushed garlic and bay leaf. Cover and simmer for 1 hour. Add the whole potatoes, carrots and the turnips. Simmer for 35 minutes. Stir in the peas and cook for 10 minutes.

Pork

Pork is now a year-round meat, thanks to refrigeration, and is an economical and versatile meat.

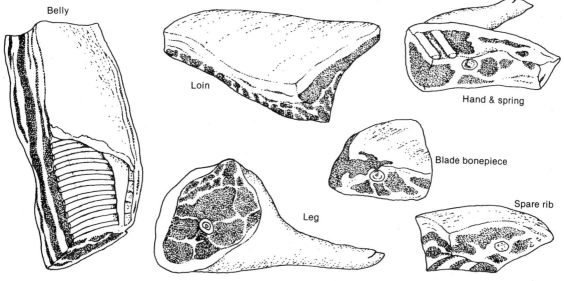

Belly
Loin
Hand & spring
Blade bonepiece
Leg
Spare rib
Pork

ECONOMICAL CUTS

Shoulder is a large joint which may be boned and rolled. The meat may be divided into *blade* and *spare rib*. Blade is an economical roasting joint which is good boned and filled with savoury stuffing, but it is also ideal for braising and stewing. Spare rib is lean and economical for roasting with little top fat and skin, and the meat may be chopped for home-made pork pies. Spare rib chops are good for grilling, frying or braising.

Hand and spring form a large joint for roasting whole, but is often divided into *hand* and *shank*. The hand can be boned and roasted, or used for boiling, while shank is good for casseroles.

Belly (sometimes known as draft or flank) may be rolled and stuffed for roasting, or cooked flat on top of a tasty stuffing, so that it yields plenty of crisp crackling. The cut may also be used for stewing or boiling, and boiled belly pork may be pressed until firm, then cut into thin slices for an old-fashioned breakfast. Slices of belly make economical grilling or frying slices, and also make very good pâté and meat loaves.

BETTER CUTS

Leg is succulent for roasting, and may be divided into *fillet* and *knuckle end*. The fillet end is a thick slice from the top of the leg which is good for roasting or may be sliced into steaks for grilling and frying. Knuckle end is a roasting joint which may be boned and stuffed.

Loin may be roasted on the bone, or boned, stuffed and rolled. It may be divided into *loin* chops and *chump* chops. The loin chops may have the kidney in, while chump chops are large and meaty. Tenderloin is a lean cut found on the inside of the loin bone, and is the equivalent of fillet steak. It is sometimes known as pork fillet, but should not be confused with fillet end from the leg. It may be split, stuffed and roasted or cut across in thin slices for beating flat into 'escalopes' which may be crumbed and fried or else lightly fried and then simmered in a sauce of mushrooms and cream or with either mushrooms, peppers or tomatoes.

SCOTTISH CUTS

Some cuts in Scotland have slightly different names and are cut differently. A shoulder of pork includes hand and spring, blade and ribs. The shoulder is usually cut in half, boned and rolled. Leg is known as gigot, and the shank end is called hough end. Hand and spring, minus shank, is called runner, and belly is sometimes called flank.

ACCOMPANIMENTS

However the meat is cut, remember that pork is a versatile meat and goes well with many different flavourings. Basil, sage, marjoram, parsley, thyme and rosemary are the herbs which may be used with roasts, grills or stews. A hint of paprika, cloves, curry powder or ginger may be rubbed into the skin before roasting, or added to sauces. Apple sauce, onion sauce, and cranberry sauce are traditional accompaniments. Include fruit in stuffings too, using apple, orange, apricot, prune or pineapple for special occasions.

ROASTING PORK

Pork should *never* be served underdone, so make sure that when a skewer is stuck into the meat any juice which runs out is colourless rather than pink. A cooking time of 30 minutes per 1 lb (450 g) and 30 minutes over at moderate oven temperature is recommended. Season pork joints before roasting, and for good crackling try brushing the scored skin with oil and rub over with a generous helping of salt. Put into a dry roasting tin and keep the rind uppermost, and never baste pork during cooking. Put a sprig of rosemary and a couple of split garlic cloves under the joint and another sprig of rosemary on top for a subtle and delicious flavour.

FRENCH PORK CASSEROLE   *Serves 4*

4 pork chops
1 garlic clove
8 juniper berries
2 tbsp lard
1½ lb (675 g) potatoes
1 medium onion
Salt and pepper
A pinch of ground nutmeg
6 bacon rashers
4 tbsp white wine or cider

Cut the garlic into four pieces and insert one piece of garlic and 2 juniper berries close to the bone of each chop. Brown the chops in the lard on both sides. Peel and slice the potatoes and onions thinly and put half the potatoes and onions into an ovenware dish. Season with salt, pepper and nutmeg. Put the chops on top and cover with remaining potatoes and onions. Season well and cover with bacon rashers. Pour in wine or cider. Cover and cook at 300°F/150°C/gas mark 2 for 2½ hours. Drain off surplus fat and continue cooking without a lid for 15 minutes until the top is brown.

SPANISH BARBECUED PORK   *Serves 6*

3 lb (1.5 kg) thick end of belly pork
2 oz (50 g) butter
Salt and pepper
1 tsp sugar
1 tsp ground ginger
1 tsp ground mixed spice

Sauce
1 tbsp Worcestershire sauce
2 tsp sugar
2 tsp malt vinegar
8 tbsp tomato ketchup
2 tbsp soy sauce
2 garlic cloves
A dash of Tabasco sauce
2 bay leaves
3 oz (75 g) stuffed green olives

The skin of the pork must be well scored. Mix butter, salt, pepper, sugar, ginger and spice and spread all over the meat. Roast at 400°F/200°C/gas mark 6 for 1 hour, basting from time to time. Drain all the fat from the meat. Mix all the sauce ingredients, crushing the garlic before adding. Pour over the meat and continue cooking for 15 minutes. Add halved olives to the sauce just before serving.

PORK AND APPLE CASSEROLE   *Serves 4*

4 spare rib pork chops
2 onions
2 cooking apples
$\frac{1}{2}$ pt (300 ml) stock
Salt and pepper
4 tomatoes

Put the chops into a shallow ovenware dish and season well. Slice the onions and apples in rings and arrange on the chops. Pour over the stock with the seasoning, cover and bake at 350°F/180°C/gas mark 4 for 1 hour. Add sliced tomatoes and continue cooking for 15 minutes. Remove the lid and continue cooking for 15 minutes.

PORK CRUMBLE   *Serves 4*

$1\frac{1}{2}$ lb (675 g) hand or shoulder pork
Seasoned flour
1 lb (450 g) potatoes
2 leeks
$\frac{1}{2}$ pt (300 ml) dry cider
1 tsp mixed herbs
Salt and pepper
3 oz (75 g) breadcrumbs
3 oz (75 g) grated cheese

Cube the pork and toss in seasoned flour. Fry in a little hot fat until golden. Put meat in casserole with sliced potatoes and leeks. Add cider, herbs and seasonings. Cover tightly and bake at 350°F/180°C/gas mark 4 for 1 hour. Mix the breadcrumbs and cheese and sprinkle over the meat. Return uncovered to the oven and cook for 30 minutes.

Poultry and Game

Before choosing or preparing poultry and game, take a little time to look at pages 27-8 to make sure that the bird or animal is suitable for the meal you want to cook. The recipes which follow the basic cooking instructions give some idea of the range of dishes which may be made from versatile poultry and game which can provide a great deal of variety to both everyday and special meals.

CHICKEN

It is always worth buying a bird which is larger than necessary for one meal, as the leftovers may be used for soup, salad and many second-day dishes. To roast a chicken, weigh the bird, and allow 15 minutes per 1 lb (450 g) at 400°F/200°C/gas mark 6. The bird may be simply dotted with butter

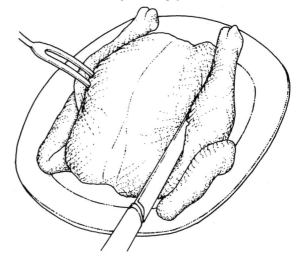

and sprinkled with salt and pepper before roasting; flavour is improved if a bunch of mixed herbs or tarragon is placed in the cavity. A chicken may be stuffed (see Stuffings, pages 58 & 134) and the bird should be weighed when stuffed so that a longer cooking time is calculated. The traditional accompaniments are small bacon rolls, chipolata sausages and bread sauce.

TURKEY

Always make sure that the turkey will fit your oven before buying a bird. A quickly roasted bird will be crisper, but slower cooking reduces shrinkage and gives a moister bird. Roasting in foil gives a moist, tender bird, but can sometimes result in a slightly stewed taste as the steam is retained in the bird. The best compromise is to put a turkey in a hot oven set at 425°F/220°C/gas mark 7 for 20 minutes, then to reduce heat to 375°F/190°C/gas mark 5 for remaining cooking time. Cover the breast with bacon rashers, or with plenty of butter and a piece of greaseproof paper so that it does not brown too quickly, and baste the bird with pan juices at regular intervals.

For a bird under 14 lb (7 kg) allow 15 minutes per 1 lb (450 g) and 15 minutes over. For a larger bird, allow 10 minutes per 1 lb (450 g) and 10 minutes over. Cut the string around the drumsticks after an hour's cooking, when they should be set, and this will allow the heat to circulate and ensure that the dark meat is cooked through. Test by inserting a skewer into the thickest part of a drumstick to see if cooking is finished; this will be when the skewer goes in easily, but no liquid runs out. The traditional accompaniments are stuffing, bread sauce, cranberry sauce, bacon rolls and sausages. The bird may have a sausage stuffing inserted in the cavity and chestnut stuffing at the neck.

GOOSE

This is a wasteful bird as it looses about half its weight in cooking. Rub the goose all over with flour to give a crisp skin and cook the bird on a rack in a large tin. After 20 minutes cooking time, prick the skin with a fork to allow fat to run out, and drain off some of the fat during the cooking, using a little to baste the bird two or three times. Start the bird at 450°F/230°C/gas mark 8 for 30 minutes, and then at 400°F/200°C/gas mark 6 for remaining cooking time, allowing 15 minutes per 1 lb (450 g) and 15 minutes over. Serve with apple sauce or fried apple rings, or use a stuffing which contains fruit such as prune or apple. Red cabbage is good served with goose — it offsets the fatness of the meat.

DUCK

Try to choose a broad-breasted bird which will carve well as it is difficult to get many portions from a duck. Rub salt into the breast and roast in a pan with $\frac{1}{2}$ in (1.25 cm) water in the base and no extra fat (this will help to give a really crisp skin). Prick the skin after 20 minutes so that surplus fat runs out. Start the bird at 450°F/230°C/gas mark 8 for 10 minutes, and then reduce heat to 350°F/180°C/gas mark 4 for remaining cooking time, allowing 15 minutes per 1 lb (450 g). Duck is best left unstuffed, but a peeled orange or apple may be inserted in the cavity which will give a subtle flavour during roasting. Sage and onion stuffing may be prepared and baked separately. Other traditional accompaniments are apple sauce or a salad of sliced oranges.

GROUSE

One young bird will be enough for 2 people; a larger older bird should be enough for 3. Roast grouse if it is young, but casserole very old or badly shot birds. Roast for 20-25 minutes at 400°F/200°C/gas mark 6 with pieces of bacon tied over the breast. Serve on pieces of toast spread with the cooked liver mashed with a little stock, and accompany with gravy, bread sauce, fried breadcrumbs and wafer potatoes. Watercress is a traditional garnish, and rowanberry jelly is very good with grouse.

PHEASANT

As with other game birds, young ones are best for roasting. The hen bird is smaller but less dry and more tender with good flavour. One large bird is enough for 4 people, and a pheasant should be hung in feathers for at least a week after shooting so that the flesh becomes tender and full of flavour. Roast at 400°F/200°C/gas mark 6 for about 45 minutes, according to the size of the bird. Tie some bacon over the breast and baste with a little butter or red wine during roasting. Serve with clear gravy, bread sauce, fried potatoes and wafer thin potatoes. Celery, sprouts, mushrooms and chestnuts are all good with pheasant.

PARTRIDGE

One bird will serve 2 people. Roast at 350°F/180°C/gas mark 4 for 25 minutes, with bacon on the breast and basting with butter. Serve split in two with clear gravy, watercress and wafer potatoes.

PIGEON

Only fat, young birds should be roasted, as older birds are lean and dry. When roasting, cover the breast with bacon, but do not baste or put hot fat on pigeons as the flesh is delicate and the hot fat will toughen it and destroy the flavour. Roast at 350°F/180°C/gas mark 4 for 30 minutes and put a piece of crustless toast under the birds 10 minutes before the end of cooking time so that the pan juices are absorbed — serve this toast under the roast pigeon.

HARE AND RABBIT

Hare has a rich, strong flavour and is most popular when 'jugged' in a casserole, or made into a pâté. It is a large animal which will feed 8-10 people. The rabbit is more suitable for small families and is excellent for pies and casseroles. Soak rabbit pieces in salted water for an hour before cooking so that the flesh is whitened.

MOROCCAN LEMON CHICKEN   *Serves 4*

1 lemon
$1\frac{1}{2}$ oz (40 g) raisins
A pinch of saffron
A pinch of ground allspice
1 tsp pepper
$\frac{1}{2}$ tsp curry powder
1 tsp salt
$\frac{1}{4}$ tsp sugar
4 lb (1.8 kg) chicken
A bunch of fresh herbs
4 tbsp oil
$2\frac{1}{2}$ oz (65 g) butter

Cut the lemon in quarters and put it into a screwtop jar with the raisins, saffron, allspice, pepper, curry powder, salt and sugar. Cover, shake well and leave it to stand. Put the chicken into a pan with water to come three-quarters of the way up the chicken. Add a pinch of salt, herbs and oil, cover and bring it to the boil. Reduce the heat and simmer for 45 minutes. Take off the lid, increase the heat and cook for 20 minutes until the water has evaporated. Melt the butter in a roasting tin until it is just browned. Put the drained chicken into the tin and strain over the lemon liquid from the jar, retaining the lemon pieces. Roast it at 375°F/190°C/gas mark 5 for 15 minutes, basting with the pan juices. Just before serving, squeeze over the remaining liquid from the lemon pieces. Serve with rice or plain boiled potatoes.

CIDER CHICKEN   *Serves 4*

$3\frac{1}{2}$ lb (1.5 kg) chicken
Salt and pepper
1 clove garlic
1 oz (25 g) butter
2 tbsp oil
8 oz (225 g) tomatoes
2 medium onions
1 oz (25 g) black olives
$\frac{3}{4}$ pt (450 ml) dry cider
$\frac{1}{2}$ oz (15 g) plain flour
2 tbsp tomato purée

Sprinkle the chicken with salt and pepper and rub it all over with the crushed garlic. Brown it on all sides in the butter and oil and put it into a casserole. Skin the tomatoes and slice them. Put them into the casserole with the sliced onions and stoned olives. Pour on the cider. Cover and cook at 375°F/190°C/gas mark 5 for $1\frac{1}{2}$ hours. Strain the liquid into a saucepan. Mix the flour with a little water and stir it into the saucepan with the tomato purée. Bring this to the boil and simmer for 5 minutes, stirring well. Pour it over the chicken and vegetables.

WINE MERCHANT'S CHICKEN   *Serves 4*

4 chicken joints
5 tbsp oil
2 oz (50 g) butter
2 oz (50 g) mushrooms
2 shallots (or 1 small onion)
1 clove garlic
4 oz (100 g) lean bacon
1 oz (25 g) flour
$\frac{1}{2}$ pt (300 ml) stock
$\frac{1}{2}$ pt (300 ml) red wine
Salt and pepper

Wipe the chicken joints. Heat the oil in a thick-bottomed pan and brown the chicken. Add a pinch of salt and lower the heat. Put on a lid, but leave it slightly aslant so that the chicken pieces are not completely covered and air gets in. Cook for 25 minutes until the chicken is cooked through. Meanwhile, melt the butter and cook the chopped mushrooms, shallots or onions, crushed garlic and chopped bacon until golden. Stir in the flour and cook for 1 minute. Add the stock and wine gradually and cook this gently until smooth and creamy. Season to taste. Serve the pieces of chicken with the hot sauce poured over them.

TURKEY IN A SALT CRUST   *Serves 10-12*

5-8 lb (2.2-3.6 kg) turkey
4 oz (100 g) butter or margarine
1 tbsp grated lemon rind
1 shallot
4 whole cloves
1 tsp thyme
1 tsp marjoram
3 lb (1.5 kg) coarse salt

Wash the turkey inside and out. Dry it with paper towels, and put 2 tablespoons butter, the lemon peel, shallot, cloves and half the thyme and marjoram inside the turkey. Close the opening with skewers. Brush the turkey all over with the rest of the butter. Sprinkle it with the rest of the thyme and marjoram. Put 1 lb (450 g) salt in the bottom of a large oval casserole. Sprinkle this with $\frac{1}{2}$ pt (300 ml) water. Arrange the turkey on the salt. Cover it completely with the rest of the salt and sprinkle it with 1 pt (600 ml) water. Mould the wet salt to cover the turkey so that no skin shows. Bake uncovered at 450°F/230°C/gas mark 8 for 20 minutes per 1 lb (450 g) plus 20 minutes. The salt will form a hard crust. At serving time, take the casserole to the table. With a sharp knife cut around the edge of the casserole. Lift off the crust. Lift the turkey onto a dish. If necessary, wipe off any salt with a damp paper towel. Carve the bird into serving slices.

PHEASANT IN CIDER   *Serves 4*

1 old pheasant
1 lb (450 g) cooking apples
8 oz (225 g) onions
2 oz (50 g) butter
$\frac{1}{2}$ pt (300 ml) cider
A bunch of mixed herbs
1 clove garlic
Salt and pepper

Wipe the pheasant thoroughly inside and out. Cut the apples into quarters after peeling and put into a casserole. Slice the onions and cook in butter until soft and transparent. Put the pheasant on top of the apples and cover with onions. Pour in the cider, and put in herbs, crushed garlic and seasoning. Cover tightly and cook at 325°F/160°C/gas mark 3 for $2\frac{1}{2}$ hours. Serve immediately, or sieve the onions and apples in the sauce, reheat and pour over the bird.

PARTRIDGE CASSEROLE   *Serves 4*

2 old partridges
Butter
2 onions
2 carrots
1 savoy cabbage
4 oz (100 g) streaky bacon
Salt and pepper
$\frac{1}{2}$ pt (300 ml) stock
Thyme and parsley
8 oz (225 g) chipolata sausages

Cut the onions and carrots into neat pieces and brown them in a little butter, together with the partridges. Cut the cabbage into quarters and cook in boiling water for 5 minutes with the bacon. Drain well. Cut bacon and cabbage into small pieces. Put half the cabbage into a casserole, season with salt and pepper and put on the partridges. Cover with bacon and vegetables, chopped herbs and the rest of the cabbage. Pour in the stock, cover with a lid and cook at 300°F/150°C/gas mark 2 for 3 hours. Grill the sausages lightly and add 30 minutes before serving time.

The addition of a glass of dry cider and a little less stock makes a good variation to the dish.

PIGEONS WITH CABBAGE   *Serves 4*

1 large firm cabbage
8 rashers fat bacon
Salt and pepper
Parsley, thyme and bay leaf
Butter
2 pigeons
$\frac{1}{2}$ pt (300 ml) beef stock

Blanch a large, firm cabbage in boiling water for 10 minutes, drain very well and chop finely. Mix with 4 rashers of chopped bacon and put into a greased fireproof dish. Season with salt and pepper and put in a sprig each of parsley and thyme, and a bay leaf. Brown pigeons in a little butter and put them into the dish, covering with the remaining rashers of bacon. Add some stock just to cover, cover tightly and simmer for 2 hours. Split the birds in half and serve on a bed of cabbage.

HARE JUGGED IN BEER   *Serves 8-10*

1 hare (with blood)
Seasoned flour
Beef dripping
1 onion stuck with cloves
1 pt (600 ml) beer
1 good wineglass port or sherry

This is somewhat easier to tackle than the usual jugged hare. Flour portions of hare and brown in dripping. Put into a large casserole with the drippings from the pan and the blood. Add the onion and beer, cover and cook in a slow oven for 5 hours until the meat leaves the bones easily. Just before serving, take out the onion and pour in the sherry or port. Serve with red current jelly.

HUNTER'S RABBIT   *Serves 4*

1 rabbit
1 small hard cabbage
1 lb (450 g) chipolata sausages
1 small onion
4 bacon rashers
Thyme, parsley and bay leaf
Salt and pepper
$\frac{1}{4}$ pt (150 ml) stock (can be made with a beef cube)
$\frac{1}{2}$ pt (300 ml) dry cider
Cut rabbit in pieces and soak, then dry thoroughly.

Cut cabbage lengthways into 6 or 8 pieces, and boil in very little water for 5 minutes, draining well. Fry sausages and sliced onion. Put cabbage in a casserole then put in rabbit pieces, followed by sausages and onion and the chopped, uncooked bacon. Add herbs and seasoning, pour in stock and cider and cover tightly. Cook at 325°F/160°C/gas mark 3 for $2\frac{1}{2}$ hours.

Fish

A wide range of fish and shellfish is available fresh and frozen, but fish often suffers from poor cooking, and particularly from over-cooking. The following methods are all suitable for successful fish cooking. A *court bouillon* is often recommended for boiling or poaching fish and gives a much finer flavour than plain water. This is a kind of aromatic stock which may be prepared in advance and it is well worth taking a little trouble to prepare.

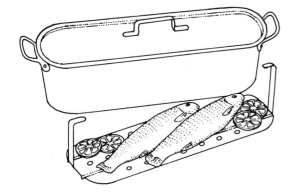

COURT BOUILLON

2 pt (1.2 litre) water
3 oz (75 g) onion
1 garlic clove
1 medium carrot
1 celery stick
$\frac{1}{2}$ bay leaf
1 sprig parsley
1 clove
2 tsp salt
4 peppercorns

For an even finer flavour, use half water and half white wine mixed. Add all the remaining ingredients and place in a saucepan. Cover and simmer for 30 minutes. Strain and keep in a covered bowl in the refrigerator until used. Do not keep longer than 3 days.

Boiling is only suitable for large pieces of fish or whole fish. A fish-kettle may be necessary so that the fish may be lifted out without breaking; if not, the fish must be tied in a piece of muslin and placed on a plate at the bottom of a large saucepan. Before cooking rub over the fish with lemon juice to keep it white and firm. Put into enough salted water or *court bouillon* to cover. Bring to the boil and then simmer very slowly with a lid on, until the fish is cooked, i.e. when the flesh comes away easily from the bone. About 10 minutes to the 1 lb (450 g) plus 10 minutes will be enough, timing from the minute when the liquid boils. Drain very well before serving.

Poaching is the method for whole small fish and pieces of fish. If using thin fillets, fold them or roll up. Heat sufficient milk and water, or *court bouillon* in a pan to half-cover the fish. When the liquid is simmering, add the fish, cover and simmer very gently, allowing 10 minutes per 1 lb (450 g). Lift out carefully and drain well.

Steaming is best for thin fish or fillets. Rub over with lemon juice and place large cuts or whole fish in a steamer. Small fillets or thin cutlets may be placed on a greased, deep plate with a tablespoon of milk and seasoning, and put over a saucepan of boiling water, then covered with a lid or plate. Allow 15 minutes per 1 lb (450 g) and 15 minutes over for large fish, but a total of 20 minutes for fillets.

Shallow frying may be used for whole, flat fish, such as sole, or for thick slices such as cod steaks. Put just enough fat or oil into a frying pan to prevent the fish sticking. When the fat is just smoking add the fish and cook quickly until golden brown on one side. Reduce the heat, turn over the fish and continue cooking gently for about 6 minutes until the flesh is loose on the bone. Fish may be prepared with a light coating just before frying. The simplest method is to coat the fish with flour seasoned with salt and pepper. A slightly thicker coating is obtained by dipping in flour, then milk, and then in flour again. A crisper coating is achieved by dipping the fish in flour, then beaten egg and finally fine breadcrumbs.

Deep frying is suitable for fish coated in batter or in egg and breadcrumbs. The principles of deep-frying are explained on page 69. Prepare fish or shellfish in batter only for deep-frying just before cooking. Dip fish in lemon juice and season with salt and pepper, and dust with flour before dipping into batter. Drain surplus batter before frying the fish. Fish which is to be coated with egg and breadcrumbs may be prepared beforehand as the coating will dry and the fish will fry more crisply.

Grilling is good for thick fish fillets and cutlets and for whole flat fish such as plaice and sole or oily fish such as mackerel and herring. Season and sprinkle with lemon juice and brush liberally with melted butter. Whole fish should be washed and scaled first, then scored with a sharp knife in 3 or 4 places on each side. Grill fish slowly and turn once or twice during cooking. Time will vary from 3-10 minutes on each side, depending on thickness; the fish is done when a knife inserted next to the bone comes out cleanly and the flesh comes away easily.

Baking is for whole fish such as cod or haddock and cutlets or fillets. To cook the fish, placed in a greased dish, season well and sprinkle with lemon juice. Pour a little milk or water around and cover with greased paper. Bake in a moderate oven at 325°F/160°C/gas mark 3 until flesh is white and firm and comes away easily from the bone. A whole fish may be stuffed before baking, using a breadcrumb stuffing well flavoured with herbs. Fish may also be baked without liquid, after brushing with melted fat and sprinkling with breadcrumbs. Fillets and cutlets are sometimes baked in a sauce. Small salmon and sea trout are particularly good if baked in foil. Keep the fish whole and insert a complementary herb, such as fennel, in the cavity, with a seasoning of salt and pepper and a small piece of butter and a squeeze of lemon juice. Wrap the fish in a loose parcel of foil which has been generously buttered inside, and with more herb sprigs, seasoning and lemon juice. As the foil protects the fish from excess heat, use a higher oven temperature of 350°F/180°C/gas mark 4. Allow 20 minutes per 1 lb (450 g) and 20 minutes over.

BAKED MUSTARD HERRINGS   *Serves 4*

4 herrings
3 oz (75 g) butter
1 tsp mustard powder
Salt and pepper

Split the herrings down one side and remove the backbone. Open them out flat, skin side down. Cream the butter, mustard, salt and pepper and spread on the fish. Fold the fish in half and wrap each one in kitchen foil. Put on a baking sheet and bake at 375°F/190°C/gas mark 5 for 25 minutes. Serve with boiled potatoes, or with brown bread and butter. Tomatoes may be baked in the oven with the fish if liked to serve as an accompaniment.

MACKEREL WITH GOOSEBERRIES   *Serves 4*

4 mackerel
4 oz (100 g) butter
2 oz (50 g) fresh breadcrumbs
1 small bunch watercress
Salt and pepper
1 lb (450 g) gooseberries, fresh or canned
2 oz (50 g) sugar

If fresh gooseberries are not available, canned ones may be used. Split the mackerel down one side and remove the backbone. Cream 3 oz (75 g) butter and work in the breadcrumbs. Reserve a few watercress sprigs for garnish, and chop the remaining leaves. Add the chopped leaves to the butter mixture and season well. Spread on the mackerel and fold them in half. Put into a greased ovenware dish and bake at 375°F/190°C/gas mark 5 for 30 minutes. While the fish is cooking, prepare the sauce. If using fresh gooseberries, simmer them in just enough water to cover until tender. Sieve and stir in the sugar and remaining butter. If using canned gooseberries, heat the fruit in syrup, sieve and add the butter, but you will not need all the sugar. Pour over the mackerel just before serving and garnish with reserved watercress. Serve with boiled or creamed potatoes. For a more simple dish, just grill the split mackerel which has been well-seasoned with salt and pepper, and serve with the gooseberry sauce.

LEMON BUTTERED PLAICE   *Serves 4*

8 plaice fillets
1 egg
5 oz (125 g) fresh breadcrumbs
1 tsp finely grated lemon rind
Salt and pepper
3 oz (75 g) butter
Parsley for garnish

Dip the fillets in beaten egg. Mix the crumbs, lemon rind and seasoning and coat the fish in the breadcrumbs, pressing the crumbs in well. Melt the butter and fry the fish gently for a few minutes on each side until golden. Drain well and garnish with parsley. Serve with boiled or fried potatoes and peas. Tartare or melted butter sauce may be served (see page 132).

COD IN CIDER   *Serves 4*

$1\frac{1}{2}$ lb (675 g) cod fillets
4 oz (100 g) back bacon
4 oz (100 g) button mushrooms
$\frac{1}{2}$ pt (300 ml) dry cider
2 oz (50 g) butter
Salt and pepper

Cut the fish into $1\frac{1}{2}$ in (3.75 cm) cubes. Dice the bacon and quarter the mushrooms. Put into a casserole and add the cider and butter cut into flakes, with the seasoning. Cover and bake at 375°F/190°C/gas mark 5 for 45 minutes. Serve with boiled potatoes and peas or carrots.

SMOKED HADDOCK WITH POACHED EGGS
Serves 4

$1\frac{1}{2}$ lb (675 g) smoked haddock
$\frac{1}{2}$ pt (300 ml) milk
$\frac{1}{2}$ pt (300 ml) water
1 oz (25 g) butter
1 oz (25 g) plain flour
2 oz (50 g) grated Cheddar cheese
Salt and pepper
4 eggs

Cut the haddock into 4 pieces and put into a large frying pan. Cover with milk and water, bring to the boil and then simmer for 10 minutes. Strain off the liquid and keep the fish on a warm serving dish. Melt the butter and add the flour. Take off the heat and add the cooking liquid. Return to the heat and stir well until the sauce is smooth and creamy. Take off the heat and stir in the cheese and seasoning. While the sauce is cooking, poach the eggs.

Pour the sauce over the fish and put a poached egg on each one. For a simple breakfast or supper dish, the fish may be cooked and topped with the eggs, and the sauce may be omitted.

BAKED CRAB WITH CHEESE

Serves 4 as a main course (or 6-8 as a first course)

1 lb (450 g) crabmeat
$1\frac{1}{2}$ oz (40 g) butter
$1\frac{1}{2}$ oz (40 g) plain flour
$\frac{3}{4}$ pt (450 ml) milk
4 oz (100 g) grated Cheddar cheese
Salt and pepper

The crabmeat may be fresh or frozen. Put into a bowl and mix the brown and white flesh together lightly with a fork. Melt the butter over low heat and work in the flour. Take off the heat and gradually add the milk, beating well. Cook for 2-3 minutes, stirring well until the sauce is creamy and smooth. Take off the heat and stir in the crabmeat and 3 oz (75 g) cheese. Season well. Put into 4 individual ovenware dishes and sprinkle with remaining cheese. Put under a hot grill until the cheese is golden and bubbling and serve at once with brown bread and butter or toast fingers, and a salad.

Pasta

Pasta is made from durum or hard wheat, milled to a fine semolina and then mixed with water to give a firm, smooth dough. The kneaded dough is rolled out or extruded through shaped moulds then dried. This dried pasta keeps well in a sealed packet, tin or jar and provides the basis of inexpensive but tasty and nourishing dishes. Dry pasta falls into four categories: (1) long pasta such as spaghetti and long macaroni; (2) short pasta such as cut (or elbow) macaroni, wheels and other shapes; (3) folded pasta such as vermicelli and noodles; (4) sheet pasta or lasagne. The pasta may be of the traditional white variety, or made from wholewheat which makes it coffee-brown in colour. One or two shapes such as lasagne and tagliatelle are also obtainable coloured green with vegetable juice.

To cook pasta allow at least 6 pt (3.5 litre) water to each 1 lb (450 g) pasta. Bring the water to the boil in a large saucepan and add 1 tablespoon salt. Also add 1 tablespoon oil to prevent the water from boiling over. For long pasta (e.g. spaghetti), coil the pasta into the pan, keeping the water on the boil. For short and folded pasta, feed it gently into the boiling water. Stir gently occasionally with a

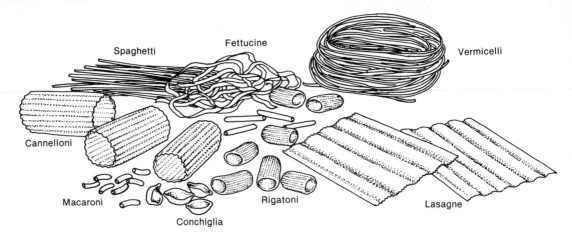

Spaghetti   Fettucine   Vermicelli

Cannelloni

Macaroni   Conchiglia   Rigatoni   Lasagne

wooden spoon or fork. Cook for the given length of time, always keeping the water at a good boil. Long pasta takes 8-15 minutes, depending on the thickness and shape. Short-cut shapes take 6-12 minutes; lasagne 15 minutes; vermicelli and noodles 2-6 minutes. To test if the pasta is cooked, take a little from the pan and bite it — the pasta should be just firm or *al dente* which is neither too hard nor too soft. Drain in a sieve or colander. Toss again in the saucepan in a little melted butter or oil and season with pepper. Serve hot with butter and grated cheese, or cold in salad.

For salads, pasta shapes (wheels, shells, etc.) or short-cut macaroni should be cooked until firm but not too soft, then refreshed by running under cold water in a colander. After cooling, the pasta may be dressed with oil and vinegar dressing, soured cream, curry sauce, mayonnaise or seafood sauce. The pasta may be mixed with chopped raw or cooked vegetables, dried, canned or fresh fruit, chopped chicken, ham or other cooked meat, fish or seafood.

SPAGHETTI CARBONARA   *Serves 6*

1 lb (450 g) spaghetti
3 tbsp oil
6 oz (150 g) bacon
4 tbsp dry white wine or stock
4 eggs
3 oz (75 g) grated Parmesan cheese
3 oz (75 g) grated strong Cheddar cheese
Salt and pepper
6 tbsp double cream

Cook the spaghetti in a large pan of boiling water and 1 tablespoon oil until just tender, about 10 minutes. Meanwhile, fry the chopped bacon in the remaining oil until crisp. Add the white wine and

cook briskly until the liquid has evaporated. Beat the eggs with the cheeses and seasoning. Drain the cooked spaghetti and return it to the pan with the bacon. Add the egg and cheese mixture and stir quickly. There should be sufficient heat in the spaghetti to cook the eggs. Add the cream and stir for 30 seconds over a gentle heat. Serve immediately, sprinkled with a little chopped parsley if liked.

SPAGHETTI BOLOGNESE   *Serves 4*

8 oz (225 g) spaghetti
1 oz (25 g) butter
2 oz (50 g) Parmesan cheese

Sauce
2 tbsp oil
1 medium onion
1 garlic clove
1 lb (450 g) minced raw beef
15 oz (425 g) can peeled tomatoes
$2\frac{1}{2}$ tbsp tomato purée
A pinch of mixed herbs
Salt and pepper
$\frac{1}{4}$ pt (150 ml) beef stock
$\frac{1}{4}$ pt (150 ml) red wine

Heat the oil in a pan and sauté the chopped onion and garlic until lightly browned. Add the minced beef and cook until browned on all sides. Stir in the tomatoes, tomato purée, mixed herbs and seasoning. Add the stock and wine and slowly bring to the boil. Simmer on a low heat for 45 minutes, stirring occasionally. Meanwhile, cook the spaghetti in boiling, salted water. Drain and add the butter. Arrange around the outside of a heated serving dish. Fill the centre with the Bolognese sauce and sprinkle with Parmesan cheese.

LASAGNE   *Serves 4-6*

6 oz (150 g) lasagne
Bolognese sauce (see Spaghetti Bolognese)

Cheese sauce
$1\frac{1}{2}$ oz (40 g) butter
$1\frac{1}{2}$ oz (40 g) plain flour
1 pt (600 ml) milk
3 oz (75 g) grated Cheddar cheese
2 tsp French mustard
Salt and pepper

Cook the lasagne in boiling salted water for 10 minutes, and drain well. Rinse in cold water and drain on kitchen paper. Grease an ovenware dish. Preheat the oven at 350°F/180°C/gas mark 4. Make the cheese sauce by melting the butter and stirring in the flour. Cook for 1 minute, then take off the heat and gradually work in the milk. Cook over low heat, stirring well until thick and creamy. Add half the cheese and the mustard, and season with salt and pepper. Line the dish with one-third lasagne and top with half the meat sauce. Spread on one-third cheese sauce. Cover with half of the remaining lasagne, the remaining meat sauce and one half of the remaining cheese sauce. Finish with the remaining lasagne and cheese sauce. Sprinkle with the remaining cheese. Bake for 45 minutes and serve at once.

MACARONI CHEESE   *Serves 4*

4 oz (100 g) short-cut macaroni
2 oz (50 g) streaky bacon
1 small onion
$1\frac{1}{2}$ oz (40 g) butter
$1\frac{1}{2}$ oz (40 g) plain flour
1 pt (600 ml) milk
A pinch of mustard powder
A pinch of cayenne pepper
4 oz (100 g) grated Cheddar cheese
1 oz (25 g) grated Parmesan cheese

Cook the macaroni in boiling salted water for about 10 minutes until tender and drain well. Chop the bacon and onion finely and soften in the butter for 5 minutes until golden. Sprinkle in the flour and stir well, cooking for 1 minute. Remove from the heat and work in the milk and then bring to the boil, stirring well, until smooth and creamy. Season with mustard and cayenne pepper. Remove from the heat and stir the macaroni into the sauce. Mix the cheeses together and stir three-quarters into the sauce. Put into a greased ovenware dish and sprinkle with remaining cheese. Put under a hot grill until the cheese has melted and the top is golden and crisp. If liked, the bacon and onions may be omitted.

Vegetables

A selection of vegetables, either raw or cooked, is essential in the daily diet. While they are often considered to be mere accompaniments to protein, vegetables have their own dietary value as roughage, as well as contributing a variety of colour and texture to meals. Many of the following dishes are also suitable for eating as a first or main course without further additions.

Artichoke, Globe

Artichokes are usually served on their own as a first course or as a light main dish when stuffed. They go stale very quickly and should be used immediately after cutting. Take off the outer leaves and trim the stalks and leave the artichokes to soak, tips downwards, in plenty of cold water, for an hour before cooking. Dig carefully into the artichokes and remove the hairy 'chokes' and trim the points from the leaves with sharp scissors. Put the artichokes into a large pan of lightly salted boiling water and boil gently for 40 minutes until a leaf pulls out easily. Drain very well and eat hot with melted butter or hollandaise sauce, or cold with French dressing or mayonnaise. If you have a large number of artichokes, take off all the leaves, rub the hearts with lemon juice and cook for 15 minutes and serve in a salad mixed with mushrooms or seafood or hot in a cheese sauce.

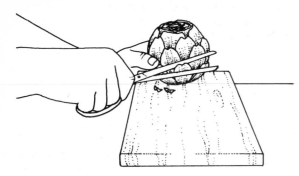

STUFFED ARTICHOKES   *Serves 4*

4 globe artichokes
4 oz (100 g) cooked ham
2 oz (50 g) mushrooms
1 small onion
1 garlic clove
$\frac{1}{2}$ pt (300 ml) stock or white wine
2 oz (50 g) butter
Salt and pepper

Prepare and cook the artichokes until just tender.
Mince the ham and mix with finely chopped mushrooms and onion and crushed garlic. Fill the
artichokes and put them in an ovenware dish with
the stock or wine. Cover and bake at 350°F/180°C/
gas mark 4 for 25 minutes. Put artichokes on
serving plates. Melt the butter in the cooking
liquid, season well and serve as a sauce.

Artichoke, Jerusalem

For those who love the flavour of artichokes in
cooking, the Jerusalem artichoke is invaluable, as
the life of the summer globe artichoke is so limited.
They may be peeled or boiled first and skinned
when hot, and used for recipes in which artichoke
hearts are specified, or for potato recipes,
Jerusalem artichokes are delicious baked around a
joint of beef, or served as a creamy purée. A very
good artichoke soup can be made be cooking the
tubers in chicken stock, sieving and thinning the
purée with milk.

ARTICHOKES WITH CHEESE   *Serves 4*

$1\frac{1}{2}$ lb (675 g) Jerusalem artichokes
$\frac{1}{2}$ pt (300 ml) white sauce
Salt and pepper
A pinch of nutmeg
3 oz (75 g) grated cheese

Peel the artichokes thinly and boil them in just
enough water to cover for about 20 minutes until

tender. Drain but keep $\frac{1}{4}$ pt (150 ml) cooking liquid.
Cut the artichokes in slices and arrange in a
shallow ovenware dish. Mix the sauce with the
cooking liquid and season well with salt, pepper
and nutmeg and pour over the vegetable. Sprinkle
on the cheese and grill until golden-brown. Serve
with roast meat, or with chicken.

Asparagus

Use asparagus immediately after picking as it goes
stale quickly, and grade it for size before cooking.
Trim off woody portions and tie into small bundles
of even-size spears. Cook in boiling water until just
tender, keeping the tips at the top of the pan so that
they only steam while the stems are cooking more
thoroughly. If you have different sized spears, start
cooking the thicker ones first and add the bundles
of thinner ones at intervals. Mix the sizes together
before serving with melted butter, French dressing
or hollandaise sauce. If you have a lot of
trimmings, or any leftover cooked asparagus,
make a purée to use as asparagus soup with
chicken stock. A pinch of nutmeg helps to bring out
the flavour. Cold asparagus can be served with
French dressing and a sprinkling of sieved hard-
boiled egg, or the tips may be dressed with mayonnaise or hollandaise sauce. A few asparagus tips
make a colourful and tasty garnish for chicken or
fish, or they can be added to mixed salads. Thick
tender asparagus is delicious served on buttered
toast, or as an omelette filling.

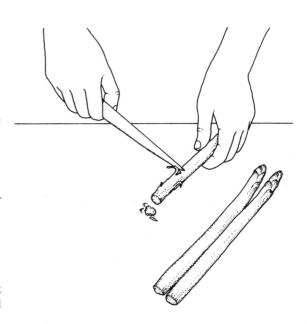

ASPARAGUS FLAN   *Serves 4*

8 oz (225 g) shortcrust pastry
1 lb (450 g) asparagus
$\frac{1}{2}$ pt (300 ml) milk
3 eggs
Salt and pepper
3 oz (75 g) grated cheese

Line a tin with pastry, prick well, line with foil and baking beans and bake at 400°F/200°C/gas mark 6 for 10 minutes. Cook and drain the asparagus and cut in 2 in (5 cm) lengths. Mix milk, eggs, salt and pepper and cheese. Put the asparagus into the pastry case, pour on milk mixture and bake at 350°F/180°C/gas mark 4 for 30 minutes.

Aubergines

Aubergines are most useful for adding a touch of glamour to all sorts of dishes. They go particularly well with lamb, and partner onions, peppers and tomatoes in a variety of recipes. Before cooking aubergines do not peel them, but split them lengthwise or cut across in slices. Sprinkle well with salt and leave to stand for an hour. Drain well before using. Aubergines are very good stuffed with meat, vegetables and rice, and a tomato sauce is delicious with them. Plain slices may be fried in oil, or buttered and fried to serve as a vegetable, or they can be strung on skewers with onions, mushrooms and lamb to make kebabs. If you have a surplus of aubergines, cook them with onions, peppers and tomatoes in olive oil very gently to make Ratatouille which can be eaten hot or cold.

AUBERGINE SAVOURY   *Serves 4*

1 large aubergine
2 rashers bacon
1 medium onion
2 sticks celery
4 oz (100 g) tomatoes
1 egg
Salt and pepper
4 oz (100 g) fresh breadcrumbs
2 oz (50 g) grated cheese

Peel the aubergine and cut the flesh into cubes. Steam over boiling water for 5 minutes and put into a bowl. Cut the bacon in small pieces and fry without additional fat until crisp. Add the bacon and the fat that runs out to the aubergines. Add the chopped onion and cook for 5 minutes until soft. Add the finely chopped celery. Skin the tomatoes, remove the pips and cut the flesh in pieces. Add to the aubergine together with the beaten egg. Put

into a greased ovenware dish and sprinkle with mixed breadcrumbs and cheese. Bake at 325°F/ 160°C/gas mark 3 for 30 minutes.

Broad Beans

Broad beans are at their best served small and young, when their skins can be slipped off after cooking, before serving hot or cold. They are very good tossed in butter with a little crisply cooked crumbled bacon or dressed with parsley sauce. Beans are particularly good served with boiled bacon which is also traditionally served with parsley sauce. Cooked broad beans make an unusual salad if covered with French dressing with plenty of pepper and finely chopped parsley, chives or winter savory.

BROAD BEAN SOUP   *Serves 4*

$1\frac{1}{2}$ lb (675 g) shelled broad beans
3 pt (1.75 litre) water
2 rashers bacon
1 small onion
1 oz (25 g) butter
1 oz (25 g) plain flour
Salt and pepper
1 tsp chopped parsley

Cook the beans in the water for 10 minutes and then drain, reserving the liquid. Remove the skins from the beans. Chop the bacon and the onion and cook in the butter until golden. Work in the flour and add the cooking liquid. Stir over gentle heat until smooth and then add the beans. Simmer for 10 minutes and then put the mixture through a sieve, or into an electric blender. Season with salt and pepper, reheat and serve sprinkled with parsley. If liked, the soup can be garnished with a little extra bacon, cooked until crisp and then crumbled. An alternative garnish can be small cubes of fried or toasted bread.

Beans, Dried

Dried beans can be used as individual types or as mixtures in soups and stews. Traditionally, they were soaked overnight before using, but in fact three hours soaking is enough. If you are really in a hurry to start cooking the beans, don't soak them, but bring them to the boil, remove from heat, leave for 40 minutes then drain and use in a recipe. They can be cooked in the water in which they have been soaked, or in stock (bacon stock is particularly good). It is important not to salt bean dishes until the end of cooking or the beans will harden. Cooked beans are useful when cold as they mix well in French dressing with plenty of seasoning to make an unusual salad. Dried beans go particularly well in lamb and pork dishes.

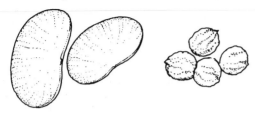

PORK AND BEAN CASSEROLE *Serves 4*

12 oz (350 g) dried beans
2 large onions
2 carrots
2 cloves
Salt and pepper
1 tbsp oil
8 oz (225 g) lean pork
1 oz (25 g) black treacle
6 rashers bacon
6 pork sausages
8 oz (225 g) garlic sausage
$\frac{1}{4}$ pt (150 ml) red wine

Soak the beans for 3 hours in enough water to cover. Do not drain but put into a large pan with the diced onions and carrots, cloves, salt and pepper and $1\frac{1}{4}$ pt (750 ml) water. Cover and simmer for $1\frac{1}{2}$ hours. Meanwhile, cut the pork in pieces and brown on all sides in the oil. Put the oil into the bottom of a large casserole and put on half the beans then the pork and the remaining beans. Add the black treacle and top with bacon. Cover and bake at 300°F/150°C/gas mark 2 for 4 hours. Grill the sausages, cut into pieces and stir in the beans, with the garlic sausage cut in chunks and the wine. Cover and continue cooking for 30 minutes.

Beans, Dwarf

Try to use dwarf beans while they are young and still pencil-thin so that they can be cooked whole. Otherwise they must be cooked in chunks, but they should never be shredded. Dwarf beans may be dressed with butter and seasoning, or a little grated onion or crushed garlic can be added. This vegetable mixes well with others and looks attractive served with a garnish of thinly sliced mushrooms cooked in butter. Cold beans make a good salad mixed with sliced tomatoes in a French dressing.

CREAMED BEANS *Serves 4*

1 lb (450 g) dwarf beans
1 small onion
1 small green pepper
2 rashers bacon
Salt and pepper
3 tbsp single cream

Cut the beans in chunks and cook until tender. Meanwhile, chop the onion, green pepper and bacon finely. Put the bacon into a pan and heat until the fat begins to run. Add the onion and pepper and cook gently for 5 minutes. Add the beans with $\frac{1}{4}$ pt (150 ml) cooking water and cover tightly. Simmer for 15 minutes, watching carefully so that the beans do not burn. Season well with salt and pepper. Remove from the heat and stir in the cream. These beans are good with poultry or with ham.

BEAN SALAD *Serves 4*

1 lb (450 g) dwarf beans
French dressing
3 oz (75 g) can anchovies
2 hard-boiled eggs

Cut the beans into chunks and cook until tender. Cool slightly, then toss in French dressing. Arrange in a serving dish and garnish with drained anchovies and finely chopped eggs.

Beans, Runner

Traditionally, these beans are finely shredded before cooking, but this often means a mushy result and loss of flavour. It is better to cook young runner beans whole or to slit them in half lengthwise or to cut them coarsely. Season runner beans well when cooked and dress with butter. They go particularly well with chicken and with roast or grilled meats, but runner beans are not so versatile as the dwarf and broad varieties and do not make such good dishes on their own.

BEANS WITH MUSHROOMS *Serves 4*

1 lb (450 g) runner beans
1 small onion
1 small green pepper
2 rashers bacon
9 oz (250 g) mushrooms
3 oz (75 g) butter
A pinch of nutmeg
2 fl oz (50 ml) single cream

Remove the tips from the beans and cut them in half if they are large. Chop the onion, pepper and bacon in small pieces. Put the bacon in a thick pan and heat gently until the fat runs. Add the onion and pepper and cook until soft and golden. Add the beans and $\frac{1}{4}$ pt (150 ml) water, cover tightly and cook gently for 15 minutes until the beans are tender. Meanwhile, wipe the mushrooms and cook them in the butter for 5 minutes. Drain off liquid from the beans and mix them with the mushrooms. Season with nutmeg and stir in the cream. This is particularly good served with boiled bacon or roast chicken. If liked, some grated cheese may be sprinkled over the beans and mushrooms, and the dish cooked under the grill or in the oven until the top is golden brown and bubbling.

Beetroot

Beetroot is usually served as a salad, cold and sliced into vinegar, but it also makes an excellent hot vegetable. Traditionally, beetroot is boiled until tender, and it is important not to break the skin or cut off the stems too close or the vegetable will 'bleed' into the water. Beetroot cooked in this way can be served hot in a white sauce, or the beetroot may be cooled and sliced into vinegar. It is very good mixed with celery, which provides a textual contrast. If beetroot is mixed with other vegetables in a salad, it tends to stain everything pink, so it is better served in a separate bowl. Cold boiled beetroot may be frozen or can be bottled in vinegar for winter use. If you really enjoy beetroot try baking instead of boiling to save all the flavour. Choose small beetroot of even size, wash them well, and leave about 1 in (2.5 cm) stems. Put into an ovenware dish without liquid and bake at 350°F/ 180°C/gas mark 4 for 30 minutes then at 325°F/ 160°C/gas mark 3 for 1 hour. When they are tender, peel the beetroot and serve with melted butter, salt and pepper.

BEETROOT SOUP   *Serves 4*

8 medium beetroot
1 small onion
$\frac{3}{4}$ pt (450 ml) chicken stock
Salt and pepper
Juice of 1 lemon
1 tbsp honey
A pinch of ground cloves

Wash the beetroot well and simmer until tender. Peel and sieve them with $\frac{1}{2}$ pt (300 ml) cooking water (use an electric blender if you like). Mix with the remaining ingredients and simmer for 5 minutes. Serve plain, or with a little sour cream and chopped chives.

Broccoli and Calabrese

All types of broccoli are delicious cooked until just tender and served with plenty of butter. Slightly warm broccoli and calabrese make a good salad well seasoned with salt and pepper and French dressing accompanied by a bowl of sliced tomatoes. Broccoli may also be served with hollandaise sauce.

CREAMED BROCCOLI   *Serves 4*

1 lb (450 g) broccoli
8 fl oz (200 ml) soured cream
$\frac{1}{2}$ oz (15 g) plain flour
$\frac{1}{2}$ oz (15 g) grated horse-radish
1 tsp wine vinegar
Salt and pepper

Clean and wash the broccoli and cook in boiling water for 15 minutes. Drain well. See that the soured cream is at room temperature or it may curdle when heated. Mix the cream and flour together and put into a bowl over boiling water or the top of a double saucepan. Cook until warm and smooth, stirring all the time. Add the remaining ingredients and pour over the hot broccoli. A few oven-browned almonds may be scattered on top of the sauce. Serve with ham, pork or veal.

ITALIAN BROCCOLI   *Serves 4*

1 lb (450 g) broccoli
2 garlic cloves
2 tbsp olive oil
2 oz (50 g) cooked ham
Salt and pepper
1 oz (25 g) Parmesan cheese

Clean and wash the broccoli and cook in boiling water for 15 minutes. Drain well. Crush the garlic cloves and warm in the olive oil. Stir in the finely chopped ham and season well. Pour over the broccoli and sprinkle on the grated cheese.

Brussels Sprouts

Sprouts are best eaten when small and firm and they should be cooked only until tender, but still crisp. Their flavour has an affinity with chestnuts, onions and celery and they are good dressed with cream and with cheese so that a good vegetable course can be prepared without meat. Sprouts quickly smell unpleasant if left in the refrigerator, but it is worth cooking some extra ones to be used later with potatoes in Bubble and Squeak to which they lend a special flavour.

SPROUT SOUP   *Serves 4*

2 lb (1 kg) Brussels sprouts
$2\frac{1}{2}$ pt (1.5 litre) chicken stock
1 oz (25 g) butter
1 oz (25 g) plain flour
1 tbsp lemon juice
A pinch of nutmeg
Salt and pepper
Grated cheese

Clean the sprouts and simmer them in stock for 10 minutes. Reserve 10 small sprouts and put the rest though a sieve with the cooking liquid. Melt the butter and work in the flour. Add the sieved sprouts gradually and heat gently, stirring well until the mixture is creamy and smooth. Add the lemon juice and seasonings and simmer for 5 minutes. Serve very hot with a garnish of whole sprouts and some grated cheese (Parmesan is best for this).

Cabbage

Cabbage is often despised, but with proper cooking it can be one of our most delicious vegetables. Cabbage should be cooked in boiling salted water or steamed only until tender, but still crisp. It must be drained thoroughly and served hot with plenty of butter and seasoning. Firm-hearted cabbage is very good shredded and served raw with a dressing, while cooked cabbage may be dressed with a white sauce. Whole cabbage heads or large leaves are good stuffed with a meat and rice filling, and they may be finished with a white or tomato sauce.

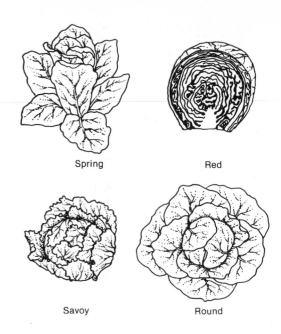

Spring   Red

Savoy   Round

STUFFED CABBAGE   *Serves 4*

1 firm cabbage
2 oz (50 g) long-grain rice
1 small onion
1 tbsp chopped parsley
1 lb (450 g) pork sausagemeat
Salt and pepper

Put the cabbage into a bowl and remove any discoloured or bruised leaves. Pour on boiling water and leave to stand for 15 minutes. Drain, cover with boiling water and leave again for 15 minutes. Drain thoroughly. Meanwhile, cook the rice in boiling water for 12 minutes and drain well. Mix the rice, chopped onion, parsley and sausagemeat together and season well. Cut the stalk out of the cabbage and put in some mixture. Fold over 2 or 3 leaves and cover with more mixture. Continue until each layer is stuffed. Tie in a cloth, put in a pan of beef or chicken stock and simmer for $1\frac{1}{2}$ hours. Put cabbage in a dish and serve with butter. If liked, the cabbage may be cooked in a casserole in a moderate oven (350°F/180°C/gas mark 4).

Carrot

Carrots are at their best when young and tender, and they should be cooked in the minimum of water until tender, before dressing with butter. They mix well with other vegetables such as peas, beans and sweet corn kernels, and are an important ingredient in stews. Raw carrots are delicious coarsely grated and dressed with lemon juice.

BRAISED LAMB AND CARROTS   *Serves 4*

$2\frac{1}{4}$ lb (1 kg) shoulder lamb
1 crushed garlic clove
1 large onion
1 green pepper
4 tbsp olive oil
$\frac{1}{4}$ pt (150 ml) tomato juice
$\frac{1}{2}$ pt (300 ml) stock
12 oz (350 g) young carrots
1 tsp marjoram
1 tbsp cornflour
6 tbsp white wine

Cut the lamb into cubes. Dice the onion and the green pepper. Heat the olive oil in a thick pan and put in the garlic, onion and green pepper. Stir and cook for 1 minute, then add the lamb and cook gently for 5 minutes stirring well. Season to taste with salt and pepper and add the tomato juice and stock. Cover and simmer for 30 minutes. Scrub the carrots and cut into short lengths. Cook them in a little water for 2 minutes, drain and add to the lamb with the marjoram. Cover again and simmer for 45 minutes. Add the wine and the cornflour mixed with a little water. Cover and simmer for 15 minutes. This is a good dish to start on the top of the stove and then to transfer to the oven set at 325°F/160°C/gas mark 3 for complete cooking. Garnish with a little chopped parsley or more marjoram.

Cauliflower

Small cauliflowers can be cooked whole, but it is better to break larger ones into sprigs. Cook sprigs for 10 minutes, but allow 15-20 minutes for whole heads in boiling water with a squeeze of lemon juice. Drain well and serve with butter or cheese or white sauce. If a sauce is not suitable with the rest of the course, dress the cauliflower with a sprinkling of browned breadcrumbs, crumbled crisp bacon and grated cheese. Cooked cauliflower is particularly good for salads and for second-day dishes such as soup and cauliflower cheese.

CAULIFLOWER CHEESE   *Serves 4*

1 medium cauliflower
$\frac{1}{2}$ pt (300 ml) white sauce (see page 129)
$\frac{1}{2}$ tsp salt
1 tsp made mustard
A pinch of nutmeg
4 oz (100 g) grated cheese
1 tbsp browned crumbs

Cook the cauliflower whole or in sprigs as preferred. Heat the white sauce, remove from the heat and stir in the seasonings and most of the cheese. Put the cauliflower in a dish, and cover with the sauce. Sprinkle on the remaining cheese and crumbs and brown under a hot grill. Serve very hot.

CAULIFLOWER SALAD   *Serves 4*

1 small cooked cauliflower
4 oz (100 g) cooked broad beans
4 oz (100 g) cooked peas
1 oz (25 g) capers
4 hard-boiled eggs
Mayonnaise

Mix together the cauliflower sprigs, beans, peas, capers and eggs cut into quarters. Dress with mayonnaise thinned with a little lemon juice if liked.

Celeriac

This vegetable has all the concentrated flavour of celery, and can be used to intensify flavour in celery soup and in casseroles. It is, however, delicious in its own right, both raw and cooked. Coarsely grated celeriac in French dressing or mayonnaise makes an excellent salad. It may also be cooked in boiling water or stock until tender and served dressed with butter or white sauce. Celeriac also makes a good purée with cream and seasonings added and it can also be mixed in equal quantities with potato purée.

CELERIAC CASSEROLE *Serves 4*

$1\frac{1}{2}$ lb (675 g) celeriac
8 oz (225 g) onions
8 oz (225 g) tomatoes
1 carrot
3 oz (75 g) butter
1 crushed garlic clove
Salt and pepper
2 slices bread

Peel the celeriac and cut it into slices. Simmer in stock or water for 10 minutes. Peel and slice the onions. Peel the tomatoes, take out the pips and cut the flesh into pieces. Peel and slice the carrot. Melt the butter and fry the onions, tomatoes and carrot lightly until the onion pieces are soft and golden. Add the drained celeriac pieces and the garlic. Season with salt and pepper, and add enough of the liquid used in cooking the celeriac to cover the vegetables. Cover and simmer until the vegetables are tender. Just before serving, cut the bread into triangles and fry in oil until golden. Use to garnish the casserole, which can be served on its own, or with meat or fish.

Celery

Celery is good raw and cooked, and its crispness provides a useful texture in many dishes. To prepare celery for eating raw with cheese, separate the stalks and wash them well, removing any blemishes. Leave a few of the young leaves on the stalks. Put the stalks into iced water containing a few ice cubes and leave in the refrigerator for 2 or 3 hours before serving. Drain well and serve very cold. Chopped raw celery is good in green salads, or mixed in seafood cocktails. Short lengths of celery can be stuffed with cream cheese and garnished with chopped chives as a cocktail snack. Short lengths of celery may be used in casseroles, while long stalks or whole hearts can be braised in butter and stock to serve as a vegetable. It is worth drying some celery leaves to use like herbs to give a hint of celery flavour to dishes, or to augment the vegetable's own flavour.

CELERY SOUP *Serves 4*

1 large head celery
1 large onion
2 oz (50 g) butter
1 carrot
1 large potato
1 tsp brown sugar
Salt and pepper
$\frac{1}{2}$ pt (300 ml) chicken stock
1 pt (600 ml) creamy milk

Clean the celery and cut into small pieces. Chop the onion. Melt the butter, add the celery and onion and stir over gentle heat for 4 minutes. Add diced carrot and diced potato and cook for 2 minutes. Add sugar, salt and pepper and $\frac{1}{2}$ pt (300 ml) water and simmer until vegetables are tender. Put through a sieve or liquidise. Add stock and milk and simmer for 10 minutes. Garnish with chopped herbs.

Chicory

Chicory is equally good raw or cooked, although some people dislike its slight bitterness. The heads should be used when the tips are pale yellow and white — when they begin to turn green the vegetable is getting old. Allow one head of chicory for each person in a salad, but two heads as a cooked accompaniment. To serve as a salad, remove outer leaves, or cut across into circular slices. Use immediately after cutting, as chicory discolours very quickly and never leave to soak in water which increases the bitterness. Serve chicory in a French dressing, or add to a mixed salad, or mix with orange slices and black olives (very good with duck). Chicory should never be boiled to serve as a vegetable, but is best braised with a little lemon juice, salt and pepper, a large knob of butter and a few spoonfuls of chicken or beef stock. It will take about 30 minutes in a tightly covered saucepan, or in a casserole in a moderate oven. White sauce and cheese sauce may be served with chicory.

CHICORY AND HAM ROLLS *Serves 4*

8 chicory heads
Lemon juice
8 thin slices cooked ham
1 pt (600 ml) white sauce (see page 129)
2 oz (50 g) grated cheese
Salt and pepper
1 oz (25 g) fresh breadcrumbs
1 oz (25 g) butter

Cook the chicory in water with a squeeze of lemon juice for 15 minutes and drain very thoroughly. Wrap each head in a slice of ham, and put in a buttered, shallow ovenware dish. Mix cheese with white sauce, season and pour over chicory. Sprinkle with breadcrumbs and dot with butter. Bake at 375°F/190°C/gas mark 5 for 30 minutes.

Cucumber

The cucumber is one of our most refreshing and attractive salad vegetables, but it may also be cooked and makes excellent pickles. Cucumbers should not be peeled before slicing as they are more digestible with the skin on and the skin contains the main food value. Thick chunks of cucumber can be hollowed out and filled with seafood or cream cheese as cocktail snacks or light first courses. Thinly sliced cucumber makes refreshing sandwiches, dressed with a little lemon juice between slices of white or brown bread. Cubed or sliced cucumber is an attractive addition to salads and to chilled summer soups, or may be dressed with sour cream to make a tempting salad. Small cucumbers may be cooked in the same way as courgettes, and are particularly good stuffed with a creamy ham and onion stuffing topped with cheese and baked until tender. Dill gives a special flavour to cucumber salad and can be added to white sauce to serve with lightly poached cucumber cubes as a cooked accompaniment. Outdoor cucumbers with rough skins are particularly useful for cooking as pickles.

CUCUMBER PICKLE   *Serves 4*

8 large cucumbers
2 oz (50 g) cooking salt
10 oz (250 g) soft brown sugar
1 tbsp mustard seed
5 cloves
2 cinnamon sticks
$1\frac{1}{2}$ pt (900 ml) white vinegar

Peel the cucumbers and cut in $\frac{1}{2}$ in (1.25 cm) slices. Remove the seeds, sprinkle with the salt and leave to stand for 24 hours. Drain in a sieve for 1 hour. Mix the remaining ingredients, and boil for 5 minutes. Add cucumber slices and simmer for 25 minutes. Put in hot preserving jars and seal.

Leeks

Leeks are very much appreciated for their light oniony flavour. They must always be very carefully cleaned as fine earth tends to get between the layers of skins. To prepare leeks, trim off most of the green tops, leaving about 1-2 in (2.5-5 cm) green and wash in cold running water, separating the edges of the skins so that loose earth is washed out. Thinly sliced leeks are good in a winter salad with chicory, celery and shredded cabbage with French dressing. Leeks may be braised in butter and beef or chicken stock to use as an accompaniment with a dressing or butter or white sauce. Leeks are also good cooked and served cold with hollandaise sauce or French dressing. As a garnish, thick circular slices of leeks can be fried in butter, and they are particularly good with grilled meat or fish. Leeks are very popular as a soup ingredient, and go particularly well with chicken stock and with potatoes — they are best cooked lightly in butter before adding to soups. Like many mild-flavoured vegetables they make a good dish on their own served as a savoury flan.

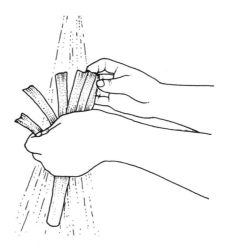

CREAMY LEEK PIE   *Serves 4*

6 large leeks
$\frac{1}{2}$ pt (300 ml) milk
Salt and pepper
3 fl oz (75 ml) single cream
8 oz (225 g) shortcrust pastry

Clean the leeks, remove green tops and cut white parts into 1 in (2.5 cm) pieces. Put into the milk with salt and pepper and simmer until the leeks are just tender. Put into a pie dish and stir in the cream. Cover with the pastry and bake at 400°F/200°C/gas mark 6 for 30 minutes. Serve on its own, or with meat.

Lettuce

To most people, lettuce means salad, and it is certainly the mainstay of the salad bowl, but also makes a number of good cooked dishes. This is very useful for those who suffer from a glut crop, as the lettuce cannot be frozen or otherwise preserved, but some soups freeze very well. In addition, lettuce may be braised to eat as a vegetable, or can be cooked with fresh green peas. Lettuce soups may be served either hot or cold, and are basically made by cooking shredded lettuce with a little bacon fat or butter, then simmering in chicken stock with a herb or spice seasoning and a little onion to flavour (spring onions are good cooked with lettuce). An addition of peas or almonds can be made to lettuce soup after the cooked vegetable and liquid have been sieved to a purée. Cream or milk may also be added, but if the soup is to be frozen, it is better to prepare it without these additions which can be made during the reheating stage.

Marrows and Courgettes

Large marrows and small courgettes are both popular in the kitchen, but they need careful cooking to retain their delicate flavour and texture. Marrows are delicious stuffed whole or in rings, but to serve them as a vegetable the flesh should be steamed (rather than boiled) before serving with white or cheese sauce. Courgettes should be eaten when young and small, with tender skins which are also eaten. They may be split lengthwise and baked with a stuffing of meat or cheese, served with cheese or tomato sauce. As a vegetable, they are best cut in 1 in (2.5 cm) slices with the skins on and lightly fried in oil until golden. Courgettes go well with onions and tomatoes and are very good simmered in oil with these two vegetables and green peppers. Aubergines may also be added to the mixture.

SAVOURY MARROW   *Serves 4*

---

1 large marrow
1 lb (450 g) cold meat
2 oz (50 g) bacon
1 oz (25 g) plain flour
Salt and pepper
2 oz (50 g) fresh breadcrumbs
1 tsp chopped parsley
2 tomatoes
1 oz (25 g) dripping

Peel and cut the marrow in half lengthwise. Scoop out seeds and pulp. Mince the meat and mix with the finely chopped bacon, flour, seasoning, breadcrumbs and parsley. Skin the tomatoes, take out the pips and chop the flesh. Mix with the meat and fill the marrow. Put in a baking dish and add the dripping. Bake at 350°F/180°C/gas mark 4 for 1 hour, basting with pan juices. Serve with gravy.

Mushrooms

Mushrooms should be used when very fresh, and they should never be washed or peeled, just gently wiped to get rid of surface dirt. Only trim the ends of the stalks because the stalk holds much of the mushroom's flavour — if a recipe says use only caps, save the stalks in the refrigerator to use for a sauce or soup. For a simple garnish, poach small button mushrooms with a squeeze of lemon juice and a cover on the pan so that they remain creamy white. When cooking in butter, add a little oil to prevent the butter browning, and a squeeze of lemon juice and cook just enough to make the mushrooms tender.

Mushrooms are delicious raw in a dressing of oil and lemon juice left for about 2 hours in the refrigerator to absorb the liquid. If you have a lot of mushrooms they can be made into a concentrated paste or duxelles which will keep for weeks in the refrigerator or may be frozen. This entails softening 2 shallots or a small mild onion in 2 oz (50 g) butter, then adding 1 lb (450 g) chopped mushrooms and another 3 oz (75 g) butter and simmering gently for an hour, stirring often until the mixture is thick, then seasoning lightly.

Mushrooms of course can be added to dozens of dishes, but they make a delicious meal on their own, served on toast, or with grilled bacon.

MUSHROOMS IN CREAM   *Serves 4*

1 lb (450 g) mushrooms
3 oz (75 g) butter
1 oz (25 g) plain flour
Thyme and parsley
Salt
8 fl oz (200 ml) single cream

Wipe mushrooms and toss in butter until just soft. Sprinkle with flour and add a pinch of thyme, salt and pepper. Add cream and cook gently for 5 minutes. Sprinkle with chopped parsley.

Onions

The onion is one of our most popular flavourings, essential to many savoury dishes. Use onions as a vegetable with grilled meat or sausages, cook them with cheese, or add them to brown or white sauces as the perfect accompaniment to beef and lamb. Herb and onion stuffings are the perfect accompaniments to rich fat meats like pork and duck. Mild onions are delicious sliced and served raw in salads, or with beetroot, tomatoes, or potatoes in salad dressings. Onions make good supper dishes, cooked in their jackets in the oven like potatoes, or braised with dripping and beef stock, or made into a clear soup served with toasted bread and cheese. They are also excellent combined with pastry in savoury flans.

HERB AND ONION FLAN   *Serves 4*

8 oz (225 g) shortcrust pastry
3 medium onions
1 oz (25 g) butter
$\frac{1}{4}$ pt (150 ml) creamy milk
1 egg
1 tbsp fresh sage
1 tsp fresh parsley
4 oz (100 g) bacon
Salt and pepper

Line a flan ring or sandwich tin with the pastry. Chop the onions finely. Melt the butter and cook the onions until soft and golden. Mix the onions with the milk, beaten egg, chopped sage and parsley, chopped bacon, salt and pepper. Pour into the pastry case and bake at 400°F/200°C/gas mark 6 for 35 minutes. Serve hot with vegetables, or with a green salad. Some grated cheese may be sprinkled on top before baking if liked. If using a flan ring, remove the ring 5 minutes before the end of cooking to brown the pastry.

Parsnips

This slightly sweet vegetable is not to everybody's taste, but the flavour is so good with meat and poultry and mixed with other vegetables that it can be an asset in the kitchen. Parsnips are particularly good part-boiled, then roasted or fried, and they can be cooked around a joint like potatoes. Parsnips are also excellent mashed, either on their own, or mixed with carrots or potatoes. Always use plenty of butter with them, or a sprinkling of grated cheese.

PARSNIP BALLS   *Serves 4*

1 lb (450 g) parsnips
4 oz (100 g) butter
1 tbsp milk
Salt and pepper
1 egg
4 oz (100 g) breadcrumbs

Cook the parsnips, mash them and mix with the butter, milk and seasoning. Heat and stir until the mixture is thick. Cool and beat in a little of the egg to give a smooth mixture. Shape into balls and roll in the remaining egg, then dip into breadcrumbs. Fry in hot fat until golden, and serve hot.

Peas

Eat peas while they are young, tender and sweet. Their flavour will be enhanced by a little mint and a pinch of sugar in the cooking water. Peas go very well with other vegetables and can be served in a mixture with young carrots, small pieces of dwarf beans and sweet corn kernels. They are also good served cold as part of a salad. Sugar peas with edible pods should be eaten when the pods are just beginning to swell. They should be cooked only until just tender, and served with plenty of melted butter as a first course, or as a separate vegetable.

FRENCH PEAS *Serves 4*

1 oz (25 g) butter
12 spring onions
1 small lettuce
1 lb (450 g) peas (shelled)
Salt and pepper
A pinch of nutmeg
1 tsp honey
Tarragon, thyme and chervil

Melt the butter in a thick saucepan. Chop the onions and lettuce finely and put into the pan, topped with the peas. Season well with salt and pepper, nutmeg and honey. Chop the herbs and add about 1 tablespoon of them. Add 3 tablespoons (45 ml) water, cover tightly and cook very gently for 12 minutes. Serve very hot.

Peppers

Peppers are rapidly gaining in popularity now that so many people find that they can be grown quite easily and need not cost a fortune at the green-grocer. This delicious vegetable goes with many others, particularly tomatoes and onions, can be used raw in salads, or cooked in dozens of dishes, and it makes excellent pickles.

Peppers are also excellent stuffed and baked, particularly with rice in the stuffing, and a topping of fresh tomato sauce. Finely chopped peppers are very useful to give texture to sandwich fillings — try them with eggs, mashed sardines or salmon, or minced ham or corned beef. The peppers must be carefully prepared to avoid the fiery little seeds. Cut away the stem and central core with a sharp knife and remove all the soft membrane and tiny white seeds. Use whole or in half for stuffing, or cut in strips or rings.

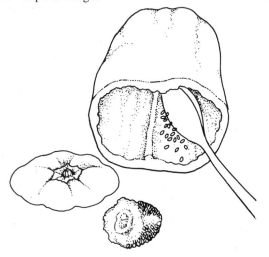

ROAST PEPPERS

4 large peppers
4 garlic cloves
4 fl oz (100 ml) olive oil
1 tsp salt

Wash the peppers and roast them at 350°F/180°C/ gas mark 4 for 20 minutes until the skin blisters and blackens and may be pierced easily with a sharp knife. Crush the garlic and heat in the olive oil, adding the salt. Skin the peppers, remove membranes and seeds and cut the flesh in 1 in (2.5 cm) strips. Put into a glass preserving jar, pour on the oil and seal. When cool, store in the refrigerator. These peppers are excellent in rice dishes, or to garnish dishes, or in salads, and are much nicer than raw peppers.

Potatoes

Potatoes are sadly mistreated in the kitchen when served plain boiled or mashed. They deserve careful cooking to make a delicious vegetable on their own. New potatoes are good cooked with mint, then drained and tossed in butter. A garnish of dill or chopped parsley helps to give them a special flavour. When slightly cool, they can be tossed in French dressing or mayonnaise for potato salad. Older potatoes are good chipped or roasted (boil potatoes for 5 minutes before roasting for the best results), or baked in their jackets. Jacket potatoes may be served with nothing more than butter and seasoning, but they can also be filled with cream cheese, with grated Cheddar cheese, with creamed fish or chicken or with crisply grilled bacon. Thinly sliced potatoes can be cooked in the oven in a covered casserole with plenty of butter, seasoning and a little milk until tender and golden to accompany whatever meat has also been cooked in the oven. Potatoes in soups and stews give bulk and help to thicken the liquid.

CHAMP *Serves 4*

8 large potatoes
6 spring onions
$\frac{1}{4}$ pt (150 ml) milk
Salt and pepper
Butter

Boil the potatoes in salted water. Drain well and dry off by putting a folded cloth on top and returning the pan to a gentle heat for a few minutes. Chop the spring onions very finely, including the green tops. Put into a bowl, pour on some boiling water and then drain them. Add to the milk and bring to the boil. Season well and pour on to the potatoes and mash them well until fluffy with salt and pepper. Put on individual plates, make a well in each pile of potatoes and put in a large lump of butter.

Spinach

Old cookery books recommend cooking spinach in huge quantities of water, but this is totally wrong. Spinach needs to be very well washed in two or three waters, then shaken dry and cooked in a covered pan with a knob of butter. The spinach needs frequent shaking or stirring so that it does not stick to the pan, and it will cook very quickly and reduce in bulk. To serve as an accompaniment or as the basis of a main dish, use 2 lb (1 kg) spinach for 4 people. It makes a good side dish served on the leaf stems and dressed with butter, but the stems may be removed before cooking and the spinach then finely chopped or made into a purée. It may also be folded into white sauce to make a very creamy purée. Spinach soup and soufflé are excellent, and a favourite dish is a purée of spinach topped with poached eggs and cheese sauce (Oeufs Florentine). Spinach beet is coarser-textured but abundant, and can be used for all spinach recipes.

SPINACH SOUP   *Serves 4*

2 lb (1 kg) spinach
1 medium onion
1 small green pepper
2 oz (50 g) butter
1 tsp sugar
Salt and pepper
1 tsp tarragon
4 fl oz (100 ml) single cream
Milk
2 bacon rashers

Strip the spinach stems from the leaves. Wash the leaves very well and drain. Chop the onion and pepper finely and soften in the butter for 5 minutes. Stir in the spinach, sugar, salt and pepper and tarragon. Cover tightly and cook until the spinach is tender. Put through a sieve, or purée in a blender. Add cream and enough milk to thin to the consistency of cream. Reheat gently and sprinkle with small pieces of crisply grilled bacon.

Swedes

Swedes have a slightly sweeter flavour than turnips and are particularly good with poultry. They are at their best cooked and made into a purée with plenty of seasoning and butter and/or single cream. Swedes blend well with potatoes in a purée, and any leftover mixture can be formed into flat cakes and fried to serve at a later meal. Turnip recipes may be used for cooking swedes.

SWEDES IN CIDER SAUCE   *Serves 4*

12 oz (350 g) carrots
12 oz (350 g) swedes
1 oz (25 g) butter
$\frac{1}{4}$ pt (150 ml) creamy milk
1 tbsp cornflour
5 tbsp cider
1 tsp caster sugar
Salt and pepper

Scrape and slice the carrots. Peel the swedes and cut into dice. Cook together in boiling salted water for 15 minutes until tender but unbroken. In a separate saucepan, melt the butter, and add the milk. Blend the cornflour with half the cider and then add to the milk together with the remaining cider. Bring to the boil, stirring well. Add the sugar, salt and pepper and simmer for 3 minutes. Drain the vegetables well and mix with the sauce. Serve hot with bacon or ham.

Sweet Corn

It is most important that sweet corn should be prepared immediately for cooking after harvesting, because at room temperature the sugar in the corn quickly becomes starch and the calorific and carbohydrate values increase rapidly. This also happens as soon as the husks are removed, so do not take them off until ready to cook the corn-cobs. The perfect cob for cooking should have plump, tender kernels, full of milk and surrounded by soft 'silk'. If you prefer to cook the kernals off the cob, scrape them off with a sharp pointed knife. Cobs may be steamed over boiling water for 15 minutes, or cooked in boiling water for just 5 minutes with a pinch of sugar and a squeeze of lemon juice. They can also be left in their husks with the 'silk' removed and a knob of butter inserted and roasted in the oven at 350°F/180°C/gas mark 4 for 35 minutes. Do not add salt to corn before cooking as this makes it tough. Corn mixes well with other vegetables, particularly tomatoes, and is useful for making fritters to serve with poultry or bacon.

CORN CHOWDER   *Serves 4*

4 bacon rashers
1 large onion
1 lb (450 g) potatoes
1½ pt (900 ml) milk
12 oz (350 g) cooked corn kernels
Salt and pepper
A pinch of rosemary
1 tsp sugar

Cut the bacon into thin strips and heat gently in a thick pan until the fat runs. Continue frying until the bacon is crisp. Drain off the fat and keep the bacon pieces on one side. Slice the onion thinly and cut the potatoes in cubes. Cook in the bacon fat, stirring gently for 3 minutes, then cover and cook until tender. Bring the milk to the boil, add the onions, potatoes and corn and seasonings. Simmer for 5 minutes, then remove from heat and leave to stand for 1 hour. Just before serving, reheat and garnish with bacon pieces.

Tomatoes

Tomatoes are used almost as widely as onions to flavour hundreds of dishes. They go well with meat, fish, eggs, and cheese; they partner rice and pasta and are invaluable for soups and sauces. Often it is recommended that tomatoes should be skinned and this is best done by holding each tomato with a fork over a flame, or by dipping them in hot and then cold water. For perfection, the pips should also be removed before using the tomatoes. Sliced tomatoes make a delicious salad, with French dressing and a garnish of chopped basil or mint. Tomatoes are also good in sandwiches, on their own or mixed with hard-boiled eggs, ham or cheese. Very large tomatoes can be sliced downwards, leaving the slices joined at the base, and the slits filled with slices of hard-boiled egg. Served with mayonnaise this is a favourite French first course or light luncheon. Another use for very large tomatoes is to cut off their tops, scoop out the pips and fill the fruit with rice salad or a seafood in mayonnaise. With a filling of chopped meat or fish, breadcrumbs and seasoning they can be baked in a little stock for a good main meal. Tomatoes can be grilled, fried or baked to accompany dishes and benefit from a good sprinkling of herbs. Green tomatoes which are just beginning to turn colour may also be grilled or fried, and both green and red tomatoes make excellent chutney.

BAKED TOMATOES AND EGGS

Large tomatoes
Eggs
Cream or grated cheese (optional)

Cut lids off tomatoes and scoop out seeds. Break an egg into each one, season and bake at 350°F/180°C/gas mark 4 for 15 minutes. Add a little cream or grated cheese before baking if liked.

Turnips

Only small, young mild turnips are worth eating, lightly cooked in water and dressed with butter and seasoning. Turnip purée is particularly good with rich fat meats such as duck, pork, ham and sausages. Turnips are good mixed with small red onions to serve with roast meat, and they may be cooked in beef stock. Part-boiled turnips may be finished off around a roasting joint, basted with the meat juices occasionally.

ROAST DUCK WITH TURNIPS   *Serves 4*

4½ lb (2 kg) duck
Butter
2 tbsp honey
1 tsp thyme
10 small turnips
10 button onions
1 oz (25 g) brown sugar
Salt and pepper
¼ pt (150 ml) red wine
¼ pt (150 ml) single cream
1 tbsp cornflour

Wipe the duck inside and out and brown it in a heavy pan in a little butter. Mix the honey and thyme and spread it over the duck skin and put the duck into a roasting tin. Peel the turnips and onions and brown them in some butter mixed with the brown sugar. Arrange round the duck, and season with salt and pepper. Add the red wine, cover and cook at 325°F/160°C/gas mark 3 for 1½ hours. Put the duck and the vegetables on to a serving dish and keep them warm. Heat the pan juices to reduce them to ½ pt (300 ml). Mix the cream and cornflour and stir gently into the pan juices. Simmer until creamy and serve separately.

Salads

The best green salad is made with lettuce and a mixture of other green stuff. This can include chicory, endive, watercress, onions, leeks, cucumber, peppers and a variety of herbs. Lettuce can also form the basis of a mixed salad with the addition of radishes, tomatoes, hard-boiled eggs, young carrots and peas. Crisp lettuce leaves often form the garnish for cold meat or fish, pâtés and other first courses. The leaves must not be limp and dull but should be crunchy and delicious enough to eat in their own right. Lettuce leaves should not be cut, but should be torn in pieces after thorough washing and drying. French dressing with a hint of mustard and sugar is the perfect accompaniment to green salad.

Mustard and cress is too often thought of as only a garnish for sandwiches, but it is very good mixed with other greenstuff in salad, or may be dressed with a French dressing to serve on its own or with an accompaniment of thinly sliced radishes or spring onions.

Radishes are very good on their own, eaten with a smear of unsalted butter (leave a little of the green stem on so that they are easy to handle).

Spring onions may be left whole for salads, with the green tips trimmed neatly, or they can be sliced in thin rings and mixed with other salad vegetables, or served in a separate bowl in French dressing. Onions are also good mixed with a little commercial soured cream seasoned with salt and pepper; a pinch of curry powder or mustard and a few thin slices of cucumber may be added. Another way of using spring onions is to chop them finely and add them to potato salad, or to sprinkle on thin slices of orange, garnished with olives and French dressing; the latter is a particularly good accompaniment to rich meats like duck and pork.

See also Bean Salad, page 118; and Cauliflower Salad, page 121.

Sauces

The basic details of sauce-making are given on page 84. These detailed recipes give the simple basic sauces and variations, along with one or two special ones which do not conform to specific rules. Remember that a sauce is designed to enhance the flavour of the food with which it is served, and must not overpower the main dish.

Roux-based sauces made with cooked butter and flour have many uses in the kitchen as they may be varied with flavourings to provide an accompaniment or finish for many savoury dishes, and may also form the basis of soups and soufflés. Warm butter sauces are made with an emulsion of egg yolks and liquid butter and provide a fine finish to simply cooked meat, poultry and fish. A variation of the emulsion method is prepared with egg yolks and oil, as in mayonnaise, for cold dishes. Melted butter sauces are quick and easy to prepare for vegetables, fish and eggs, while hard butter sauces may be savoury or sweet and can be prepared in advance.

Roux Sauces

BASIC WHITE SAUCE *Makes 1 pt (600 ml)*

1 oz (25 g) butter
1 oz (25 g) plain flour
1 pt (600 ml) milk
Salt and pepper

Melt the butter in a saucepan. Stir in the flour and cook gently for 1 minute. Remove the pan from the heat and gradually stir in the milk. Return to the heat and bring to the boil, stirring well. Add seasoning and continue cooking for a few minutes until the sauce is smooth and creamy. This gives a pouring consistency.

Coating consistency

Prepare as above, but use 2 oz (50 g) butter and 2 oz (50 g) flour to 1 pt (600 ml) milk.

Parsley sauce

Add 2 level tablespoons chopped parsley when the sauce has been cooked.

Cheese sauce

Remove cooked sauce from heat and stir in 4 oz (100 g) grated cheese and a pinch of mustard powder.

Egg sauce

Add 2 finely chopped hard-boiled eggs to the cooked sauce.

Mustard sauce

Add 3 teaspoons made mustard, 1 teaspoon wine vinegar and $\frac{1}{2}$ teaspoon chopped chives to the cooked sauce.

BÉCHAMEL SAUCE   *Makes 1 pt (600 ml)*

1 small carrot
1 small celery stick
1 shallot or small onion
1 blade mace
6 peppercorns
1 pt (600 ml) milk
2 oz (50 g) butter
2 oz (50 g) plain flour
Salt
2 tbsp single cream

Slice the carrot, chop the celery and slice the shallot or onion. Put into a pan with the mace, peppercorns and milk. Heat very gently without boiling for 8 minutes. Strain and cool. Melt the butter, add the flour and cook gently for 1 minute, stirring well. Take off the heat and gradually stir in the cooled milk. Return the pan to the heat and bring to the boil, stirring well. Adjust seasoning and continue cooking for 5 minutes. Remove from heat and stir in the cream.

Simple velouté sauce

Substitute 8 mushrooms for vegetables and use stock in place of milk. Add $\frac{1}{2}$ teaspoon lemon juice at the end of cooking.

Mornay sauce

Prepare béchamel sauce, remove from heat and stir in 4 oz (100 g) grated cheese and 1 teaspoon made mustard.

BROWN SAUCE   *Makes 1 pt (600 ml)*

1 small onion
1 medium carrot
$1\frac{1}{2}$ oz (40 g) butter
2 tsp tomato purée
$1\frac{1}{2}$ oz (40 g) plain flour
1 pt (600 ml) beef stock
Salt and pepper

Slice the onion and carrot. Melt the butter and cook the vegetables over low heat, stirring well until browned. Take off the heat and stir in the tomato purée, flour and stock gradually. Return to the heat and bring to the boil, stirring well. Season with salt and pepper. Cover and simmer for 30 minutes and then put the sauce through a sieve. Adjust seasoning if necessary and reheat before serving.

Warm Butter Sauces

These sauces made from egg yolks and butter can be a little tricky. It is most important that they never become more than barely hot, or separation will occur. If separation happens, whisk in 2 teaspoons cold water, or start again with another beaten egg yolk, and beat in the separated sauce. The secret is to whisk over hot, but not boiling, water — the water must never come to the boil.

HOLLANDAISE SAUCE   *Makes $\frac{1}{4}$ pt (150 ml)*

3 tbsp wine vinegar
6 peppercorns
1 bay leaf
A blade of mace
2 egg yolks
Salt
4 oz (100 g) butter (soft, but not melted)
2 tsp lemon juice

Put the vinegar, peppercorns, bay leaf and mace into a small heavy saucepan. Boil until the liquid is reduced to 1 tablespoon and remove the spices and bay leaf. Put the egg yolks, a pinch of salt and 1 tablespoon butter into a bowl and cream together. Put over a pan of hot, but not boiling, water. Beat with a wooden spoon while adding the reduced liquid. Beat in the remaining butter in small pieces, a little at a time, so that the sauce becomes thick and light. Take off the heat, and beat for 1 minute. Adjust seasoning and add lemon juice. Keep the sauce warm by standing the bowl over hot water, but do not let it get hot or cold. This sauce should be served warm with vegetables or fish.

Mousseline sauce
Just before serving, fold in 3 tablespoons cream whipped to soft peaks and serve with vegetables.

Herbed hollandaise sauce
Stir in 1 tablespoon each chopped fresh tarragon and chervil.

Maltaise sauce
Add the grated rind of 1 orange and $1\frac{1}{2}$ tablespoons orange juice just before serving with fish.

BÉARNAISE SAUCE   *Makes $\frac{1}{4}$ pt (150 ml)*

3 tbsp tarragon vinegar
2 small shallots
6 peppercorns
1 bay leaf
A sprig of tarragon
A sprig of chervil
2 egg yolks
4 oz (100 g) butter
Salt and pepper
1 tsp chopped tarragon
1 tsp chopped chervil

Put the vinegar into a small heavy pan with finely chopped shallots, peppercorns, bay leaf and herb sprigs. Simmer until the liquid is reduced to 1 tablespoon. Strain. Put the egg yolks into a small bowl with a pinch of salt and a small piece of the softened butter. Put over a pan of hot water, but do not allow the water to boil. Beat the egg yolks with a wooden spoon and add the strained vinegar. Beat in the butter a little at a time until the mixture is thick and creamy. Stir in the chopped herbs and adjust seasoning. Serve with fish, lamb or steak.

Choron sauce
Omit the chopped tarragon and chervil. Fold 2 tablespoons tomato purée into the finished sauce. Serve with chicken or pork.

Melted Butter Sauces

These sauces are simply made from melted butter with flavourings. Unsalted butter is best for them, as seasoning may then be more subtly added.

MELTED BUTTER SAUCE

4 oz (100 g) unsalted butter
Salt and pepper

Put the butter into a sauceboat and stand it in hot water or a warm place until melted. Season lightly and serve with vegetables or fish. When butter is heated in this way it will not become brown or spoil.

NOISETTE BUTTER

4 oz (100 g) unsalted butter
2 tbsp lemon juice
Salt and pepper

Melt the butter in a small saucepan, heating gently until it is a pale coffee brown. Put the lemon juice into a hot sauceboat, gradually pour in the butter and season to taste. Serve with fish, vegetables or eggs.

BLACK BUTTER SAUCE

3 oz (75 g) unsalted butter
1 tbsp wine vinegar
1 tbsp chopped capers

Melt the butter in a small saucepan and heat gently, shaking the pan occasionally until it turns dark brown but does not burn. Add vinegar and capers and serve at once with fish, vegetables or eggs.

Hard Butter Sauces

Flavoured butters may be prepared and kept in the refrigerator for 2 days or frozen. Savoury butters should be shaped into a cylinder and rolled in foil, then chilled before cutting in slices to place on grilled meat, fish or vegetables. Sweet butters may be chilled in small pots to serve with puddings.

MAÎTRE O'HÔTEL BUTTER

2 oz (50 g) butter
2 tsp lemon juice
1 tsp finely chopped parsley
Salt and pepper

Cream the butter and work in the lemon juice, parsley and seasoning. Form into a cylinder and chill before using.

GARLIC BUTTER

2 oz (50 g) butter
1 garlic clove
2 tbsp lemon juice
Salt and pepper

Cream butter and work in the crushed garlic, lemon juice and seasoning. Form into a cylinder and chill before using.

BRANDY BUTTER

4 oz (100 g) unsalted butter
4 oz (100 g) caster sugar
1 tsp grated orange rind
2 tbsp brandy

Cream the butter and sugar until light and fluffy. Cream in the orange and brandy very gradually until incorporated. Put into a serving dish and chill before using on puddings or pies.

Rum butter

Omit orange rind. Substitute light soft brown sugar and rum for the caster sugar and brandy.

Oil Emulsion Sauces

An oil emulsion sauce needs care in making, but is not difficult to prepare. Have all the ingredients at room temperature, and add the oil drop by drop, beating all the time. The mixture should be very thick by the time half the oil is added. If mayonnaise is made in a blender or food processor, a better result is obtained by using 1 whole egg instead of 2 egg yolks. If mayonnaise curdles, put a fresh egg yolk into a clean bowl and add the curdled mixture drop by drop, beating all the time until the sauce is smooth again.

MAYONNAISE   *Makes $\frac{1}{2}$ pt (300 ml)*

2 egg yolks
1 tsp made mustard
$\frac{1}{2}$ pt (300 ml) olive oil
A squeeze of lemon juice
1 tbsp wine vinegar
Salt and white pepper

Put the yolks and mustard into a bowl and beat well with a wooden spoon. Add the oil drop by drop, beating all the time until half the oil has been absorbed. Beat in the lemon juice. Continue adding the oil, which may be now in slightly larger quantities, and the vinegar in drops. Beat until thick and creamy and season to taste.

Tartare sauce

Add 1 tablespoon chopped gherkins, 1 tablespoon chopped capers, 1 tablespoon chopped parsley, 1 finely chopped shallot and a squeeze of lemon juice.

Green mayonnaise

Add 1 tablespoon chopped fresh dill, 1 tablespoon chopped chives and 1 tablespoon chopped parsley and process with mayonnaise in a blender.

Tomato mayonnaise

Add 2 tablespoons tomato purée, 1 teaspoon finely chopped tarragon and 1 tablespoon finely chopped chives.

Cucumber mayonnaise

Cut up $\frac{1}{4}$ cucumber, including the skin, and put into a blender with 1 onion slice and 2 teaspoons made mustard. Blend on high speed until finely chopped and add 6 tablespoons mayonnaise. Blend until just mixed.

FRENCH DRESSING

3 tbsp salad oil
1 tbsp wine vinegar
Salt and pepper

Put the ingredients into a screwtop jar and shake well. The jar should always be well shaken before using until the oil and vinegar are emulsified. A large quantity of dressing may be prepared in advance and stored in the refrigerator, where it will become slightly thicker. This dressing is sometimes known as oil-and-vinegar dressing or vinaigrette, and may be varied by using different oils such as walnut or olive, and herb-flavoured vinegars. Chopped fresh herbs are sometimes used, or a little made mustard, pinch of sugar, or crushed garlic may be added according to individual taste and the food with which it is used. When serving with a green salad, it is usual to pour the dressing over the salad and toss the leaves at the moment of service — if dressing is left on the salad, the leaves become limp and unpalatable.

Miscellaneous Sauces

These sauces comply with no sauce-making rules, but they are traditional accompaniments and worth making well.

MINT SAUCE

4 tbsp chopped fresh mint
1 tbsp caster sugar
2 tbsp boiling water
1 tbsp wine vinegar

The mint should be well washed and chopped very finely. Put the mint into a bowl with the sugar and pour on the boiling water. Leave to stand for 5 minutes until the sugar has dissolved. This hot water treatment ensures that the mint stays green and attractive. Stir in the vinegar and leave for an hour before serving. It is important to see that there is plenty of mint in the sauce, and wine vinegar gives a finer flavour than the harsher malt vinegar.

TOMATO SAUCE   *Makes $\frac{1}{2}$ pt (300 ml)*

1 medium onion
1 garlic clove
1 tbsp olive oil
1 lb (450 g) ripe tomatoes
1 tsp salt
1 tsp sugar
1 tsp paprika
1 tbsp vinegar
1 bay leaf
Pepper

Chop the onion finely and crush the garlic. Cook gently in the oil until soft and golden. Skin the tomatoes by dipping them in boiling water. Chop finely and add to the onion and garlic. Add the other ingredients, cover and simmer for 15 minutes. Remove the bay leaf and put the mixture through a sieve. Simmer for further 15 minutes and serve hot with pasta, or with meat, poultry or fish. Fresh basil or marjoram may be added to the sauce during the first cooking. If fresh tomatoes are not available, canned tomatoes with their liquid may be used.

BREAD SAUCE   *Makes $\frac{3}{4}$ pt (450 ml)*

1 medium onion
4 cloves
1 pt (600 ml) milk
Salt, pepper and nutmeg
3 oz (75 g) day-old bread
2 tbsp double cream

Peel the onion and stick the cloves into it. Put into a pan with the milk and simmer gently for 10 minutes. Take out the onion and season the milk with salt, pepper and a pinch of nutmeg. Make the bread into crumbs and add gradually to the milk. Simmer gently for 5 minutes and take off the heat. Just before serving, stir in the cream. Serve with turkey, chicken, game or sausages.

APPLE SAUCE   *Makes $\frac{1}{2}$ pt (300 ml)*

1 lb (450 g) cooking apples
2 oz (50 g) sugar
A little water or cider

Peel, core and slice the apples and put into a pan with water or cider to cover. Simmer until the apples are soft and fluffy. Put through a sieve, or smooth in a blender. Stir in the sugar and reheat before serving with pork, ham or sausages. Cider gives a very good flavour to the sauce, and a few seedless raisins may be added during the reheating process. It is best to use an apple like Bramley's Seedling which goes fluffy when cooked. If the apples are just cut into pieces without peeling and coring they can be sieved after cooking and the flavour will be stronger.

CRANBERRY SAUCE   *Makes $\frac{1}{2}$ pt (300 ml)*

8 oz (225 g) cranberries
$\frac{1}{2}$ pt (300 ml) water
4 oz (100 g) sugar

Wash the cranberries and put into a pan with the water. Simmer until the berries burst but retain their shape. Stir in the sugar until dissolved and remove from the heat. Serve hot or cold with turkey, pork or ham. If liked, the sauce may be sieved and served as a purée. A little grated orange rind will give a delicious flavour to the sauce, which may be stored in the refrigerator or freezer.

CUMBERLAND SAUCE   *Makes $\frac{1}{2}$ pt (300 ml)*

1 orange
1 lemon
1 shallot
8 oz (225 g) red currant jelly
$\frac{1}{4}$ pt (150 ml) port
$\frac{1}{2}$ tsp made mustard
$\frac{1}{2}$ tsp ground ginger
A pinch of cayenne pepper

Peel the orange and lemon very thinly so that no white pith is taken from the fruit. With a very sharp knife, cut the peel into needle-thin shreds. Chop the shallot very finely and pour on a little boiling water. Leave to stand for 1 minute and drain well. Put the fruit peel and shallot into a pan. Squeeze out the juice from the orange and lemon and strain into the pan. Add the remaining ingredients and simmer for 10 minutes. Leave to cool and serve with ham.

CUSTARD SAUCE   *Makes $\frac{1}{2}$ pt (300 ml)*

$\frac{1}{2}$ pt (300 ml) milk
$\frac{1}{2}$ oz (15 g) sugar
$\frac{1}{2}$ vanilla pod
2 egg yolks

Put the milk, sugar and vanilla pod into a pan and bring slowly to the boil. Put the egg yolks into a bowl and beat enough to break them up. Take the vanilla pod out of the milk and pour the hot milk on to the egg yolks, stirring all the time. Return to the pan and stir over gentle heat until the mixture thickens and coats the back of a spoon, but do not let it boil or it may curdle. If you find it difficult to lower the heat enough, cook the custard in a bowl over hot water, or in the top of a double saucepan. If a vanilla pod is not available, add a few drops of vanilla essence just before serving hot or cold.

CHOCOLATE SAUCE   *Makes $\frac{1}{4}$ pt (150 ml)*

4 oz (100 g) caster sugar
$\frac{1}{4}$ pt (150 ml) water
2 oz (50 g) cocoa powder

Put the sugar and water into a saucepan and stir over a low heat to dissolve the sugar. Bring to the boil and simmer for 1 minute. Add the cocoa and whisk until the sauce is smooth. Bring back to the boil and take off the heat. Stir occasionally as the sauce cools and thickens. The sauce may be stored in the refrigerator or freezer, and may be served cold or hot over ices and puddings.

Mocha sauce
Add $\frac{1}{2}$ teaspoon instant coffee powder, or a few drops of coffee essence.

Stuffings

A variety of stuffings can complement savoury foods and add flavour and moisture to dishes, as well as extending portions. Full details of preparing and using stuffings are on page 58, but the following recipes give some idea of the range of ingredients which may be used. Bread is the basis of most stuffings, but rice is sometimes used, particularly for filling vegetables, and flavour is added with fruit, onions, herbs and seasonings. When stuffing poultry or rolled joints, do not overfill, as the stuffing will expand during cooking, but bake any surplus mixture in a separate ovenware dish, or roll into small balls and fry in butter.

HERB STUFFING

2 oz (50 g) butter
2 oz (50 g) streaky bacon
1 medium onion
8 oz (225 g) day-old breadcrumbs
1 tbsp chopped parsley
1 tsp thyme
Grated rind of 1 lemon
$\frac{1}{2}$ tsp ground nutmeg
Salt and pepper
Chicken liver
Egg or stock

Melt the butter and cook the finely chopped bacon and onion until soft and golden. Add the breadcrumbs and stir until the fat is absorbed. Remove from heat and add the herbs, lemon rind, nutmeg, salt and pepper. Fry the chicken liver in a little butter until just coloured, and then chop it and add to the stuffing, together with any cooking juices. Moisten with a little beaten egg or stock made from the chicken giblets, but do not make the stuffing wet, as it will absorb a lot of liquid from the poultry. Mix well and use for a 3-4 lb (1.5-2 kg) chicken.

Celery stuffing
Add 2 celery sticks, very finely chopped.

Mushroom stuffing
Add 4 oz (100 g) chopped mushrooms cooked in a little of the butter.

Fruit and nut stuffing
Add 2 oz (50 g) chopped seedless raisins and 2 oz (50 g) chopped walnuts.

CHESTNUT STUFFING

2 lb (900 g) chestnuts
1 pt (600 ml) stock or milk
4 oz (100 g) day-old white breadcrumbs
Grated rind of $\frac{1}{2}$ lemon
1 egg
2 oz (50 g) melted butter
2 tbsp single cream
Salt and pepper

If fresh chestnuts are not available, use 1 lb (450 g) can chestnut purée, and omit the stock or milk in the recipe. To prepare fresh chestnuts, use a very sharp pointed knife to slit the shells at each end. Boil in water for 10 minutes. Take off shells and inner brown skins, and simmer the nuts in stock or milk until tender. Drain, and then put the nuts through a sieve, or make them into a purée in a blender or food processor. Put the chestnut purée, breadcrumbs and lemon rind into a bowl and stir in the egg, butter, cream and seasoning. Mix well and use to stuff a 5-6 lb (2.5-3 kg) chicken, or the neck cavity of a turkey.

WATERCRESS STUFFING

3 oz (75 g) butter
2 celery sticks
1 medium onion
1 large bunch of watercress
10 oz (300 g) day-old white breadcrumbs
1 egg
Salt and pepper

Melt the butter and fry the finely chopped celery and onion until soft and golden, which will take about 5 minutes. Chop the watercress leaves and a few of the thin stalks. Add to the onion with the breadcrumbs and continue frying, stirring well for 5 minutes. Cool and mix in the egg and seasoning. Use to stuff a 3-4 lb (1.5-2 kg) chicken or make into 20 small balls and fry in butter to serve with chicken, turkey or pheasant.

APPLE STUFFING

3 oz (75 g) butter
2 cooking apples
4 oz (100 g) day-old white breadcrumbs
$\frac{1}{2}$ oz (15 g) caster sugar
Pinch of ground cinnamon
Salt and pepper

Peel and core the apples and chop them coarsely. Melt the butter, add the apples and cook over low heat for 10 minutes. Stir in the breadcrumbs,

sugar, cinnamon, salt and pepper. Cool and use to stuff a 3-4 lb (1.5-2 kg) chicken, duck, or joint of pork. This stuffing is also very good if placed in a greased ovenware dish, topped with a few small pieces of butter and baked at 350°F/180°C/gas mark 4 for 25 minutes, to serve with roast pork or poultry.

ORANGE STUFFING

2 oz (50 g) butter
1 medium onion
5 oz (125 g) day-old white breadcrumbs
2 tsp chopped parsley
2 oranges
1 oz (25 g) walnuts
Salt and pepper

Melt the butter and fry the finely chopped onion until soft and golden. Stir in the breadcrumbs and parsley. Grate the rinds and squeeze out the juice from the oranges. Stir into the breadcrumbs, with the chopped walnuts and seasoning. Cool and use to stuff a boned shoulder or breast of lamb.

RICE STUFFING FOR VEGETABLES

3 oz (75 g) long-grain rice
4 oz (100 g) butter
4 lambs' kidneys
1 small onion
2 oz (50 g) mushrooms
Salt and pepper

Cook the rice in boiling salted water for 12 minutes and drain well. Melt the butter and cook the finely chopped kidneys, onion and mushrooms in it for 5 minutes. Season well and stir in the rice. The kidneys may be omitted and the stuffing may be flavoured with tomato purée if preferred. Use to stuff peppers, aubergines or courgettes.

Fruit

A very wide range of fruit is available in shops and markets as well as from gardens or pick-it-yourself farms. Although a few fruit such as bananas and citrus fruits are available year-round, most are at their best in limited seasons and then represent good value for money.

Apples

For cooking purposes, apples fall into two categories — crisp and fluffy. Use crisp apples for pies or any dish in which the shape of slices is important. Use fluffy apples which break up in cooking for purées, mousses, cakes and apple sauce. For a special flavour cook apple slices in butter and sugar instead of water (allow 2 oz (50 g) butter to 1 lb (450 g) apples, plus sugar to taste). Other complementary flavourings for apples are with the traditional cloves, or with cinnamon or ginger, a little lemon or orange rind and juice or some rose-hip syrup. Team apples with blackberries or raspberries, quinces, plums or apricots for sweet recipes. For savoury dishes, use apples with pork, goose, duck and pheasant and add a little grated apple to the horse-radish sauce served with beef.

DORSET APPLE CAKE

8 oz (225 g) self-raising flour
A pinch of salt
4 oz (100 g) margarine
12 oz (350 g) eating apples
4 oz (100 g) sugar
2 oz (50 g) currants
Milk
3 oz (75 g) butter
1 oz (25 g) soft brown sugar

Sift together the flour and salt and rub in the margarine until the mixture is like fine breadcrumbs. Peel and core the apples and chop them up roughly. Mix them with the flour and stir in the sugar and currants. Add enough milk to make a stiff dough and stir well together. Put into two greased 7 in (17.5 cm) sponge tins and bake at 425°F/220°C/gas mark 7 for 15 minutes. Reduce heat to 300°F/150°C/gas mark 2 and bake for 1 hour. While warm, sandwich together with two-thirds of the butter. Cut the remaining butter in small pieces, mix with brown sugar and spread on top. Eat warm and fresh.

Apricots

Apricots must be really golden and ripe to eat raw, but slightly under-ripe fruit can be poached in a heavy sugar syrup or cooked in the oven with sugar. A little Kirsch, Curaçao or rum goes well with apricots and may be added to many puddings. The apricot is a good fruit for accompanying ham, pork and poultry. If only a few fruit are available, they can be mixed with apples to give their flavour to pies and puddings. This is a versatile fruit which makes excellent jam and pickles, and bottles and freezes well.

APRICOT AND APPLE PIE   *Serves 4*

1 lb (450 g) shortcrust pastry
$1\frac{1}{2}$ lb (675 g) cooking apples
4 oz (100 g) granulated sugar
3 oz (75 g) soft brown sugar
$1\frac{1}{2}$ oz (40 g) plain flour
Juice of 1 lemon
1 tsp ground cinnamon
$\frac{1}{2}$ tsp ground nutmeg
$\frac{1}{4}$ tsp salt
1 lb (450 g) fresh apricots
$\frac{1}{2}$ tsp almond essence
1 oz (25 g) butter

Roll out the pastry and line a pie dish with half of it. Peel the apples and slice thinly. Mix with the granulated and brown sugars, flour, lemon juice, spices and salt, and put into the pie dish. Cut the apricots in half, remove stones, and put the fruit cut side down on the apples. Sprinkle with the essence and put on small pieces of butter. Cover with pastry and bake at 400°F/200°C/gas mark 6 for 20 minutes. Reduce heat to 350°F/180°C/gas mark 4 and bake for 25 minutes. If liked, sweet shortcrust pasty (see page 145) may be used for this pie, which is good hot or cold, preferably with thick cream.

Avocados

The avocado or alligator pear is a sub-tropical fruit, dark green and pear-shaped with a slightly rough skin and large conical seed. It is rich in vitamins and oil, while the sugar and carbohydrate contents are very low; this richness has caused the avocado to be nicknamed 'midshipman's butter' by sailors in tropical waters and 'poor man's butter' in Central America.

The fruit can be used for a variety of spreads, dressings and savoury dishes, and is particularly good for the appetiser course. One avocado will serve two people. To test for ripeness the thumb and finger should be applied as to a peach. If the fruit 'gives' or feels soft the avocado is ready for serving. Tomatoes bring out the flavour and also fresh lime or lemon juice. Lemon juice also prevents discolouration if the fruit is prepared some time before a meal.

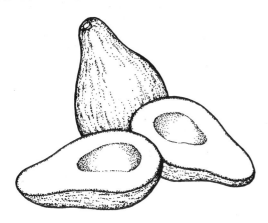

The avocado may most simply be served by being cut in half lengthwise and the stone removed. Each half is then sprinkled with salt and pepper, or sugar and vinegar, lemon or orange juice. A half avocado can also be served with 1 tablespoon of sherry poured into the cavity left by the stone.

The pulp of the fruit can be scooped from the skin, seasoned with salt and pepper and served on hot buttered toast. Seasoned with lemon juice, the pulp can be spread on small salt cocktail biscuits.

AVOCADO CRAB SALAD *Serves 4*

2 avocados
3 tsp lemon juice
4 oz (100 g) crabmeat (fresh or canned)
6 tbsp mayonnaise
A pinch of curry powder
2 tbsp breadcrumbs
1 oz (25 g) butter

Cut the avocados in half, remove stones and brush surfaces with 2 teaspoons lemon juice. Bind crabmeat with mayonnaise, remaining teaspoon lemon juice and curry powder. Warm this mixture and fill avocado halves. Top with breadcrumbs and a dab of butter and put under grill for 3 minutes.

Bananas

The banana is a popular dessert fruit with a high calorific content and it is particularly enjoyed by children. Some people like bananas mashed with sugar and cream, or jam, honey or chocolate. In America, the banana is often used with meat or poultry — particularly chicken — or is made into pies, fritters or ices. Cooked bananas lose much of their flavour, but are popular in West Indian cooking, and their natural accompaniments seem to be brown sugar and rum. Other complementary flavourings include brandy, ginger, walnuts, lemon juice and rind.

BANANA AND WALNUT CAKE

8 oz (225 g) plain flour
A pinch of salt
1 level tsp bicarbonate of soda
5 oz (125 g) butter
4 oz (100 g) caster sugar
3 eggs
2 bananas
1 oz (25 g) chopped walnuts
2 tbsp milk
1 tbsp lemon juice

Sift the dry ingredients. Cream butter and sugar until light and fluffy, then beat in eggs, one at a time, adding a tablespoon of flour with each. Stir in mashed bananas, and nuts, then gently fold in the rest of the flour alternately with the milk and lemon juice. Turn into a well-greased 7 in sq (17.5 cm sq) cake tin, lined on the bottom with greaseproof paper. Bake in the centre of a moderate oven at 350°F/180°C/gas mark 4 for 50-60 minutes or till the cake is well risen and firm.

Black currants

Blackcurrants are excellent for all kinds of pies and puddings, and the flavour is heightened with a few drops of Cassis, the black currant liqueur. Try a pinch of ground cinnamon in any accompanying pastry too. The fruit has good seting qualities and makes a pleasant jam, while black currant syrup is worth making for the freezer.

BLACK CURRANT SHORTCAKE   *Serves 4-6*

1 lb (450 g) black currants
4 oz (100 g) sugar
4 oz (100 g) butter
4 oz (100 g) caster sugar
2 eggs
4 oz (100 g) self-raising flour
A pinch of salt
$\frac{1}{2}$ pt (300 ml) double cream

Strip the currants from their stems and cook the currants with the sugar and 4 tablespoons (60 ml) water until just tender, then cool. Cream the butter and caster sugar until light and fluffy. Beat the eggs lightly and add to the butter mixture alternately with the flour sifted with salt. Put into two 7 in (17.5 cm) sandwich tins and bake at 325°F/160°C/gas mark 3 for 25 minutes. Cool, and sandwich together with black currants and whipped cream.

Cherries

For cooking purposes, the Morello cherry is the most suitable, but black or white eating cherries can of course be eaten raw or cooked. Cooking in red wine gives them good flavour and colour, and their flavour is enhanced by Cherry Brandy or Kirsch. Cherries are a favourite garnish with duck and can be made into a good salad to serve with poultry.

CHERRY COMPOTE   *Serves 4*

1 lb (450 g) cherries
$\frac{1}{2}$ pt (300 ml) red wine
7 oz (175 g) sugar
$\frac{1}{2}$ tsp ground cinnamon
$\frac{1}{2}$ tsp ground nutmeg
A pinch of ground cloves
2 tbsp red currant jelly

Stone the cherries and put them into the wine with the sugar and the spices. Cook until the fruit is just tender but not broken. Drain the cherries and put them into a serving bowl. Return the syrup to the saucepan and boil until thick. Stir in the red currant jelly and cool, and then pour over the cherries. Serve very cold with whipped cream. If liked, the mixture can be served hot over vanilla ice cream. Black cherries are best for this, but Morello cherries can be used with a little more sugar to taste.

CHERRY AND WALNUT SALAD   *Serves 4*

8 oz (225 g) black cherries
2 oz (50 g) walnut halves
$\frac{1}{4}$ pt (150 ml) French dressing
2 tbsp double cream
A squeeze of lemon juice

Stone the cherries and put into a serving dish. Drop the walnut halves into boiling water, skin them and chop roughly. Mix with the cherries and pour over the French dressing. Drain off the surplus dressing and top the salad with cream to which the lemon juice has been added. Serve with poultry or ham.

Figs

Figs must be eaten when they are freshly picked because they are very perishable. They are good just peeled and sliced but cream may be served with them, plus a little lemon or orange juice, or a spoonful of rum. Figs can be frozen in syrup, but they are a surprisingly good basis for jam and pickles.

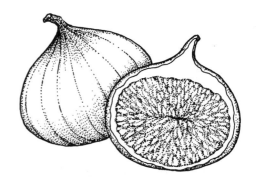

FIG JAM   *Makes approx. 2 lb (1 kg)*

1 lb (450 g) fresh figs
8 oz (225 g) apples
3 lemons
A piece of cinnamon stick
A piece of root ginger
2 cloves
1 lb (450 g) sugar

Peel the figs and blanch them in boiling water for 1 minute. Drain them, rinse in cold water and cut in thin slices. Put into a thick pan with peeled and sliced apples. Add the juice of 3 lemons and the grated rind of 1 lemon. Put the spices in a piece of muslin and suspend in the pan. Cover and cook gently until the fruit is tender. Add the sugar and stir until dissolved. Boil rapidly for 15 minutes then pour into small hot jars and cover.

Gooseberries

Large ripe eating gooseberries are splendid eaten raw, or cut in half and served with a sprinkling of sugar. Most of the crop however remains hard and green, but the berries are very popular cooked in pies and puddings, in sauce for savoury dishes and in jam and chutney. Gooseberries bottle and freeze well. In sweet dishes their flavour is enhanced by a head of elderflowers, which gives the fruit a hint of muscat.

GOOSEBERRY SAUCE   *Makes $\frac{1}{2}$ pt (300 ml)*

$1\frac{1}{2}$ oz (40 g) butter
1 oz (25 g) plain flour
8 oz (225 g) gooseberries
Salt, pepper and sugar

Melt half the butter and stir in the flour. Cook gently until light brown. Gradually add $\frac{3}{4}$ pt (450 ml) water and cook to make a thin sauce. Top and tail the gooseberries and add to the sauce. Simmer until the berries are soft and then sieve. Reheat gently and season to taste with salt, pepper and sugar. Add the remaining butter just before serving. This is the traditional sauce to serve with mackerel, but is good with any oily fish.

Grapefruit

The grapefruit is a refreshing variety of citrus fruit with a slight tang which makes it most useful for appetising first courses and fruit salads. It can be used in many ways like the orange but does not benefit from cooking, although a little grapefruit in a marmalade recipe gives a good flavour. When grapefruit is used in a salad or as an ice, a little chopped mint is a pleasant garnish.

HOT FRUIT SALAD   *Serves 4*

1 large grapefruit
2 bananas
Juice of $\frac{1}{2}$ lemon
1 oz (25 g) soft brown sugar
2 oz (50 g) sultanas
2 tbsp rum

Peel the grapefruit, and cut it between the sections to remove flesh but not the skin around sections. Put into a lightly buttered ovenware dish. Cut the bananas into halves across and then downwards to make four pieces. Roll in lemon juice. Put bananas into dish, sprinkle with sugar and sultanas and add the rum. Cover and bake at 375°F/190°C/gas mark 5 for 15 minutes. Serve hot with cream.

Grapes

Perfect grapes make an elegant finish to a meal and are rarely cooked. They do however make a good garnish for fish — sole and haddock in particular — or can be added to rabbit dishes. Plainly roasted pheasant tastes better than ever if simply stuffed with fresh grapes before cooking, which melt away leaving a rich pan juice. If there is a glut of grapes which are not quite perfect for the table, they can be made into a very good jam to use for tarts, or on toast.

TOFFEE GRAPES   *Serves 4*

1 lb (450 g) grapes
2 oz (50 g) caster sugar
$\frac{1}{2}$ pt (300 ml) double cream
3 oz (75 g) soft brown sugar

Use large juicy grapes, either black or green. Peel them and remove the pips. Put into an ovenware dish and sprinkle with caster sugar. Whip the cream to soft peaks and spread lightly over the fruit. Chill the dish in the refrigerator for 2 or 3 hours. Just before serving, spread the brown sugar on top and place under a hot grill until the sugar melts and turns to a hard crisp caramel. Serve at once. This recipe may be used for many other types of fruit or a mixture of them. Raspberries, strawberries, peaches and apricots are particularly good, and a little appropriate liqueur may be added to the fruit base before adding the cream and caramel topping.

Lemons

Lemons provide one of the most popular of all kitchen flavourings. Lemon rind and juice are indispensable in a huge variety of recipes from salad dressings and savouries through to cakes and ices. A squeeze of lemon juice enhances fish and veal, is essential to mayonnaise and gives a zip to pastry. Lemon juice helps in the preparation of such fruit as melons, apples, plums and rhubarb and helps to preserve the delicate colouring of peaches and avocados. It is also a useful addition to such puddings as treacle tart where it counteracts the sweetness.

LEMON CAKE

$1\frac{1}{2}$ oz (40 g) butter
6 oz (150 g) caster sugar
3 egg yolks
$\frac{1}{4}$ tsp lemon essence
6 oz (150 g) self-raising flour
$\frac{1}{4}$ pt (150 ml) less 2 tbsp milk
A pinch of salt

Icing
1 tbsp grated orange rind
3 tbsp soft butter
12 oz (350 g) icing sugar
2 tbsp lemon juice
1 tbsp water
A pinch of salt

Cream the butter until light and gradually add the sugar, egg yolks and lemon essence. When the mixture is soft and fluffy, add the flour alternately with the milk. Add the salt and beat well. Bake in two 8 in (20 cm) round tins, greased and bottom-lined with greased paper at 350°F/180°C/gas mark 4 for 25 minutes. Prepare the icing and ice between the layers and on the top and sides of the cake. Make the icing by adding the orange rind to the butter and creaming well. Cream in one-third of the icing sugar with the salt. Mix the lemon juice and water and add to the mixture alternately with the remaining icing sugar. Beat well until smooth.

LEMON FLUMMERY   *Serves 4*

$\frac{3}{4}$ oz (20 g) butter
1 lemon
1 oz (25 g) plain flour
4 oz (100 g) caster sugar
1 egg
2 oz (50 g) biscuit or macaroon crumbs

Grate the lemon peel. Boil the butter with $\frac{1}{2}$ pt (300 ml) water and the grated peel. Mix the flour and sugar in a bowl and make a well in the centre. Pour in the hot liquid, whisking to avoid lumps. Mix the egg yolk with a little of the hot flour mixture, add to the contents of the bowl and then return all the liquid to the pan. Bring slowly to the boil and cook gently for 10 minutes. Remove from the heat and add the juice of the lemon. Pour into a bowl and fold in the stiffly whisked egg white. Cool and then scatter the crumbs over the surface. Serve very cold with cream.

Loganberries

These berries are very similar to raspberries but slightly more acid. This makes them more suitable for cooking than for eating raw, and loganberries may be used for any raspberry, blackberry or mulberry recipe. The fruit goes well with apples and with other summer fruits so it may well be added to give a rich colour and slightly sharp flavour to a variety of puddings and jams.

LOGANBERRY SPONGE   *Serves 4*

2 oz (50 g) butter
6 oz (150 g) caster sugar
2 eggs
4 oz (100 g) self-raising flour
12 oz (350 g) loganberries
1 large eating apple

Cream butter and sugar. Beat the eggs lightly and work into the mixture alternately with the flour. Add the loganberries and the peeled, cored and sliced apple and fold in carefully. Put into a greased pudding basin, cover and steam for $1\frac{1}{4}$ hours. If preferred the pudding may be put into an ovenware dish and baked at 350°F/180°C/gas mark 4 for 1 hour. Serve with custard or cream.

Melons

Many varieties of melon are available, according to the season of the year, although most are imported during the summer. The cantaloupe melon has a ribbed, warty skin, and flesh which is either dark orange or pale green, juicy and sweet. The smaller honeydew melon has a lace-patterned pale skin and is more watery and sweet. The charantais melon looks like a miniature pumpkin, and has a rich

orange flesh and a strong musky scent and flavour. The water melon comes from very hot countries and is like a large dark green football with bright pink flesh and dark brown seeds scattered throughout. It is very watery and refreshing, with little flavour.

While melons are occasionally cooked as a vegetable, or made into jam or pickles, they are best served well chilled at the beginning or end of a meal. The flesh blends well with oranges and the two fruits can be combined in a refreshing cocktail. Melon can be eaten alone with a little sugar and nutmeg or ginger, but is more refreshing served with a little salt and even pepper. Lemon rind and juice can also be served with melon or a few drops of Crème de Cacao or port. A slice of melon is excellent with cold pork or ham, particularly raw Parma ham, and it is also good with Roquefort cheese.

Peaches

The best peaches to eat raw must be large, soft and juicy. If they are a little smaller and harder, they are excellent cooked in the same ways as apricots. This is another fruit which goes well with savoury food, particularly pork, ham, bacon and cream cheese. They make excellent jam, bottle and freeze well. It is worth putting a few spoonfuls of brandy into the heavy syrup when bottling peaches to provide a treat for winter parties.

PEACH DUMPLINGS *Serves 4*

8 oz (225 g) shortcrust pastry
4 peaches
2 oz (50 g) butter
12 oz (350 g) soft brown sugar
A pinch of ground nutmeg

Roll out the pastry and cut into four squares. Peel the peaches and take out the stones, leaving the fruit as whole as possible. Fill each cavity with butter and sugar, and sprinkle with nutmeg. Put a peach in the centre of each pastry square, form into parcels and seal the edges with a little water. Put the brown sugar in a saucepan with 8 tablespoons (120 ml) water and heat for 5 minutes to make a thick syrup. Spoon some over the dumplings and bake at 425°F/220°C/gas mark 7 for 10 minutes. Reduce heat to 350°F/180°C/gas mark 4 and continue baking for 30 minutes, basting with more syrup every 10 minutes. Serve warm or cold with cream.

GRILLED PEACHES *Serves 4*

4 peaches
Butter and sugar

Peel and halve the peaches. Brush with melted butter and sprinkle with sugar. Grill and serve with ham, pork or chicken.

Pears

Juicy dessert pears are suitable for eating raw, or for lightly poaching to serve with chocolate or raspberry sauce. A fresh ripe pear is delicious eaten with a piece of Brie or Camembert cheese. Pears can be rather insipid, and when bottled or frozen they need a little extra flavouring such as vanilla, cloves or rum. Pears may be cooked slowly in red wine and the hard winter cooking pears may be left to cook in wine for many hours in a slow oven until they become deep red and tender.

HONEY PEARS *Serves 4*

4 ripe pears
Juice of 2 lemons
6 oz (150 g) honey
1 tsp ground cinnamon
1 oz (25 g) butter

Peel and core the pears, and cut in half. Put in a greased ovenware dish, cut side up. Mix the lemon juice and honey and pour over the pears, then sprinkle with cinnamon and dot with butter. Bake at 350°F/180°C/gas mark 4 for 20 minutes. Serve hot or cold with cream.

Pineapple

The pineapple, traditional symbol of hospitality, is also one of the most delicious of dessert fruits. A simple slice of pineapple can be served sprinkled with Kirsch; a half pineapple makes a container for ice-cream or even for a sweet-and-savoury salad. Fresh pineapple has the finest flavour, but the canned fruit is useful for recipes although rather insipid in flavour. For a dish which requires gelatine canned pineapple should always be used, as fresh pineapple contains an enzyme which inhibits the setting quality of gelatine. For sweet dishes, pineapple is enhanced by rum as well as Kirsch and for ending a meal a piece of fresh pineapple is delicious with Roquefort cheese. Those who like a combination of savoury flavours with fruit find that pineapple enhances the flavour of ham, pork, chicken and shrimps.

GRILLED PINEAPPLE

1 small fresh pineapple
2 oz (50 g) brown or white sugar
2 oz (50 g) butter

Peel the pineapple and cut into thick rings. Sprinkle well with sugar and dot with flakes of butter. Grill to a toffee brown, basting with melted butter. Serve with ham or turkey.

Plums

Large ripe plums are delicious eaten raw, and they can also be halved and sprinkled with sugar and a little Kirsch or Cherry Brandy. It is a mistake to stew plums in water — they are better arranged in layers in a casserole with sugar and a sprinkling of cinnamon or a little lemon or orange rind. Add a little water or red wine to come half way up the plums and cook them in a slow oven (300°F/150°C/ gas mark 2) until the juice runs. Plums bottle and freeze well and make a useful jam.

SPICED PLUM TART   *Serves 4-6*

12 oz (350 g) sweet shortcrust pastry
$1\frac{1}{2}$ lb (675 g) plums
7 oz (175 g) sugar
1 tsp ground cinnamon
1 tbsp lemon juice
1 oz (25 g) butter

Roll out the pastry to line a 9 in (22.5 cm) pie plate, fluting the edges. Cut the plums in half and take out the stones. Put the fruit cut side down on the pastry. Mix the sugar and cinnamon and sprinkle half on the plums. Pour over the lemon juice and dot with the butter. Bake at 350°F/180°C/gas mark 4 for 40 minutes. Sprinkle with the remaining sugar and cinnamon. Serve hot or cold with cream.

Raspberries

Fresh raspberries are delicious served plainly with caster sugar and cream, and they mix well with other summer fruit such as strawberries, red-currants and peaches. A pinch of cinnamon brings out the flavour of raspberry dishes and so does a pinch of ground coffee in the accompanying pastry. Raspberries lose their flavour and shape when they are stewed and are not good for bottling. They freeze very well and make excellent jam and jelly.

RASPBERRY PUDDING   *Serves 4*

1 lb (450 g) raspberries
4 oz (100 g) caster sugar
1 oz (25 g) butter
4 oz (100 g) fresh white breadcrumbs
3 large eggs

Put the raspberries into a thick saucepan with the sugar and heat gently until the juice runs. Sieve the fruit and juice and return to the saucepan with the butter. Reheat gently and pour over the bread-crumbs. Leave to stand for 30 minutes. Beat the eggs lightly and mix in with the raspberry purée. Put into an ovenware dish and bake at 350°F/ 180°C/gas mark 4 for 1 hour. Serve hot or cold dusted with icing sugar and with cream. Frozen raspberries may be used, and should be thawed before use.

Rhubarb

Young pink sticks of rhubarb are the best to use for pies and puddings while the older thicker ones are excellent for making into jams and chutneys. The best way to cook rhubarb is to cut the sticks into short pieces and cook them in a saucepan or in the oven in a little raspberry or plum jam or marmalade. This colours the rhubarb and supplements the flavour far better than the traditional water and sugar. Only cook the fruit until it is tender, but still keeps a good shape. Rhubarb mixes well with oranges and with dried fruit, and the flavour is delicious with the addition of candied angelica or ginger.

RHUBARB FOOL *Serves 4*

1 lb (450 g) rhubarb
8 oz (225 g) marmalade
$\frac{1}{2}$ pt (300 ml) single cream
A pinch of ground ginger

Cut the rhubarb in pieces and simmer with the marmalade until tender. Sieve and cool. Stir in the cream and ginger and serve chilled.

Strawberries

Always eat strawberries freshly gathered but do not hull them until immediately before eating. Some people eat them with salt, or a shake of pepper, but the traditional caster sugar and cream are probably the most popular accompaniments to strawberries. Gourmets swear by serving them in orange juice or with claret, port or Champagne poured over them. The strawberry changes in both texture and flavour when cooked but strawberry jam is always a great favourite. Great care must be taken when freezing strawberries to achieve a good result.

STRAWBERRY SHORTCAKE *Serves 4-6*

8 oz (225 g) plain flour
2 tsp baking powder
$\frac{1}{4}$ tsp salt
4 oz (100 g) butter
4 fl oz (100 ml) milk
$1\frac{1}{2}$ lb (675 g) strawberries
4 oz (100 g) sugar
$1\frac{1}{2}$ oz (40 g) butter
$\frac{1}{4}$ pt (150 ml) double cream

Sift together the flour, baking powder and salt and work in the butter thoroughly. Lightly mix in the milk to make a soft dough and divide into two pieces. Put each portion into an 8 in (20 cm) sandwich tin and prick with a fork. Bake at 400°F/ 200°C/gas mark 6 for 15 minutes. Meanwhile, hull the strawberries. Lightly crush half of them and

sprinkle with sugar. When shortcakes are cooked spread butter on top of one. Cover with crushed berries and top with second shortcake. Cool slightly then top with whipped cream and whole berries.

Pastry

The difference between one type of pastry and another depends on the proportion of fat to flour, and on the way the action of the gluten is controlled. For short pastry the gluten is broken up by rubbing the fat into the flour so that each grain is covered and the fat keeps the grains separate when the water is added. For flaky, rough puff and puff pastry, the results must be layers of flakes. This is achieved by adding the fat in pieces, rather than rubbing it in; and by repeated folding and rolling, layers of dough are covered by layers of fat.

Plain flour is recommended for short pastry, and strong plain flour (bread flour) gives excellent results when making flaky, rough puff and puff pastry.

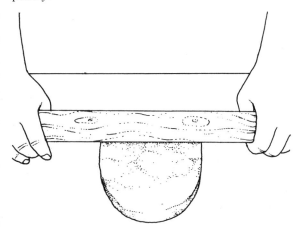

Pastry may be made with butter, margarine or lard, or specially formulated white fat. Hard block margarine used on its own gives excellent results as it does not melt as quickly as the other fats at the high temperature used for baking pastry, so that the flakes or crumbs of pastry remain light and separate. Many people like to use a mixture of hard margarine and lard, which gives a more tender result. Soft margarine should not be used for pastry as it will give a 'cakey' result. Be careful to use the proportion of fat to flour stated in a recipe; too little fat makes pastry hard, and too much makes it unmanageable and very short. The fat should be just soft enough, but not too soft, to rub in easily using the tips of the fingers and thumbs, until the mixture looks like fine breadcrumbs. If pastry is over-rubbed, the pastry will break when rolled out. You will recognise that the mixture is over-rubbed when the 'crumbs' start to become bigger rather than smaller. The water added to pastry should be ice-cold, and usually 2 table-spoons is enough for 8 oz (225 g) flour. Sprinkle in all the water at once to give a firm, but not sticky, dough. If the pastry is too dry, it will crack.

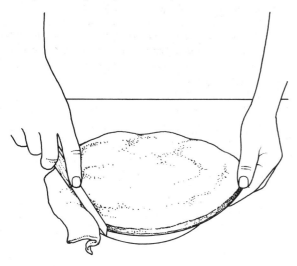

Everything used for making pastry should be cool, including your hands, the mixing bowl and the ingredients, and the kitchen atmosphere. Pastry should be handled as little as possible so that it does not become warm, and fat may be worked into the flour with a knife or special pastry mixer. Shape the pastry into a round, square or oblong, according to requirements, before rolling out, and then roll evenly and quickly in one direction only. If covering a pie, make the pastry a little larger than required and trim it when in place, as pastry which is stretched will shrink away from the edge of the dish when cooking. To avoid tears, lift rolled pastry by rolling it loosely around the rolling pin and raising it into place.

Pastry may be made very successfully with an electric mixer or a food processor. Watch the mixing carefully, as the pastry can quickly become over-worked with tough results. When using a food mixer, switch off immediately the water has been incorporated and a ball of dough formed.

Always preheat the oven for about 15 minutes to the temperature stated in the recipe. Put a baking sheet into the oven to heat at the same time. Put a flan tin or pie plate directly onto this as it will help to spread heat evenly and ensure a crisp base to the pastry. When lining a flan ring or pie plate, be sure

to press the pastry firmly against the base to push out air, or the air will expand in the hot oven and push the pastry up through the filling. If pastry browns too quickly, cover with a sheet of foil or greaseproof paper. Bake pastry until golden brown, and then cool items such as tartlets, flan cases and vol-au-vents on a wire tray so that steam escapes and the pastry remains crisp.

Knocking up means sealing the edges of pastry by dampening one edge with water, pressing lightly to the other side to seal them then sharply tapping with the back of a knife. The edges may then be cut at short intervals with a knife, pressed with a fork, or pinched between finger and thumb to provide a decorative finish.

Baking blind is a technique often required by a recipe, and it means cooking a pastry case without filling. The uncooked case should be lined with foil or greaseproof paper and filled with baking beans or crusts of bread to prevent the bottom rising during cooking. Alternatively the base may be pricked with a fork before lining with foil and then beans or crusts are not needed. Take out the weighting ingredients and lining 5 minutes before the end of cooking time so that the base becomes firm and crisp.

Baking glazes make pastry look more appetising. For savoury pies, brush the top evenly with an egg wash made from equal quantities of egg and water and a pinch of salt which heightens the glaze. Egg yolks only may be used in the mixture, or a whole egg. For sweet pies, brush the top with milk or water and sprinkle with caster sugar before baking. Alternatively, egg white may be brushed on and sprinkled with caster sugar 10 minutes before the end of baking.

EMERGENCY PASTRY

Prepared pastry may be kept in a refrigerator for 3 days or in the freezer for 3 months. It must be wrapped in polythene or foil to prevent the surface drying. Rubbed-in fat and flour may be kept in a sealed polythene bag or jar in the refrigerator for 3 months. It should be taken out of the refrigerator for 30 minutes before water is added and the pastry completed.

WHOLEMEAL PASTRY

Pastry made with brown flour may be used for all pastry dishes, but it is particularly good for meat pies and sausage rolls. It is best made with 81 per cent flour, or a mixture of 81 per cent and 100 per cent wholemeal flour (see page 12 for definitions of flour). One hundred per cent wholemeal flour on its own has a high proportion of coarse bran and is therefore not so good for pastry. Use the same proportion of fat and flour as for white pastry, but add water carefully as wholemeal flour soaks up a great deal of moisture, and too much liquid will make the pastry hard and biscuit-like.

The following basic pastry recipes give a guide to the proportion of ingredients and methods necessary for most recipes. To know the quantity which will result, simply add the total flour and fats and any other weighed ingredients such as sugar. Eight ounces (225 g) flour with half weight of fat will yield approximately 12 oz (350 g) pre-pared pastry; if 4 oz (100 g) cheese is added, there will be about 1 lb (450 g) cheese pastry. The recipes in this book specify the quantity of prepared pastry needed so that the ingredients may be easily calculated. In old recipe books, where, for instance, 8 oz (225 g) pastry is specified, it actually means the amount of pastry which can be made from 8 oz (225 g) flour, so that the quantity of pastry needed is in fact. nearer 12 oz (350 g).

The temperatures given in the basic pastry recipes are the ideal ones for preparing everyday dishes. In some composite recipes, temperatures may vary slightly according to the fillings being used.

Pastry Quantity Checklist

Dish	Made pastry quantity	Yield and size
Oval pie dish	8 oz (225 g) covers	1×1 pt (600 ml) dish
	10 oz (300 g) covers	$1 \times 1\frac{1}{2}$ pt (900 ml) dish
	12 oz (350 g) covers	1×2 pt (1 litre) dish
	1 lb (450 g) covers	1×3 pt (1.8 litre) dish
Pie plate	8 oz (225 g) lines *or* covers	1×7 in (17.5 cm) plate
	10 oz (300 g) lines *or* covers	1×9 in (22.5 cm) plate
	12 oz (350 g) lines *and* covers	1×7 in (17.5 cm) plate
	1 lb (450 g) lines *and* covers	1×9 in (22.5 cm) plate
Tartlets	12 oz (350 g) makes	$18 \times 2\frac{1}{2}$ in (6.75 cm) tarts
Flan ring	8 oz (225 g) lines	1×7 in (17.5 cm) ring
	10 oz (300 g) lines	1×8 in (20 cm) ring
		or
		1×6 in (15 cm) ring
		and
		$6 \times 2\frac{1}{2}$ in (6.75 cm) tarts

SHORTCRUST PASTRY

8 oz (225 g) plain flour
$\frac{1}{2}$ tsp salt
2 oz (50 g) hard margarine
2 oz (50 g) lard
2-3 tbsp cold water

Use for sweet and savoury pies, flans and tarts. Sift together the flour and salt and rub in the margarine and lard until the mixture is like fine breadcrumbs. Add the water and mix to a firm dough. Turn on to a lightly floured board and form into required shape. Roll out in one direction to required thickness. Bake at 425°F/220°C/gas mark 7 for 20-25 minutes for a pie or flan. When baking tartlets and thin pastry cases, bake at 400°F/200°C/gas mark 6 for 10-15 minutes.

SWEET SHORTCRUST PASTRY

6 oz (150 g) plain flour
$\frac{1}{4}$ tsp salt
3 oz (75 g) butter
1 oz (25 g) caster sugar
1 egg yolk
1 tbsp cold water

Use for sweet flans and tartlets. Sift together the flour and salt. Rub in the butter until the mixture resembles fine breadcrumbs. Stir in the sugar evenly. Mix the egg yolk and water together and add to the flour, mixing to a firm dough. Shape on a lightly floured board and roll out carefully as this is a delicate pastry. Roll out to required shape. Bake at 400°F/200°C/gas mark 6 for 20-25 minutes; small tartlets will only take 10-15 minutes.

CHEESE PASTRY

8 oz (225 g) plain flour
$\frac{1}{2}$ tsp salt
A pinch of cayenne pepper
4 oz (100 g) hard margarine or butter
4 oz (100 g) finely grated hard cheese
1 egg yolk
2 tsp cold water

Use for savoury pies and flans. Use dry, finely grated cheese with a strong flavour (a mixture of Cheddar and Parmesan is good). Soft, sticky or coarsely grated cheese will not mix evenly and makes the pastry difficult to handle. Sift together the flour, salt and cayenne pepper. Rub in fat until the mixture is like fine breadcrumbs. Add the grated cheese and stir in to mix thoroughly. Mix the egg yolk and water together and add to the flour, and mix to a firm dough. Shape on a lightly floured board and roll out. Bake at 425°F/220°C/gas mark 7 for 20-25 minutes.

Rich Pastries

Flaky, puff and rough puff pastry are a little more difficult to make than shortcrust, but they are delicious and very worth while for savoury and sweet dishes. Use a firm fat, i.e. hard margarine or butter, in the proportion given in the basic recipe. When the dough has been formed, knead the pastry until it is elastic. Roll it out evenly, keeping the pastry straight at the sides and ends, and if the fat breaks through, put the pastry in a cold place so that it hardens again. Roll rich pastry fairly thinly so that it will expand well and cook through and refrigerate for at least 30 minutes before baking. If the pastry has to be cooled during making, be sure that it is covered with foil or polythene to prevent drying out. Bake in a hot oven at first to expand the air in the pastry and make it rise, and then cover and reduce the heat until any filling is cooked. If using up trimmings of rich pastry, do not squeeze them together, but keep flat and place one on top of the other before pressing with a rolling pin, folding, and rolling them out lightly to the required shape.

If rich pastry leaks fat, the dough is too soft, or the fat was too soft during rolling and folding. The rolling and folding may have been uneven, or the oven too cool. A cool oven can also result in badly risen pastry. If the pastry is soggy in the middle, it means too high an oven, under-baking, or insufficient fat rolled in. Hard, tough pastry can mean that it was over-handled, or not kept cool during rolling. Too much water, insufficient fat, or too much flour used during rolling can have the same effect. When pastry does not rise well with light flakes, it may be because the flour dough was too stiff and badly kneaded, the fat was unevenly distributed, or too warm, or the pastry has not been rested between rollings.

PUFF PASTRY

1 lb (450 g) plain flour
1 tsp salt
1 lb (450 g) hard margarine
2 tsp lemon juice
$\frac{1}{2}$ pt (300 ml) less 1 tbsp cold water

Sift together flour and salt. Divide fat into four, and rub one-quarter into flour. Mix to a dough with lemon juice and water. Knead on a lightly floured board until smooth. Cover and leave for 15 minutes in a cool place. Form the remaining fat into a slab 5 in (12.5 cm) square on a floured board. Roll dough into a rectangle 11 × 6 in (27.5 × 15 cm). Put the piece of fat at the top end of the dough, leaving a margin about $\frac{1}{2}$ in (1.25 cm) along the sides and top. Fold remaining dough over, placing top ends together, and brush off surplus flour.

Turn pastry so that the folded edge is on left-hand side. Press three open edges together with a rolling pin to seal them. Press dough across about 5 times with rolling pin to flatten. Roll out to 12 × 6 in (30 × 15 cm), keeping edges straight.

Fold pastry in three by folding bottom third upwards and top third downwards and over to cover it. Turn so that folded edge is again on the left. Seal edges and roll as before. Fold, turn, and seal edges. Cover and leave in a cold place for 20 minutes.

Roll out four more times, always turning and

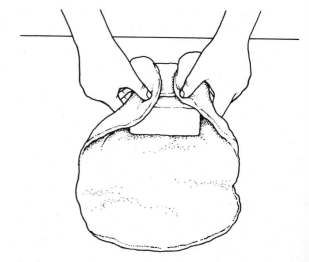

sealing dough as before, and resting 20 minutes between each rolling. If any patches of fat show, give dough another rolling. Rest dough before finally rolling into place. Bake at 425°F/220°C/gas mark 7 for 20-25 minutes, according to recipe.

ROUGH PUFF PASTRY

8 oz (225 g) plain flour
$\frac{1}{2}$ tsp salt
3 oz (75 g) lard
3 oz (75 g) hard margarine
7 tbsp cold water

Sift the flour and salt into a basin. Cut up the lard and margarine roughly in $\frac{1}{4}$ in (6 mm) cubes. Add to the flour and mix to a soft dough with water. Roll out on a lightly floured board into a rectangle 12 × 6 in (30 × 15 cm). Fold the bottom third upwards and top third downwards and over it. Turn the dough so that the folded edge is on the left-hand side and seal the edges. Roll, fold and seal edges twice more, keeping folded edge always to the left. If the pastry becomes too soft, chill between rollings. Roll out to required size. Bake at 425°F/220°C/gas mark 7 for 20-25 minutes, according to recipe.

FLAKY PASTRY

1 lb (450 g) plain flour
1 tsp salt
12 oz (350 g) hard margarine
1 tsp lemon juice
$\frac{1}{2}$ pt (300 ml) less 1 tbsp cold water

Divide the fat into four portions. Sift the flour and salt together and rub in one-quarter of the fat. Mix to a dough with lemon juice and water. Roll out dough into a rectangle 12 × 6 in (30 × 15 cm), keeping the edges straight. Cut one piece of fat into small pieces and place in lines over top two-thirds of dough, leaving margin of $\frac{1}{2}$ in (1.25 cm) around edges. Fold bottom uncovered third upwards and top third downwards and over to cover it. Turn dough so that folded edge is on left-hand side. Press edges together with rolling pin to seal. Roll out into a rectangle 12 × 6 in (30 × 15 cm), and place on second portion of fat as before. Fold, turn and seal edges. Wrap and rest in a cool place for 20 minutes. Roll out again, using remaining fat in same way, and fold, turn and seal. Repeat the folding and rolling again without fat, then fold and wrap before leaving to rest for 20 minutes. Roll out to required size. Bake at 425°F/220°C/gas mark 7 for 20-25 minutes, according to recipe.

RABBIT PIE   *Serves 6*

1 large rabbit
Salt and pepper
1 tbsp chopped fresh parsley
1 small onion
12 oz (350 g) streaky bacon
4 oz (100 g) pork sausagemeat
$\frac{1}{2}$ oz (15 g) plain flour
$\frac{1}{2}$ pt (300 ml) chicken or beef stock
12 oz (350 g) made shortcrust pastry

Put the rabbit joints into a bowl and pour on cold salted water. Leave to stand for 4 hours, drain and dry on kitchen paper. Preheat oven to 425°F/220°C/gas mark 7. Put the rabbit pieces into a 2 pt (1 litre) pie dish. Sprinkle with salt, pepper and parsley. Chop the onion and bacon finely and sprinkle on the rabbit. Form the sausagemeat into 8 small balls and tuck them in between the rabbit joints. Mix the flour with a little stock to a paste and then stir in remaining stock. Pour over the rabbit. Cover with pastry and bake at 425°F/220°C/gas mark 7 for 15 minutes. Reduce heat to 375°F/190°C/gas mark 5 and continue baking for 1 hour. If the pastry becomes very brown, cover with a piece of foil after the first 30 minutes.

SPINACH TART   *Serves 6*

12 oz (350 g) made shortcrust pastry
2 lb (1 kg) fresh spinach
3 oz (75 g) butter
$\frac{1}{4}$ pt (150 ml) double cream
Salt and pepper
3 oz (75 g) Gruyère cheese

Preheat oven to 400°F/200°C/gas mark 6. Line a 9 in (22.5 cm) flan tin with pastry. Prick the pastry well and bake at 400°F/200°C/gas mark 6 for 15 minutes. Remove stems from the spinach and wash the leaves well. Put the leaves into a pan with only the water which clings to the leaves; cover and simmer for 15 minutes. Press out all the moisture. Soften the butter slightly without melting. Stir butter and cream into the spinach and season well with salt and pepper. Pour into the pastry case. Cut the cheese into small thin slices and arrange on top of the spinach. Bake at 400°F/200°C/gas mark 6 for 20 minutes. Serve very hot.

STEAK AND KIDNEY PIE   *Serves 6*

1 oz (25 g) plain flour
Salt and pepper
1½ lb (675 g) chuck steak
8 oz (225 g) ox kidney
1 oz (25 g) lard
1 medium onion
4 oz (100 g) button mushrooms
1 pt (600 ml) beef stock
12 oz (350 g) made puff or flaky pastry
Beaten egg for glazing

Put flour with plenty of salt and pepper into a polythene or paper bag. Cut the steak and kidney in cubes and place in the bag. Shake until the meat is coated with flour. Lift out the meat, reserving flour in the bag. Melt the lard and fry the chopped onion over low heat until soft and golden. Add meat and brown quickly on all sides. Cut mushrooms in half and add to pan. Cook for 1 minute. Stir in reserved flour and add stock. Bring to the boil, cover and simmer gently for 1½ hours until the meat is tender. Put into a 2 pt (1 litre) pie dish and pour in enough of the gravy to come halfway up the pie dish. Roll out pastry all round to fit the lightly-greased rim of the dish. Moisten the top of this strip with a little water, and put on the pastry lid. Seal by pinching together between thumb and finger. Brush with beaten egg and bake at 425°F/220°C/gas mark 7 for 20 minutes. Reduce heat to 350°F/180°C/gas mark 4 and continue baking for 20 minutes. Serve with any surplus gravy which has been reheated. A few raw oysters or mussels (which may be frozen or canned) may be added before the pastry is put on to the pie, and will give added richness and flavour.

ONION TART   *Serves 6*

12 oz (350 g) made shortcrust pastry
1½ lb (675 g) onions
2 oz (50 g) butter
1 tbsp olive oil
3 eggs
3 tbsp double cream
3 oz (75 g) grated Gruyère cheese
Salt and pepper
A pinch of nutmeg
6 black olives

Preheat oven to 400°F/200°C/gas mark 6. Line a 9 in (22.5 cm) flan tin with pastry. Prick the pastry well and bake at 400°F/200°C/gas mark 6 for 15 minutes. Peel the onions and cut them into thin slices. Heat the butter and oil in a large saucepan, until the butter has melted. Add the onions, cover and cook over low heat for 20 minutes until soft and yellow. Take off the heat. Beat the eggs and cream together and beat into the onions. Add the cheese and mix well. Season with salt and freshly ground black pepper and nutmeg. Put into the pastry case and arrange olives on top. Bake at 375°F/190°C/gas mark 5 for 30 minutes. Eat hot or cold.

INDIVIDUAL CHICKEN PIES   *Serves 6*

12 oz (350 g) made puff pastry
1 lb (450 g) chicken
4 rashers streaky bacon
4 oz (100 g) button mushrooms
4 hard-boiled eggs
1 medium onion
1 tbsp wine vinegar
1 tsp chopped parsley
½ tsp salt
½ tsp Worcestershire sauce
Beaten egg for glazing

Cut the flesh from the chicken and chop into small neat pieces. Put the carcass into a saucepan, cover with water, put on a lid and simmer for 1 hour. Preheat oven to 425°F/220°C/gas mark 7. Put the chicken pieces into a bowl, and mix with chopped bacon, sliced mushrooms, chopped eggs, finely chopped onion, vinegar, parsley, salt and sauce. Divide between 6 individual pie dishes. Half-fill each dish with the stock made from the carcass. Cover each dish with pastry, and brush with a little beaten egg. Cut a small slit in the top of each lid. Bake at 425°F/220°C/gas mark 7 for 20 minutes. Reduce heat to 350°F/180°C/gas mark 4 and continue baking for 40 minutes.

STEAK PASTIES   *Serves 6*

1 lb (450 g) made shortcrust pastry
8 oz (225 g) minced raw lean beef
6 oz (150 g) streaky bacon
4 oz (100 g) lamb's kidneys
1 large onion
Salt and pepper
½ tsp Worcestershire sauce
Beaten egg for glazing

Preheat oven to 425°F/220°C/gas mark 7. Roll out the pastry and cut into six 7 in (17.5 cm) rounds. Put the beef into a bowl. Chop the bacon, kidneys and onion finely. Mix into the steak with the salt, pepper and Worcestershire sauce. Put the mixture on to half of each round and fold over pastry. Pinch the edges together. Brush the top surface with beaten egg. Place on a lightly greased baking sheet. Bake at 425°F/220°C/gas mark 7 for 15 minutes. Reduce heat to 350°F/180°C/gas mark 4 and continue baking for 45 minutes. Serve hot or cold.

ALMOND TARTLETS   *Makes 18*

8 oz (225 g) made shortcrust pastry
3 tbsp jam
2 egg whites
5 oz (125 g) caster sugar
4 oz (100 g) ground almonds

Preheat oven to 350°F/180°C/gas mark 4. Roll out the pastry and cut into 18 rounds to fit small tartlet tins. Put a little jam at the bottom of each pastry case. Whisk the egg whites to stiff peaks and fold in the sugar and almonds. Put on top of the jam in each pastry case. Bake at 350°F/180°C/gas mark 4 for 20 minutes.

BAKED LEMON CHEESECAKE   *Serves 6-8*

8 oz (225 g) made shortcrust pastry
2 oz (50 g) butter
2 oz (50 g) caster sugar
8 oz (225 g) cream cheese
1 oz (25 g) plain flour
2 oz (50 g) seedless raisins
1 lemon
2 tbsp single cream
3 eggs
1 oz (25 g) icing sugar

Preheat oven to 400°F/200°C/gas mark 6. Line a loose-bottomed 9 in (22.5 cm) flan tin with pastry. Cream butter, sugar and cream cheese together until light and fluffy. Work in the flour, raisins, grated rind and lemon juice and cream. Separate eggs, and beat the egg yolks into the cheese mixture. Whisk the egg whites to stiff peaks and fold into the mixture. Spoon into the pastry case. Bake at 400°F/200°C/gas mark 6 for 50 minutes until well-risen, golden and springy to the touch. Cool in the tin and remove carefully, placing the tin base on a serving plate. Dust the top with sieved icing sugar.

TREACLE CREAM TART   *Serves 4-6*

8 oz (225 g) made shortcrust pastry
8 oz (225 g) golden syrup
2 oz (50 g) butter
1 egg
5 tbsp single cream
$\frac{1}{2}$ tsp grated lemon rind

Preheat oven to 400°F/200°C/gas mark 6. Line an 8 in (20 cm) flan tin with pastry. Put the syrup and butter into a pan and warm gently until the butter has melted. Break the egg into a bowl and mix lightly with the cream and lemon rind. Pour in the syrup mixture and beat well together. Pour into the pastry case. Bake at 400°F/200°C/gas mark 6 for 30 minutes. This is very good hot or cold.

DEEP APPLE PIE   *Serves 4-6*

12 oz (350 g) made shortcrust pastry
$1\frac{1}{2}$ lb (675 g) cooking apples
3 oz (75 g) granulated sugar
$\frac{1}{2}$ oz (15 g) plain flour
$\frac{1}{4}$ tsp ground cloves
$\frac{1}{2}$ tsp ground cinnamon
1 tbsp cold water
1 oz (25 g) butter
$\frac{1}{2}$ oz (15 g) caster sugar
A pinch of ground cinnamon

Preheat oven to 425°F/220°C/gas mark 7. Peel and core the apples and cut them into thin even slices. Place in a deep $1\frac{1}{2}$ pt (900 ml) pie dish and sprinkle with granulated sugar, flour, cloves and cinnamon. Turn the apples with a spoon so that they are well coated with the sugar mixture. Sprinkle with water and dot with flakes of butter. Roll out the pastry to cover the dish and overlap. Trim off surplus and place a strip of pastry all round the greased rim of the dish. Damp the top edge of this pastry with a little water and place the pastry lid on top. Finish the edge of the lid by pressing lightly with a fork and use any trimmings to make decorative leaves and fix to lid with a little water. Bake at 425°F/220°C/gas mark 7 for 15 minutes. Reduce heat to 350°F/180°C/gas mark 4 and continue baking for 25 minutes. Mix the caster sugar and cinnamon and sprinkle on the pie just before serving.

Banbury apple pie
Omit cloves. Add 2 oz (50 g) chopped mixed candied peel, 3 oz (75 g) currants.

Blackberry and apple pie
Add 8 oz (225 g) blackberries and additional 2 oz (50 g) sugar.

Four fruit pie
Instead of apples, use 8 oz (225 g) desert pears, 8 oz (225 g) blackberries, 8 oz (225 g) cooking apples and 12 oz (350 g) plums. Peel, core and slice pears and apples, and stone plums.

SPECIAL MINCEMEAT PIE   *Serves 6*

12 oz (350 g) made shortcrust pastry
1 lb (450 g) fruit mincemeat
8 oz (225 g) eating apples
2 oz (50 g) stem ginger
2 tbsp fine white breadcrumbs
Grated rind of 1 orange
Grated rind of 1 lemon
$\frac{1}{2}$ oz (15 g) caster sugar

Preheat oven to 425°F/220°C/gas mark 7. Line a lightly greased 8 in (20 cm) pie plate with three-quarters of the pastry. Put the mincemeat into a bowl. Peel and core the apples and chop them finely. Chop the stem ginger into small pieces. Mix the apples, ginger, crumbs and rind into the mincemeat and then put onto the pastry. Roll out the remaining pastry to form a lid and place over the filling. Seal the edges by pressing with a fork or pinching with thumb and finger. Brush the top with water and dust with caster sugar. Bake at 435°F/220°C/gas mark 7 for 15 minutes and then reduce heat to 350°F/180°C/gas mark 4 for 15 minutes. Serve hot or cold with cream or ice-cream.

APRICOT PIE   *Serves 4-6*

12 oz (350 g) made shortcrust pastry
1$\frac{1}{2}$ lb (675 g) fresh apricots
6 oz (150 g) granulated sugar
$\frac{3}{4}$ pt (450 ml) water
1 egg white
$\frac{1}{2}$ oz (15 g) caster sugar

Preheat oven to 425°F/220°C/gas mark 7. Cut the apricots in half and remove the stones. Crack two of the stones and remove the kernels. Put the apricots into a 1$\frac{1}{2}$ pt (900 ml) pie dish with the kernels, which will give an almond flavour. Put the sugar and water into a pan and heat gently until the sugar has dissolved. Simmer for 5 minutes and pour over the apricots. Leave until cold. Roll out the pastry to cover the dish and overlap. Trim off surplus and place a strip of pastry all around the greased rim of the dish. Damp the top edge of this pastry with a little water and place the pastry lid on top. Finish the edge by pressing lightly with a fork, or pinch edges between finger and thumb. Bake at 425°F/220°C/gas mark 7 for 15 minutes. Reduce heat to 350°F/180°C/gas mark 4 for 15 minutes. Whisk the egg white to stiff peaks and brush over the pastry. Sprinkle with caster sugar. Continue baking for 10 minutes. This pie is particularly good served just warm, or cold, with cream or ice-cream.

Cakes and Biscuits

Although many people do not want to makes cakes for teatime, it is useful to have a few basic recipes, as some types of cake form part of other sweet courses.

Fresh, high quality ingredients are essential for cakes, to give good flavour, colour and texture. Eggs should be used at room temperature, and when separated, the whites must be completely free of yolk or the volume of beaten white will be less, and the texture will change. Butter and margarine may be substituted for each other. Butter gives the best flavour, and unsalted butter is best for very delicately flavoured cakes. Margarine gives a light texture and the flavour is masked in strongly flavoured cakes such as chocolate or coffee.

Caster sugar is best for most cakes, as the fine grains dissolve quickly in whisked and creamed mixtures. Brown sugar gives a rich flavour and colour to gingerbread and fruit cakes. Flour should be plain when specified, and this is very important in rich mixtures which require little raising agent.

All ingredients for cake making are best used at room temeprature so that they are easily and evenly mixed. The basis of all methods is to incorporate air through beating or whisking, so it is important not to knock out this air again when finishing off the mixture. Final ingredients should be folded in with a knife or metal spoon, using a sharp clean action like cutting a cake, lifting the heavier substances from the bottom of the bowl. Lighter mixtures should be folded into heavier ones, and flour into creamed mixtures so that air is not pressed out.

The consistency of mixtures is very important

and often specified in recipes. A soft dropping consistency means that the mixture should be too stiff to pour, but will drop from a spoon without being shaken. A stiff dropping consistency means that the mixture is too soft and sticky to handle, but stiff enough to keep its shape when shaken from a spoon.

All cakes must be baked at the specified temperature, in the centre of the oven. If the correct tin size is not used, the depth of the mixture will affect cooking time. A cooked cake should be well-risen, golden and firm but springy when pressed lightly with a finger. A thin skewer or knife will come out clean if used to pierce the cake when the specified cooking time has expired. A cooked cake will also shrink slightly from the edges of the baking tin. Cakes should be left to firm up for a few minutes before being turned out of the tin to cool on a wire rack; some rich fruit cakes are best left in the tin until cool as they break easily if turned out too quickly.

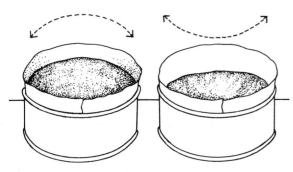

Successful & failed cakes

Gingerbread is made by melting the soft ingredients before adding flour, eggs, etc. Most other cakes are made by the rubbed in or creamed methods. The introduction of soft margarine has encouraged the use of the one-step method in which all the ingredients are placed in a bowl together and beaten for a short time before baking. The rubbed in method is used for plain cakes, and the fat is cut into small pieces and added to the sieved dry ingredients. The mixture is rubbed together with the fingertips until the texture is like fine breadcrumbs, and then the liquids are added and beaten well. In a creamed mixture, the fat should be soft but not melted and must be beaten until soft and light with a wooden spoon or mixer. When the sugar is added and beaten, the mixture will be very light and fluffy. Eggs are added alternately with flour to prevent the mixture curdling.

SCONES   *Makes 12-15*

Scones are quickly made and economical. They may be served freshly baked and warm, but they freeze well, so it is worth making a large batch while the oven is on. When they have been frozen, they can be reheated in a moderate oven (350°F/ 180°C/gas mark 4) for 5 minutes while still frozen, and will be exactly like freshly baked scones.

Measure ingredients carefully, especially the liquid. If too little is used the scones will be small and close; and if too much is used, they will be heavy and doughy. Sour milk makes particularly light scones. The dough before baking should be soft and elastic, and it is a good idea to mix with a knife so that air is retained in the flour. Knead the mixture very lightly with the fingertips for about 30 seconds. This will give a smooth dough, but over-kneading gives tough, hard scones. Roll out the dough very lightly to $\frac{1}{2}$ in (1.25 cm) thickness as they will be like biscuits if rolled out any thinner.

8 oz (225 g) plain flour
2 heaped tsp baking powder
$\frac{1}{2}$ tsp salt
2 oz (50 g) margarine or butter
$\frac{1}{4}$ pt (150 ml) milk

Preheat oven to 425°F/220°C/gas mark 7. Sieve the flour, baking powder and salt together in a bowl. Cut the fat into small pieces and rub into the flour with the tips of the fingers until the mixture looks like breadcrumbs. Add the milk and mix with a knife to a soft dough. Knead and then roll out lightly on a floured board to $\frac{1}{2}$ in (1.25 cm) thickness. Cut into 2 in (5 cm) rounds with a cutter. Placed on a greased baking sheet so that they just touch. The scones will then rise evenly and have soft sides. Press any remaining pieces of dough together, roll out again and cut into rounds and place on the baking sheet. Brush the scones lightly with a little extra milk. Bake at 425°F/220°C/gas mark 7 for 15 minutes. Cool on a wire rack.

Wholemeal scones
Replace 4 oz (100 g) white flour with the same quantity of wholemeal flour. Add 1 oz (25 g) sugar if liked.

Cheese scones
Add 2 oz (50 g) grated cheese, pinch of mustard powder and pinch of cayenne pepper to white or wholemeal flour.

Fruit scones

Add 1 oz (25 g) sugar and 2 oz (50 g) mixed dried fruit, or seedless raisins or sultanas.

DROP SCONES   *Makes 36*

Sometimes known as Scotch Pancakes or Flap-jacks, these are like small, thick round pancakes. They may be eaten with butter and jam, honey or syrup or served with maple syrup or with bacon. They are cooked on a griddle (girdle) which is a thick flat metal plate, or in a thick frying pan, which should be placed over moderate heat and brushed lightly with melted lard or oil. As soon as they are cooked, they should be placed on a clean cloth, and covered with another one. This keeps the scones warm and moist until served, and they are best eaten when freshly cooked.

8 oz (225 g) plain flour
3 heaped tsp baking powder
A pinch of salt
1 oz (25 g) caster sugar
1 egg
7 fl oz (200 ml) milk

Sieve the flour, baking powder and salt into a bowl. Stir in the sugar. Beat the egg lightly with the milk. Pour gradually into the flour, stirring all the time with a wooden spoon and then beating until the mixture is creamy and smooth. Place the griddle or frying pan over moderate heat and brush lightly with melted lard or oil. Drop a tablespoonful of batter on to the hot surface and follow with a further tablespoonful, keeping them well apart. Cook for about 2 minutes until the tops of the scones have set and are covered with bubbles on top. Turn with a palette knife and cook for 2 minutes on the other side. The scones should be golden brown on both sides. Place on a clean cloth and cover with another one. Continue until all the batter has been used.

FATLESS (WHISKED) SPONGE

3 eggs
3 oz (75 g) caster sugar
3 oz (75 g) plain flour
A pinch of salt
Jam for filling
Caster sugar

Preheat the oven at 350°F/180°C/gas mark 4. Grease and base-line two 7 in (17.5 cm) sponge tins and sprinkle lightly with caster sugar and flour, which will give a slight 'crust' to the finished cake.

Put the eggs and sugar into a bowl and place it over a pan of simmering water. Whisk until light, thick and fluffy. If an electric mixer is used, it is not necessary to use this heating method. Take the bowl from the heat, and continue beating until the mixture is cool. Sieve the flour and salt together and fold into the mixture with a metal spoon. Do not beat again, otherwise the air will be knocked out of the mixture. Divide the mixture between the tins and bake in the centre of the oven for 30 minutes. When the cakes are cooked, they will be pale gold in colour and will have slightly shrunk from the edges of the tins. Turn out on a wire cake rack to cool. Fill with jam and sprinkle caster sugar on the top of the cake. A fatless sponge is best eaten freshly made as it will not keep well in a tin or freezer. It is not suitable for added flavourings such as chocolate.

VICTORIA SANDWICH

4 oz (100 g) butter
4 oz (100 g) caster sugar
2 eggs
4 oz (100 g) self-raising flour
Jam for filling
Caster or icing sugar

Preheat the oven at 350°F/180°C/gas mark 4. Grease and base-line two 7 in (17.5 cm) sponge tins. Have the fat slightly soft, but not melted before beginning to make the cake. Put the butter and sugar into a bowl and cream together until light and fluffy and almost white. Add the eggs one at a time, beating well. Sieve the flour and fold into the creamed mixture. Divide between the tins and bake in the centre of the oven for 30 minutes. Cool on a wire cake rack. Fill with jam and sprinkle with caster or sieved icing sugar.

ONE-STAGE SANDWICH CAKE

The one-stage method of cake making has been made possible by the development of soft margarine. This is a very quick way of making a cake by hand, or with an electric mixer or food processor. Because the margarine has a bland flavour, the mixture is particularly suitable for flavouring with chocolate, coffee, etc. and for finishing with butter icing.

6 oz (150 g) soft margarine
6 oz (150 g) caster sugar
3 eggs
6 oz (150 g) self-raising flour
$1\frac{1}{2}$ tsp baking powder

Preheat the oven at 350°F/180°C/gas mark 4. Put all the ingredients into a bowl and beat hard for about 3 minutes until the mixture is very light, soft and creamy. Divide the mixture between two greased and base-lined 7 in (17.5 cm) sponge tins and bake in the centre of the oven for 35 minutes. Cool on a wire cake rack. Fill the cake with jam and sprinkle with caster sugar or fill and top with butter icing.

Chocolate sandwich cake

Add 1 oz (25 g) cocoa powder and 2 tablespoons milk to the other ingredients. Either fill and top with chocolate butter icing *or* fill with raspberry or apricot jam and top with chocolate glacé icing.

Coffee sandwich cake

Add 1 tablespoon coffee essence to the other ingredients. Fill and top with coffee butter icing and decorate with hazelnuts or walnut halves.

Lemon or orange sandwich cake

Add 2 teaspoons grated lemon or orange rind to the other ingredients. Fill and top with lemon or orange butter icing.

PLAIN (RUBBED IN) CAKE

8 oz (225 g) plain flour
2 tsp baking powder
A pinch of salt
3 oz (75 g) butter or margarine
3 oz (75 g) sugar
1 egg
$\frac{1}{4}$ pt (150 ml) milk

Preheat the oven at 375°F/190°C/gas mark 5. Grease and line a 7 in (17.5 cm) round cake tin. Sieve the flour, baking powder and salt into a bowl. Cut the fat into small pieces and rub into the flour until the mixture is like coarse breadcrumbs. Stir in the sugar. Whisk the egg and milk together until just mixed, and gradually beat in the flour until the mixture has a soft dropping consistency. This means that a little will drop easily from a spoon when lifted in the air. Add flavourings or additional ingredients. Put into the prepared cake tin and bake in the centre of the oven for 50 minutes. Leave in the tin for 5 minutes, then turn on to a wire cake rack to cool.

Flavoured cake

Add a few drops of essence (vanilla, lemon, almond) or 1 teaspoon spice (cinnamon, ginger, mixed spice).

Fruit cake

Add 4 oz (100 g) mixed dried fruit.

Chocolate cake

Add 1 oz (25 g) cocoa powder.

RICH (CREAMED) CAKE

6 oz (150 g) butter or margarine
5 oz (125 g) caster sugar
8 oz (225 g) plain flour
1 tsp baking powder
3 eggs

Preheat the oven at 350°F/180°C/gas mark 4. Grease and line an 8 in (20 cm) round cake tin. Cream the fat and sugar until very light and fluffy. Sieve the flour and baking powder. Add a little flour to the creamed mixture and then 1 egg. Beat and add a little more flour with the next egg. Repeat and then fold in the remaining flour and flavouring or additional ingredients. Put into the tin and bake for $1\frac{1}{4}$ hours. Leave in the tin for 5 minutes, then turn onto a wire cake rack to cool.

Flavoured cake

Add a few drops of essence (vanilla, lemon, almond) or 1 teaspoon spice (cinnamon, ginger, mixed spice).

Fruit cake

Add 12 oz (350 g) mixed dried fruit.

Chocolate cake

Add 1 oz (25 g) cocoa powder.

CELEBRATION FRUIT CAKE

This cake will keep extremely well for at least 6 months in a tin, and is very good without icing. With the addition of almond icing and royal icing it makes an excellent cake for weddings and other celebrations.

8 oz (225 g) butter
8 oz (225 g) dark, soft brown sugar
1 tbsp black treacle
4 eggs
4 tbsp sherry or cold tea
Grated rind of 1 lemon
$\frac{1}{2}$ tsp vanilla essence
$\frac{1}{2}$ tsp almond essence
6 oz (150 g) plain flour
4 oz (100 g) self-raising flour
$\frac{1}{4}$ tsp salt
1 tsp ground mixed spice
A pinch of ground cinnamon
A pinch of ground nutmeg
12 oz (350 g) currants
12 oz (350 g) sultanas
8 oz (225 g) seedless raisins
2 oz (50 g) chopped mixed candied peel
2 oz (50 g) glacé cherries

Grease and line a 10 in (25 cm) round cake tin. Cream the butter and sugar until light and fluffy. In another bowl, put the treacle, eggs, liquid, lemon rind and essence. Beat with a wooden spoon only just enough to break up the eggs. Sift the flours, salt and spices into a third bowl. Add a little of the egg mixture to the fat alternately with the flour. Continue adding until all the egg and flour mixtures are used up. Do not beat the mixture but stir well until completely blended. Add the fruit, mixing just enough to distribute evenly. Put into the cake tin, level off the mixture with the back of a spoon, and leave to stand for 1 hour. Preheat the oven at 300°F/150°C/gas mark 2 and cook the cake for $4\frac{1}{2}$ hours. Leave in the tin until just warm, and then turn out on to a wire rack to cool.

GINGERBREAD

8 oz (225 g) margarine
8 oz (225 g) dark, soft brown sugar
8 oz (225 g) black treacle
12 oz (350 g) plain flour
4 tsp ground ginger
3 tsp ground cinnamon
2 eggs
$\frac{1}{2}$ pt (300 ml) milk
2 tsp bicarbonate of soda

Preheat the oven at 325°F/160°C/gas mark 3. Grease and line a 11 × 7 in (27.5 × 17.5 cm) rectangular tin. Put the margarine, sugar and treacle into a pan and warm together until the fat has melted. Sieve the flour and spices into a bowl. Stir in the warm melted mixture. Add the beaten egg and beat well. Warm the milk just to blood heat and stir in the soda. As the milk foams, pour it into the mixture and beat well. Pour into the tin, and bake in the centre of the oven for $1\frac{1}{2}$ hours. Cool in the tin for 5 minutes and then turn out on to a wire cake rack to cool.

WHOLEMEAL BISCUITS   *Makes 40*

These biscuits are suitable for eating with cheese. They are also good if the backs are coated with plain melted chocolate.

8 oz (225 g) wholemeal flour
4 oz (100 g) plain flour
$\frac{1}{2}$ tsp salt
3 oz (75 g) margarine
2 oz (50 g) lard
2 oz (50 g) light, soft brown sugar
1 egg
4 tbsp water

Preheat the oven at 350°F/180°C/gas mark 4. Sieve together the wholemeal and plain flour and salt. Cut the fat into small pieces and rub in until the mixture is like fine breadcrumbs. Mix in the sugar, beaten egg and water to give a soft dough. Roll out on a lightly floured board and cut into 2 in (5 cm) rounds with a plain cutter. Put on to a greased baking sheet and prick with a fork. Bake for 25 minutes. Lift off the baking sheet carefully on to a wire cake rack to cool.

SWEET BISCUITS   *Makes 40*

4 oz (100 g) butter or margarine
4 oz (100 g) caster sugar
1 egg
1 tbsp milk
$\frac{1}{2}$ tsp vanilla essence
8 oz (225 g) self-raising flour
$\frac{1}{2}$ tsp salt

Preheat the oven at 375°F/190°C/gas mark 5. Cream the butter and sugar until light and fluffy. Lightly beat the egg and milk together and add the essence. Sieve the flour with salt. Add the liquid mixture and flour alternately to the fat, beating until completely incorporated and mixed to a firm dough. Chill for 1 hour. Drop basic mixture in teaspoonfuls 1 in (2.5 cm) apart on a greased baking sheet, and press with a knife or fork dipped in cold water. Bake for 8 minutes, then lift off carefully on to a wire cake rack to cool. Leave plain or decorate with thin icing or sieved icing sugar.

If rolled biscuits are preferred add 2 oz (50 g) flour, chill and roll out to $\frac{1}{4}$ in (6 mm) before cutting into rounds or other shapes.

Chocolate biscuits
Add 2 oz (50 g) cocoa powder and bake at 325°F/160°C/gas mark 3.

Coconut biscuits
Add 2 oz (50 g) dessicated coconut.

Date biscuits
Add 2 oz (50 g) finely chopped dates.

Fruit biscuits
Add 2 oz (50 g) currants.

Ginger biscuits
Add 1 teaspoon ground ginger.

Lemon biscuits
Add 1 teaspoon grated lemon rind.

Nut biscuits
Add 2 oz (50 g) finely chopped nuts.

Spice biscuits
Add $\frac{1}{4}$ teaspoon each ground nutmeg and ground cinnamon.

MERINGUES   *Makes 8*

2 egg whites
A pinch of salt
4 oz (100 g) caster sugar

Preheat the oven at 250°F/120°C/gas mark $\frac{1}{2}$. Line a baking sheet with a piece of baking parchment. Put the egg whites into a bowl, making sure it is completely dry and free of fat, or else the egg whites will not become stiff and foamy. Whisk the egg whites and salt until the mixture stands in stiff peaks. It should be possible to hold the bowl upside-down without the mixture falling out or moving. Using a metal spoon, fold in the sugar very lightly. Spoon the mixture into 8 mounds on the baking sheet, rounding them slightly between two spoons. Bake for 2 hours. Remove carefully and cool on a wire cake rack. Just before serving, put meringues together in pairs with whipped cream or ice-cream. Meringues may be made in advance and stored in a tin or the freezer.

Brown sugar meringues
Use soft brown sugar instead of caster sugar. Put together with whipped cream and a little finely chopped crystallised ginger.

Meringue discs
Mark two 7 in (17.5 cm) circles on baking parchment. Spread the meringue mixture lightly on these circles. Bake as for small meringues and lift off carefully to cool on a rack. Just before serving, sandwich together with whipped cream and fruit, or ice-cream, or flavoured butter icing.

Choux Pastry

This pastry is used for savoury and sweet choux buns and for éclairs. It is very easy to make if ingredients are measured accurately and the method is followed exactly. It is most important that all the flour is tipped into the fat and water mixture at once; it is also important that the eggs are put in gradually so that the mixture remains at the right consistency, or it will become too soft to shape correctly and will remain flat when baked instead of forming light crisp cases full of air.

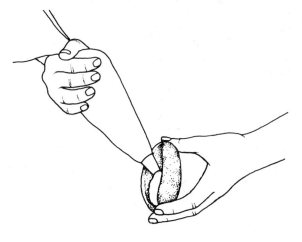

CHOUX BUNS
Makes 8 buns/éclairs or 16 small buns

2 oz (50 g) butter
$\frac{1}{4}$ pt (150 ml) water
$2\frac{1}{2}$ oz (65 g) plain flour
A pinch of salt
2 eggs

Preheat the oven at 400°F/200°C/gas mark 6. Put the butter and water into a pan and bring to the boil. Meanwhile, sieve the flour and salt on to a piece of greaseproof paper. As soon as the water mixture boils, tip in all the flour quickly and beat hard with a wooden spoon until smooth. Continue cooking over low heat for 2 minutes, stirring well until the mixture leaves the sides of the pan. Leave to cool for 15 minutes. Beat the eggs together and add a little at a time to the dough, beating well between each addition until the paste is smooth and glossy and stiff enough to stand in peaks when pulled with the back of a spoon. Do not grease a baking sheet, but hold under a running tap until damp. Spoon 8 heaps of mixture on to the baking sheet, leaving plenty of space between them. Bake for 30 minutes. Lift on to a wire cake rack and make a tiny hole in each bun so that the steam escapes. When cold, either split the buns, or make a slightly larger hole, and fill with whipped cream. This is most neatly done by piping in the cream. Sprinkle with sieved icing sugar, or coat with chocolate or coffee glacé icing.

Éclairs
Pipe mixture with plain $\frac{1}{2}$ in (1.25 cm) plain nozzle into 3 in (7.5 cm) lengths. When cold, proceed as for choux buns.

Profiteroles
Make buns half-size and cook for only 20 minutes. Fill with whipped cream or ice-cream and serve with chocolate sauce.

Savoury choux buns
Make buns half-size and cook for 20 minutes. Fill with cream cheese flavoured with plenty of chopped fresh herbs and well-seasoned.

BUTTER ICING
Enough to fill and ice 1 × 7-8 in (17.5-20 cm) cake

4 oz (100 g) butter
8 oz (225 g) icing sugar
2 tbsp hot water
Flavouring

Make sure that the icing sugar is free from lumps, and put it through a sieve. Cream the butter until very soft and light and gradually beat in the icing sugar and hot water. Add flavouring and beat until the icing is soft and creamy. Fruit juice may be used instead of hot water. If the icing is for piping, a little extra icing sugar may be added to give a firmer texture, and the icing for piping should be cool and firm.

Coffee icing
Substitute 1 tablespoon coffee essence for half the water.

Chocolate icing
Add 1 tablespoon cocoa powder to hot water *or* add $1\frac{1}{2}$ oz (40 g) melted plain chocolate.

Mocha icing
Prepare chocolate icing, using coffee essence for half the liquid.

Citrus icing
Substitute orange or lemon juice for water, and add 1 teaspoon grated orange or lemon rind. Add a little orange food colouring if necessary.

ONE-STAGE SOFT ICING
Enough to fill and ice 1 × 7-8 in (17.5-20 cm) cake

3 oz (75 g) soft margarine
8 oz (225 g) icing sugar
1 tbsp hot water

Put all the ingredients into a mixing bowl and beat hard with a wooden spoon for 3 minutes until the icing is soft and creamy. Add flavourings as for butter icing.

GLACÉ ICING
Enough to ice 1 × 7-8 in (17.5-20 cm) cake

4 oz (100 g) icing sugar
1 tbsp warm water

Put the sugar and water into a small thick pan. Add the chosen flavouring. Heat gently until just warm, stirring to dissolve the sugar. The icing will look smooth and glossy and should coat the back of a spoon quite thickly without sliding off.

Coffee icing
Add 1 teaspoon coffee essence.

Chocolate icing
Dissolve 2 teaspoons cocoa powder in the water before adding sugar. Add a few drops of vanilla essence.

Mocha icing
Make chocolate icing, but add coffee essence instead of vanilla.

Citrus icing
Use orange or lemon juice instead of water. If liked, add a few drops of orange food colouring.

ALMOND ICING
Enough to cover 1 × 8 in (20 cm) cake

4 oz (100 g) caster sugar
4 oz (100 g) icing sugar
8 oz (225 g) ground almonds
1 tsp lemon juice
A few drops of almond essence
Beaten egg to mix

Stir the sugars together, making sure that the icing sugar is free from lumps. Stir in the almonds, lemon juice and essence. Add enough egg to bind the mixture and give a firm paste (if egg white only is used, the icing will be pale and cream-coloured, which many people prefer). Knead lightly on a board dusted with icing sugar. Roll out to required thickness to put on cake.

ROYAL ICING
Enough for 1 × 8-10 in (20-25 cm) cake

4 egg whites
2 lb (900 g) icing sugar
1 tbsp lemon juice
2 tsp glycerine

Make sure the icing sugar has been sieved and is free from lumps. Whisk the egg whites until slightly frothy and stir in the sugar gradually. When half the sugar has been mixed in, add the lemon juice. Beat in the remaining sugar until the mixture forms soft peaks when pulled with a spoon. Stir in the glycerine. Keep icing in a covered bowl until used and beat lightly again before using. A little extra sugar may be necessary to give the icing he correct stiffness for piping.

Index